Con Curtis is a writer and keen photographer. After his time in Antarctica, he worked with Family Services for many years, specialising in the rehabilitation of young offenders and supporting families in crisis; he has a first-class Honours degree in Youth Justice. He lives in Yorkshire with his fiancée Sarah and Labrador Mac, plays guitar in a covers band and gets into the mountains whenever he can.

Dedication

Dedicated to the memory of my brother Ed Curtis, an inspiration to all he met; and to May and Eddie, the most wonderful parents anyone could ever have wished for.

Con Curtis

WORKING AT THE END OF THE WORLD

An Antarctic Diary

To Eleanor

Best wishes

Con Curtis

Dec 2018.

AUSTIN MACAULEY PUBLISHERS™

LONDON • CAMBRIDGE • NEW YORK • SHARJAH

A CIP catalogue record for this title is available from the British Library.

ISBN 9781788232524 (Paperback)
ISBN 9781788232531 (Hardback)
ISBN 9781788232548 (E-Book)
www.austinmacauley.com

First Published (2017)
Austin Macauley Publishers Ltd.
25 Canada Square
Canary Wharf
London
E14 5LQ

Acknowledgements

There are so many wonderful people who have supported me on this journey, far too many to mention but here's just a few:

My sister Gail, one of the strongest women I know, always smiling, always positive; my brother Damian who shares so many interests with me and has always encouraged my aspirations; James for everything that a friend should be, and more, with extra-large portions of laughter along the way; my close mates Andy, Rob, Dave, Marty, Paul, Richard and Bill for their unconditional friendships and endless support; thanks to my wonderful unique friends Phil and Carrie living their dream on the beautiful Island of Colonsay, for their kind hospitality and letting me experience what an author's retreat truly means; all my extended family – the Curtis, Dwyer, Dowling and Ford clans; and so many other loyal friends who have encouraged me to achieve this goal (I know it's a cliché but you know who you are); my writer friend and often mentor Lucy Jago for her help and advice, Bob for the same; Philip Parker for help with the initial draft of the manuscript; the band Sundogs and all my musician friends for putting up with my wailing and guitar playing; and thanks to my publishers Austin Macauley, for understanding and having a belief that such a story is worth sharing.

I also need to say thank you to the British Antarctic Survey for allowing me the privilege to experience the dramatic beauty of the great white continent and to contribute towards the important scientific research being undertaken there.

Finally, I would like to give a special thank you to my partner Sarah, an amazing woman, for always believing in me and giving me the time, love and space to accomplish my goals, while dealing so admirably with all the problems that life inevitably presents.

Contents

MAPS

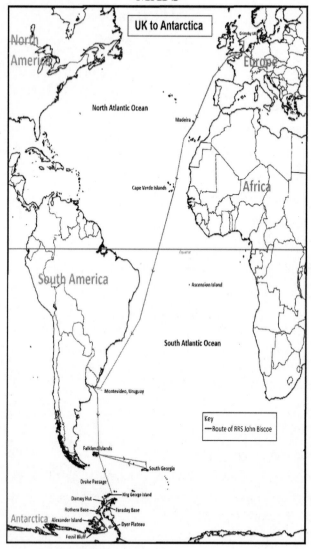

UK to Antarctica

North America

Europe

Grimsby UK

North Atlantic Ocean

Madeira

Cape Verde Islands

Africa

Equator

South America

Ascension Island

South Atlantic Ocean

Montevideo, Uruguay

Key
Route of RRS John Biscoe

Falkland Islands

South Georgia

Drake Passage

King George Island

Damoy Hut

Rothera Base

Faraday Base

Antarctica   Alexander Island

Dyer Plateau

Fossil Bluff

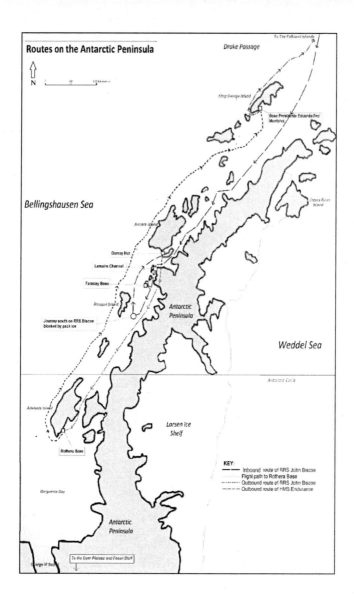

Routes on the Antarctic Peninsula

N

Drake Passage

To The Falkland Islands

King George Island

Base Presidente Eduardo Frei Montalva

James Ross Island

Bellingshausen Sea

Anvers Island

Damoy Hut

Lemaire Channel

Faraday Base

Booth Island

Journey south on RRS Biscoe blocked by pack ice

Antarctic Peninsula

Weddel Sea

Antarctic Circle

Adelaide Island

Larsen Ice Shelf

Rothera Base

Marguerite Bay

Antarctic Peninsula

George VI Sound

To the Dyer Plateau and Fossil Bluff

KEY:
Inbound route of RRS John Biscoe
Flight path to Rothera Base
Outbound route of RRS John Biscoe
Outbound route of HMS Endurance

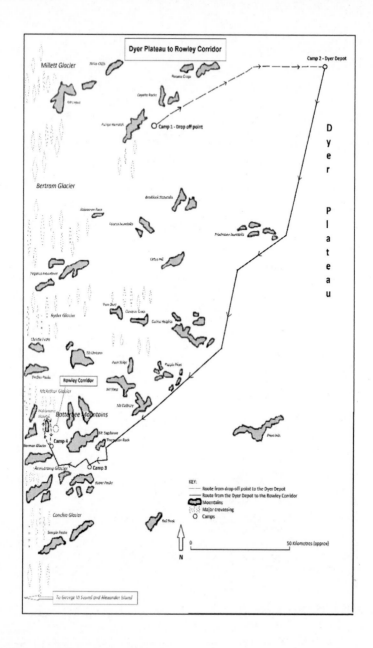

Dyer Plateau to Rowley Corridor

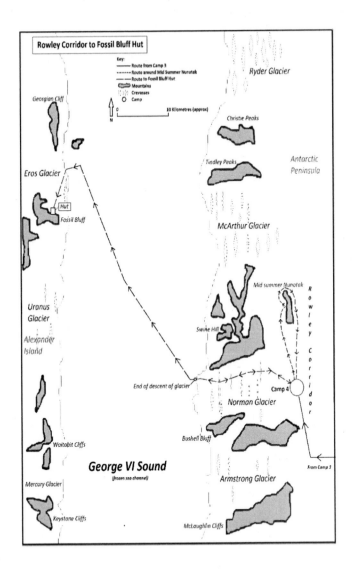

1. Introduction

'I think my snot's frozen again' was a term I often heard when I spent two austral summers working in Antarctica for the British Antarctic Survey (BAS) as a base and field assistant between 1990 and 1992 (in lay terms this role is similar to that of a 'mountain guide'). The main body of this book is the diary extracts from the first of the two field seasons combined with a retrospective account of each day. I joined a glaciology project on the Dyer Plateau in North West Antarctica which culminated in an epic 280-kilometre sled journey that had never been undertaken before, and to my knowledge, not repeated since. We travelled from our base camp high on the Plateau, through the Batterbee Mountains, carried out a first descent of the treacherous Norman Glacier, and then travelled across the George VI frozen sea channel to the sanctuary of Fossil Bluff transit hut on Alexander Island. The following year was an intensive three-month mobile geology project in North West Palmerland.

The Dyer Plateau project was a four-week trip undertaken with another field assistant; no scientific staff were involved, as our task was reasonably straightforward (even for two climbers). The previous summer, geophysicists and glaciologists from the University of Washington had participated with BAS scientists in a cooperative programme; the broad goals of the project were to assess the relationship between paleo-climate records from interior Antarctica and climate changes at lower latitudes. The team had drilled out some ice cores from depths between one hundred and three hundred metres which would provide climate records from the past one thousand years; the cores were boxed up in one-metre sections and buried in an underground snow chamber (its location marked only by a single two-metre bamboo cane with a small black flag on the top). The team had also placed a grid of aluminium glacier poles over an area of approximately 400 square kilometres, with each pole half a kilometre apart. Our task was two-fold; to measure the accumulation of snow against each individual pole and place a two-metre extension on each one. Secondly, to locate and dig out the buried ice cores and bring them to the surface for aircraft to transport back to Rothera Base (which proved quite tricky – find the single two-metre bamboo cane with a black flag atop, on a glacial plateau the size of Wales). However, although the ice cores were undoubtedly of scientific value, the trip was going to be so much more to me than just the advancement of science. It was about personal growth and development, stepping beyond mainstream goals and challenges, testing my limits, embarking on a journey of discovery, and hopefully having a fantastic time along the way.

My second summer saw a graduation to a three-month deep field geology project; these projects were much sought after by field assistants as they involved extensive travel through some of the most spectacular (and equally dangerous) scenery on the planet. This entailed travelling as a self-sufficient two-man field unit for nearly three months, taking rock samples from a variety of mountain ranges in North West Palmerland; in total, we made seven separate camps and travelled over seven hundred and fifty kilometres. However, this book concentrates on the first season, the story of the second season is to be told at another time.

2. Working in Antarctica

Antarctica is the highest, coldest and windiest continent on earth, it is roughly the size of Australia and India put together and the interior is covered by an ice sheet that is over 4,000 metres thick in places; so heavy is this ice sheet that in some areas it has pushed the rock below it underneath the sea level. Over 90% of the earth's fresh water is held within the snow and glaciers of Antarctica.

The mountains that stretch down through the Peninsula are a geological continuation of the Andes that run the length of the western side of South America, submerging below Drake Passage off Cape Horn, to reappear at the northern tip of the Antarctic Peninsula. The mountains nearer on the Peninsula are spectacular and similar to the European Alps (but without the vegetation); beneath their towering heights, impenetrable chaotic glaciers flow toward the sea, their icy cliffs often breaking off to form huge icebergs.

There is an abundance of life around the coastal regions, including seabirds such as skuas, petrels and albatross; Weddell, crabeater and leopard seals, a variety of whales including humpback, orca, minke, and numerous penguins (Adélie, chinstrap, gentoo, king, macaroni). However, once one ventures into the interior, the presence of any living thing is very rare, the climate and environment are too harsh to support much in the way of life; lichen and moss etch out a scant existence in this hostile area of Antarctica. Knowing these facts, one becomes aware of the limits of human endurance when embarking on lengthy deep field research trips. Common feelings for people returning from such an extreme environment are humility, respect and a definite feeling of insignificance.

The British Antarctic Survey (BAS) is one of the world's leading environmental research centres and is responsible for the UK's national scientific activities in Antarctica; it has an excellent reputation globally. BAS is a component of the Natural Environment Research Council (NERC), based in Cambridge, United Kingdom. It has, for almost 60 years, undertaken the majority of Britain's scientific research on and around the Antarctic continent. It now shares the continent with staff from over thirty countries.

BAS employs over 400 staff, and at present supports two year-round research stations beneath the Antarctic Circle; these are at Rothera Base on Adelaide Island and Halley Base on the Brunt Ice Shelf, there are also summer-only forward logistic stations within the Antarctic Circle at Fossil Bluff on Alexander Island, and Sky Blu at Eastern Ellsworth Land. The other year-round bases north of the Antarctic Circle are at Signy Island in the South Orkneys, Bird Island just west of South Georgia, and King Edward Point on South Georgia. During my period of employment, there was also a year-round research station called Faraday on Galindez Island. Throughout the Antarctica summer, BAS has hundreds of staff working on the continent, including scientists, field assistants, pilots, cooks, engineers, doctors, mechanics and a whole array of support staff; the bases are kept open through the winter months by a skeleton staff.

Ice-strengthened ships sustain the Antarctic operations. The RRS James Clark Ross has advanced facilities for oceanographic research. The RRS Ernest Shackleton is primarily a logistics ship used for the resupply of stations. Four de Havilland 'Twin Otter' aircraft fitted with wheels and skis are based at Rothera station, these are the workhorses that support field parties and other research stations. Since my time there, BAS now use a wheels-only Dash-7 aircraft that provides the inter-continental air-link from Rothera to the Falkland Islands and flies inland to blue ice runways. It was in this harsh and challenging landscape that I was about to find myself spending a summer season.

3. Preparing to Depart

My yearning to travel and work in Antarctica built up following years of climbing and mountaineering in mountain ranges in Britain, the Alps, North America and New Zealand. My desire to enter into the hostile world of Antarctica was driven by the psychological and physical challenges that would undoubtedly present themselves in such an environment, and are less and less to be found in the more popular mountain regions of the world. The isolation, the extreme cold and venturing into the unknown were the tests; the reward was simple to define: to be allowed to work and travel in the most beautiful and pristine mountain environment on the planet. This was going to be a real test. However, for many years my motto has been 'life's a journey', and living for me means stepping beyond the confines of my own comfort zone and testing my limits, physically, emotionally and psychologically; being in a tent with only one other person in such a wild and remote environment was certainly outside of my, and I imagine most people's, comfortable day-to-day experiences.

The news arrived that I had been successful with my job application to BAS while I was working at a summer camp in New Hampshire in the United States. Andy Tugby, an old college friend, and I had gone across to the States to teach outdoor activities there following the completion of a year-long outdoor education course we had undertaken together in Edinburgh. I was sad to leave the good friends I had made in the States, some of whom remain loyal, close friends today, but a great adventure awaited me, so what could I do?

Arriving back in England in late September left little time to organise things for my trip south. I was also in a relationship with a wonderful girl called Sandra who had always been patient with me, and who understood and respected my desire for travel and adventure; however, having just arrived back home following four months' work in the States, I could sense I was pushing my luck with this trip. She was a stunning looking girl with many admirers and had remained loyal when I was away travelling; as I prepared for my trip, I wondered if that would remain the case.

Following an early morning tearful farewell with Sandra on a train station platform (which did feel a bit clichéd, but I guess that is just the way these things happen) I travelled east from my hometown of Leeds to Grimsby to join the Royal Research Ship (RRS) John Biscoe which was docked at the industrial fishing port there. My sense of adventure was twinned with a deep sense of sadness. The reality of leaving Sandra for such a long period of time engulfed my thoughts as I gazed from the train carriage window, the cloud covered countryside sweeping past me. As mentioned earlier, 'life's a journey' has been my mantra for many years, however, the realistic consequence of departing on this leg of the 'journey', could be losing a woman I cared a great deal about. I recall my eyes welling up with tears as I contemplated the real possibility of this, I noticed the young couple sitting across the table from me had seen me attempting to contain my emotions (in true British 'stiff upper lip' style) and asked if I was okay; I reassured them I was fine, but something stopped me from sharing with them my journey ahead. In such situations, I try not to share my adventures, particularly when back in England, and especially with people who may have a more traditional lifestyle, probably for fear of coming across as boastful and immodest. I was also honest with myself about the level of selfishness I seemed to be displaying, Sandra had looked heartbroken as the train pulled away from Leeds train station and I felt so responsible for her emotional strain; however, my drive to be in the Antarctic was strong enough to result in my heading to Grimsby to join the ship for an epic ocean journey south, I just hoped it would be worth the sacrifice I was making.

I was feeling emotionally vulnerable as I sat on the train pondering on, and critically analysing what had brought me to take up the BAS offer, even at the risk of a relationship I valued so highly. My love of pristine spectacular mountain landscapes, adventure, and global travelling were undoubtedly the most significant driving forces, but I questioned myself about what other factors were pushing my decision. Was it heavily influenced by the psychological tests ahead, was it to 'prove' anything? Although my upbringing in a tough council estate in the north of England had built a strong personal resilience, and aspiration and ambition had always been encouraged by my parents, I was aware that it was quite unusual for someone from such a humble background to be heading in the direction I was currently going. Was I proving something not only to myself, but to family and friends, and also to my peers, not in a conceited or arrogant way, but to make some kind of statement; 'Anyone can do this kind of thing if they have enough drive and self-determination, regardless of their background' However, more pragmatically though, I knew I did not have any confirmed employment when I finished the work in the States; the contract with BAS paid a reasonable salary and I had some outstanding bills to pay.

Britain has a history of ships sailing to Antarctica from the more traditional ports of Southampton, Whitby and Portsmouth, our less than glamorous departure point of Grimsby one dark and dreary morning in early October was a sobering start. My voyage south was memorable and an adventure in itself; I had been given the option of flying from England to the Falkland Islands and boarding the ship there. But how could I not embark on such an ocean adventure? Our six-week voyage would take us through the English Channel, across the Bay of Biscay, down the west coast of Africa calling at Madeira and the Cape Verde Islands, across the Atlantic passing over the equator to berth in the Uruguayan capital Montevideo. From there we would sail down the east coast of South America to the Falkland Islands, across to South Georgia, back to the Falklands, and then from Port Stanley, across the ferocious and terrifying seas of Drake Passage, to the eventual calmer ice-laden waters of Antarctica finally anchoring in Dorian Bay at Wiencke Island.

The '*Biscoe*' was the oldest of the BAS research ships and ours was the last trip south for the old workhorse; it was an ice-strengthened, ocean-going research ship that had completed many tours of the Antarctic, its first in 1959. The Captain and First Mate were chalk and cheese; one a well-spoken Oxbridge graduate, the other a tough Glaswegian, however, the combination seemed to work productively. I recall the Captain calling to us at Grimsby as we headed ashore for our last British beers before sailing south the following morning, "Gentlemen, before you go ashore, remember…'time and tide wait for no man' – we leave at 08:00 hours, sharp!" This advice differed dramatically in both its style and content to that given by the First Mate as he saw us walking off the ship towards a local bar! The rest of the thirty-plus crew consisted of a First Officer and the usual complement of cooks, engineers, electricians and a variety of deck hands.

4. Journey South

I had never travelled across the ocean by boat before. I had just experienced what many had, including trips across the Irish Sea from Liverpool or Holyhead to Dublin, or from England to Holland or Spain, so I was eagerly anticipating the voyage ahead. The RRS *John Biscoe*, named after a famous English Antarctic explorer of the 1800s (the third man to circumnavigate the Antarctic continent) was undertaking her final voyage to the Antarctic after spending over thirty years as a supply and research ship. In 1992 she would be sold to the Cypriot Fayza Shipping Co. Ltd, relinquishing her historical name, and gaining the less than grand title of 'Fayza Express'. Her final fate was a scrap yard at Aliaga Turkey in 2004.

The trip down was a fantastic adventure in itself, the six-week ocean voyage would have entailed parting with a significant amount of tourist dollars had those on board been paying customers, so I felt hugely privileged to see all the spectacular things I did during the trip and receive a salary to top things off. I did feel a certain amount of guilt at times at being paid to sit basking on the back of the ship, sailing through the tropics, watching a blood-red sun drop over the horizon with a cold beer to my lips, thinking, *I shouldn't really be getting paid for this*. However, to balance the moral equilibrium, just weeks later I was sat freezing in a small tent in a violent storm in a remote mountain range hundreds of kilometres from the base, 'enjoying' 100 kmh winds and a still air temperature of minus 35C, thinking *Is this tent going to get blown away, and am I about to perish? I really don't get paid enough for this shit!* Additionally, the crossing of Drake Passage (Mar de Hoces), the 800-kilometre stretch of sea between Cape Horn and the northern tip of the Antarctic Peninsula, was certainly 'interesting'; the ship being thrown around for two days by terrifying thirty-metre waves was an experience not to be forgotten too quickly!

I would not really want to paint a picture of a six-week trip filled just with relaxation, beers and sunsets; an agreed part of the trip was that every second day the scientists and field assistants on board would assist the crew in completing manual low-skilled tasks. Although everyone on board was employed by BAS, undertaking these duties gave us a sense of 'paying our way', and also removed the chance of getting bored, though that was never going to happen to me; I could easily sit for hours at the back of the ship watching majestic wandering albatross glide off the stern end, just skimming the surface of the ocean with their huge wingspan.

The variety of jobs given to us to undertake was dependent on a number of factors; our background; whether we were a scientist or a mountaineer; and, most importantly, who was in charge of allocating the tasks. This duty was split between the Glaswegian First Mate George and the First Officer Paul. George was a tough career seaman and something of a 'class warrior', very quiet and as hardy as they come, having been sailing to Antarctica for over thirty years. He appeared to have an innate dislike for university graduates ("Och, they've nay fuckin common sense"), was not overly fond of the English, and even less fond of those from southern England. However, I heard he had been a climber in his youth and he seemed to tolerate us mountaineers, while also seeming to have a certain degree of affinity with those of us from the north of England. Paul, on the other hand, was a Merchant Navy officer who was fair with all, regardless of their background. Consequently, when George was allocating out tasks one very hot morning a few hundred miles north of the equator, I got the pleasant enough job of renewing the '*John Biscoe*' lettering on the life-buoys with 'stick on' letters, this task undertaken as I sat comfortably in the shade at the back of the ship. Alan, on the other hand, my PhD graduate companion from Cambridge, born to affluent parents and presenting a royal-like accent, was given the task of cleaning some old thick steel cables in the depths of the engine room that were covered in sticky tar-like black lubricant, in a sweltering 40 degrees Celsius tropical heat – oh yes, he ticked all of George's resentment boxes.

The mix of scientists, field assistants and base staff was a fairly interesting combination. The scientists hitching a ride on the ship were geologists or glaciologists; the inbound field and base assistants all had one thing in common: their love of mountains, rock faces and wild environments. That said, all the scientists had a thirst for adventure, they had made a choice to apply for posts with BAS and knew that meant deep field research in isolated harsh environments. There was also a doctor called John with us on the *Biscoe,* who was taking up an eighteen-month post as the base physician at Halley Research Station on the Brunt Ice Shelf. He was a friendly guy with a dry sense of humour who coincidentally knew a close friend of mine back in England, Dave Walsh, who is something of a 'character'. They had met years ago doing some military stuff together and Dave's name came up during a conversation about crazy antics back home.

There were always funny stories to tell about Dave; he and I have had many interesting adventures together in the mountains and Dave has probably used up most of his nine lives, either in the mountains or in military shenanigans. His last close call was a lone retreat from the Petit Dru in Chamonix; he became stranded on a rock ledge for six days in a horrendous storm after becoming separated from his climbing companions following an unsuccessful attempt to climb a route up the vertical rock wall of the Dru. Eventually running out of food in his lonely isolated bivvy site, and most importantly having no water or fuel to melt snow, he braved the unrelenting storm and abseiled down onto the glacier below; to remain on his soggy perch without any water would have meant certain death. Fading in and out of consciousness, he crawled and crossed dangerous glaciers eating handfuls of snow to keep himself alive, until after two more days, he came across two climbers near the base of the glacier who managed to raise some help. Following emergency treatment at Chamonix hospital, he was very fortunate to survive, many others less resilient and fit, would likely have perished. This epic adventure was a significant point in Dave's life, he had been struggling with his sexuality for years, although at this time he already accepted that he was gay, he had not gone public; this near-death experience changed that and he 'came out'. Due to archaic Army regulations at the time, he could not remain in the Regiment; consequently, he resigned, enrolled at university where he gained a degree in Computer Science and moved to Brighton. We remain good friends today and I have never seen him happier; one cannot get in the way of nature.

A day after leaving Grimsby, the Bay of Biscay provided most of us non-crew with our first experience of sea-sickness; those who have experienced this will understand that 'once it gets you, it gets you', and that there is no escape, especially when you know you are to remain on the ship for the next six weeks. The nausea, dizziness, vomiting, disorientation and general feeling of awfulness seemed to be without cure – gazing at the horizon, wearing 'healing' wrist bands, and other mythical remedies were to no avail, laying down in one's bunk was the least unpleasant way of dealing with it. However, my first bad experience from the swells produced off the north-west coast of Spain lasted only a day or two until I developed my 'sea legs'; much worse was to come weeks later when crossing Drake Passage (when I recall not even the hardiest of the crew members escaped the dreaded sea-sickness!) There appeared to be a real mix of personalities amongst the scientific staff and field assistants and some were coping better than others in these early sea swells. Being ill was certainly not a reflection of one's inability to cope, but there was some healthy banter going around and not much sympathy for those heaving their guts over the side.

Being at sea, especially crossing a huge ocean, is a humbling experience; not seeing land for days and weeks really gives one a sense of the immensity of the oceans. The abundance of life in the sea also becomes apparent and I was fortunate to see an enormous variety of ocean dwellers; we saw every type of whale gliding majestically through the water, humpback whales were particularly impressive as they occasionally breached the surface and three-quarters of their bulk came out of the sea before crashing back in a huge splash; the keen photographers amongst us were eager to get the classic shot of a humpback's tail remaining alone on the surface just for that brief moment before it dived down into the depths. Seeing these beautiful creatures as they casually took their annual journeys of thousands of miles was so rewarding; however, it was also deeply saddening to know that in previous eras, hundreds of thousands of whales had been slaughtered indiscriminately for commercial use. On another mid-Atlantic morning, I was privileged to see a school of about one hundred hammerhead sharks just thirty yards off the port side of the ship, cruising along in crystal clear tropical waters. I am no marine biologist and until this point had always thought that sharks were more solitary creatures. I had obviously not spent enough time watching wildlife documentaries on the television featuring the oceans; I'm sure it wouldn't have surprised the legendary natural world film-maker, David Attenborough, to see such an amazing sight.

Visitors to the ship on a regular basis were dolphins; viewing them power majestically through the sea, seemingly without effort, was a sight one could never tire of; on many occasions a few of us would be jostling for a position at the front of the ship to peer over the railings and catch the best view of the dolphins, as they, too, jostled for a position with each other to get the best propulsion from the ship's bow waves, darting in and out of the clear water, their powerful dark bodies shimmering and glistening in the sunlight.

The majority of the ship's crew had spent many years sailing along this route, therefore it was mostly us scientist and mountaineer ocean 'virgins' who were captivated by the amazing sights the sea could present. One memorable experience was seeing 'flying fish' (Exocoetidae) travelling fast across the surface of the warm tropical waters. I saw this many times as the fish made powerful, self-propelled leaps out of the sea into the air, where their long, wing-like fins enable them to glide and fly above the water's surface for considerable distances; some I witnessed travelling more than fifty metres (I understand this ability is a natural defence mechanism to evade predators). On one evening, and much to our amusement, two flying fish gained too much upward push and landed on both the front and back decks of the ship within seconds of each other. Although the odd crew member suggested 'putting them in the pot', we managed to catch hold of them as gently as possible and direct them back over the side into their home habitat.

Crossing the Line

For anyone who has worked on an ocean-going ship and crossed the equator, they may be familiar with the 'crossing the line' ceremony; an initiation rite undertaken on both naval and merchant ships, which commemorates a sailor's first crossing of the equator. This naval tradition has gone on for hundreds of years and entails the uninitiated being brought before 'King Neptune and his Court'; on our voyage, this was an officer and two of the crew who were decked out in the appropriate clothing. King Neptune looking very regal and wearing a crown and makeshift robes sitting atop a 'throne', one of the crew as Davy Jones, wearing a pirate's hat with bundles of string as his hair and thin plastic tubing painted green attached to his lower face with elastic and tape to mimic tentacles, the other crewman dressed as her Highness Amphitrite, wearing make-up and lipstick, with a blonde wig and long white robes; I'm not sure where he found the blonde wig, I'm assuming it was kept on board for these occasions (or maybe he wore it every second Saturday into the mess and called himself Julie). Those to be initiated are brought before Neptune and his cronies (really, I'm not bitter about what happened) just as the ship is about to cross the line of zero degrees latitude. They then have a variety of unpleasant things happen to them to prove they can withstand hardship, pay proper homage to the god of the sea 'King Neptune' and be worthy of sailing the oceans.

Historically, on Navy ships these ceremonies have often been quite brutal, the uninitiated have been beaten with boards, wet ropes, forced to eat vile concoctions, maybe whipped and sometimes thrown over the side of the ship. However, after an Australian news network received a videotape in the 1990s showing sailors on board an Australian submarine being assaulted during the initiation ceremony, most navies now have regulations that prohibit physical attacks on sailors undergoing this 'rite of passage'. Amongst those on the RRS *John Biscoe,* there were about twelve of us who had to undergo the ceremony, which was just about all the field assistants and scientists and two of the crew; the ceremony was going to transform us from slimy 'Pollywogs' (a sailor who hasn't crossed the equator) to a 'Shellback' (a son or daughter of Neptune). We were 'subpoenaed' the evening before by 'Davy Jones', one of the leading crew, to appear before King Neptune's court the following day, dressed only in our shorts. The next day was blisteringly hot, with not a breath of wind and a searing heat of around 42 degrees Celsius. We assembled at midday on the rear deck and were to be brought one at a time before the 'King' who sat on his makeshift throne, to hear his declaration of our unworthiness, and to seek his permission to become Shellbacks, most of us having already had a beer or two in preparation for what the ceremony would bring.

A skeleton crew were manning the ship, as everyone else had the day off, and we slowly edged across the equator in the stifling heat; the remainder of the crew were around the perimeter shouting and cheering with beers in their hands, as well as directing a variety of abusive insults towards us. *This all looks like a bit of nautical fun and easy enough*, I thought. Then one of the crew produced a huge comedy-like giant clear plastic syringe about one foot long and full of a reddish coloured liquid which I felt sure was destined for our mouths and stomachs (or worse still, up our backsides – which has been known to happen occasionally on naval ships). Beside him was one of the mess crew with the large refill bucket, pouring more extra hot chilli powder and Tabasco sauce into the volcanic looking liquid. King Neptune was the First Officer Paul, and he decided what was to happen to us once we had pledged our allegiance to Neptune and the sea; it was at this point I felt a huge sense of relief that it was not the First Mate George sat on the throne - not so much for me but for the scientists; I can only imagine what type of punishments he would like to instil upon them for having been unfortunate enough to have a privileged background!

My friend Mike was the first up. He was a carpenter from Wales who was heading down to Rothera station for two seasons on the base, a terrific guy who was always smiling (but not for long…). Two of the crew took hold of him roughly by the arms and dragged him to kneel before Neptune. At this point, some rotten fruit and veg were pelted at him and then just after he had stated his allegiance to Neptune and the sea, he was held while the king of the ocean ordered him to 'drink the fiery liquid'. The syringe concoction was then pushed into his mouth and about half a pint squirted down his throat – he clearly struggled ingesting the lovely potion and vomited some back up over himself and the deck, and then had buckets of sea water thrown over him before being dragged roughly away. It was my turn next. The same thing happened to me as I was dragged through the deck, now awash with an unpleasant mixture of puke, water and the fiery-looking sauce; however, I tried to avoid the syringe containing vomit-inducing liquid from hell being forced into my mouth, much to Neptune's helper's displeasure. Their determination to force me to drink this was quite admirable, as they proceeded to chip two of my teeth as they wrestled the hard plastic syringe into my mouth while squirting liquid into my throat, plenty up my nose and some into my eyes. Growing up in a community that has a significant South Asian population generally leads one into frequenting curry houses and eating spicy food, and so I am quite partial to food with hot chilli, but the liquid I had squirted into my mouth, nose and eyes that balmy day felt like it had to be right off the Scoville scale. Laying on the deck with rotting fruit and veg being pelted at me as I looked into a blazing sun, with my face, eyes, nose, mouth and throat on fire while running my tongue over the chipped teeth assessing the damage, was something I will not forget; the 'punishment' of lukewarm seawater thrown in my face to confirm my initiation into King Neptune's world was actually something of a welcome relief.

Once I had recovered to a point I could breathe again, see things reasonably clearly and I realised the skin wasn't going to melt off my face, I thought it would be a good idea to jump over the side and have a swim in the most inviting looking crystal clear calm sea you could ever imagine. As I began to climb onto the railing, one of the more sensible members of the crew grabbed me by the back of the shorts and advised me that he had seen sharks near the boat just ten minutes earlier. The Captain was observing things from the bridge and somewhat pragmatically confirmed this through the ship's PA system, "I do not want anyone to jump into the sea, you will be eaten by the wildlife". Wisdom prevailed and I chose the smart option as the crew enthusiastically threw more buckets of water over me – a less life-threatening alternative, I guess.

The only real injury of the day happened to Bruce, another of the field assistants. As a former naval officer, the crew thought he should get special treatment during his equatorial initiation. The majority of the crew were based in the tough fishing port of Grimsby; it seemed apparent that a dislike of military officers, and in particular naval officers, was in their blood, so a golden opportunity such as this to dish out some pain to Bruce via the crossing the line ceremony was obviously too good to miss. Since Bruce left the Navy and became involved in the mountains, he had grown his hair long and sported a shiny black ponytail tied at the back of his head (it has to be said he did have lovely hair, the glossy type you see in hair product ads). Historically, there was a tradition of taking a lock of the uninitiated's hair as part of the ceremony; however, during today's nautical antics prior to Bruce going before the 'court', this hadn't happened. But now one of the crew produced a pair of scissors while Bruce was held on his knees by two other henchmen in front of Neptune. Bruce saw what was about to happen and, due to his being very fond of his uber cool ponytail, tried to grab hold of the scissors just as they were going in for the chop. He didn't lose any hair, but during the struggle, one arm of the scissors went straight through the fleshy part of his hand between his thumb and forefinger, blood now added to the liquid mixture on the deck – whoops.

Montevideo

We arrived mid-afternoon in the large industrial port of Montevideo. I had had a great night's sleep the night before so was up early to enjoy our first approach to a large mainland, and the continent of South America was certainly that. Earlier, while standing against the rail on the starboard front bow, I was rewarded with a great view of the coast of Uruguay, which was bathed in early morning light from a strong sun slowly rising behind me, I could easily pick out the large city of Montevideo with the huge estuary of Rio del la Plata (The River Plate) on its southern flank, bridging the gap between Uruguay and Argentina, which I thought I could just barely make out on the horizon in the far distance. Through the course of the morning, a variety of staff had also gathered on the decks to soak up the land ahead of us, which was slowly growing and developing in detail as we edged closer towards the coast. The plan was to stay overnight in Montevideo, re-fuel and re-stock the ship with fresh produce, and then head further south the following day; some brief discussion amongst us led to the obvious conclusion that a trip ashore to discover the delights of this great-looking city was the order of the day. As with all plans, people started dithering, so Mike and I arranged to meet some of the lads later on that evening in a bar that one of the crew had mentioned, and we took a taxi from the port and headed towards the Central

Post Office (Correo Uruguayo) to collect mail that we had been told by the First Officer would be waiting there for collection; we volunteered for this task as we knew we would at least get to see some of the city before it became 'beer o'clock'.

We planned on collecting the mail, dropping it back off at the ship while a taxi waited for us, and then heading back into town to have a look around before meeting up with the rest of the guys later; it was far too risky a plan to take a bag full of the ship's mail out drinking with us. The taxi seemed the smart option; as with most large ports in big cities, particularly industrial ones, the surrounding area looked a tad sketchy and probably not the safest of places to wander through as a visitor on foot with a pocket full of pesos; I had been in similar situations before and experienced how bravado prevailing over wisdom can lead to negative outcomes. As we exited the taxi and strolled towards the old building, it was easily noticeable how the influence of the Spanish colonials had left a lasting impression on the architecture around Montevideo; although quite a lot of the city was now modern and developed, the Spanish influence was certainly evident in the Ciudad Vieja, the old town. The post office presented a sense of dated grandeur, there were old classical style columns rising up to an ornate weather-beaten stone cornice below a well-worn entrance floor of light coloured marble.

After entering the post office, I spoke to a friendly-looking guy at the counter, trying my best with my six-word Spanish vocabulary accompanied by much gesturing, to get him to hand over our mail. This proved completely unsuccessful as his chief response was a shake of the head and a repeated, "No mail, no mail". After a bit of head scratching, more animated gesturing, some scribbling of notes and more failed attempts to communicate (while being acutely conscious of not defaulting to that very irritating 'British abroad' trait of speaking English slowly in a raised voice, in the hope that it will cause the recipient to immediately become bi-lingual), I beckoned Mike outside to re-evaluate our options. As we were pondering on our next course of action, which was increasingly leaning towards the 'cold beers in the sunshine' preference, an official-looking chap came out of the post office towards us. He had overheard my pathetic attempt at Spanish as I enquired about the mail, and in perfect English informed us that there had been a postal strike for the last four months which had led to a huge backlog of mail; okay. "No problem, so would that be organised and sorted out very soon?" I optimistically enquired.

"It is already sorted, my friend", he smiled back, and then with a hint of an apologetic face continued, "We burned it all."

Apparently, rather than go through the trouble of sorting the backlog, we were told someone in a senior position had given instructions to pile it all up at the back of the office building and torch the lot. I remain unconvinced that this really happened, however, what I am sure of is that our ship and its personnel did not receive any mail that we were told was definitely at this post office, and there had unquestionably been a postal strike in Uruguay during the months prior to our arrival. With the failure to locate our post, the 'cold beers in the sunshine' option now became increasingly attractive; Mike and I re-entered the post office, this time leaving after a far more successful mission to change some pounds into pesos, although in our case, the pesos could easily have been referred to as 'beer tokens'. We nipped to a phone box and got a message about the mail situation back to the *Biscoe* on the contact number I had been given, before heading into town, to take in some touristy sightseeing and photo stops, and then as predicted, cervezas beckoned.

The evening quickly developed into a boozy marathon; we met up with other guys from the ship, sampled many local strong beers, danced on tables, and got involved in tequila drinking competitions with some visiting US sailors. As usual with alcohol fuelled adventures that progress into the early hours, we all managed to get split up and I took the unwise option of having a 'rest' on an inviting-looking bench in a pleasant park on my wobble back to the ship. I awoke on my pew in the Plaza Independencia to the sound of birds tweeting and an early morning sun bathing my uncomfortably positioned body. Opening one groggy eye, I caught sight of some local musicians getting warmed up on their guitars for a day's busking, and the bronze statue of Uruguay's national hero, Jose Artigas, frowning down from atop his immobile metal horse at my very hungover state. A quick check for 'UDIs' (unidentified drinking injuries) found me in good shape physically, but a very fragile head reminded me not to run too fast to the ship that was, fortunately for me, docked in the port reasonably close by. I recalled the Captain's words of, "time and tide wait for no man" as I hurried back towards the *Biscoe*. On my hurried return, I also blended quite nicely into the less than salubrious area surrounding the docks, my earlier cautiousness about the safety of the area having disappeared from my hazy head. I most definitely did not want to miss the ship; presenting myself at the British Embassy, slightly dishevelled, stinking of beer and tequila, with no passport and about eight pesos in my pocket was not an appealing option.

I made it back with a few hours to spare and headed to my bunk to get some real sleep. As I had walked from the quayside up the gangway onto the *Biscoe*, the First Officer Paul greeted me, "A good night then, I assume, glad you could make it, you're all in a sorry state this morning." He didn't seem to be too aggrieved, I guess he knew we were due a bit of a blow-out having been on the ship for quite a while, and given the fact that we were heading towards relatively dangerous work in the mountains of Antarctica.

The Falkland Islands

From Montevideo, we headed out later that morning back into the South Atlantic and down towards the Falkland Islands, over a thousand miles away further south; I missed our departure due to lying in my bunk nursing a very fuzzy head and feeling slightly sorry for myself, regretting immensely those last half dozen tequila shots. The next few days sailing provided more great views of wildlife in its natural habitat. Standing on a windy deck combined with some circuit training soon cleared the Montevideo hangover and it was so enjoyable soaking up the ocean environment, watching huge wandering albatross out feeding on the wing hundreds of miles from their nesting grounds, plus many whales and dolphins breaching the surface close to the ship on their travels off the South American coast. Even though I had now been on the ship for a few weeks and already seen a whole array of wildlife that most people will not see in a lifetime, I never tired or became nonchalant about the beautiful wildlife and scenery around me.

It was a dull grey morning as we slowly sailed into the harbour at Stanley, which lay at the north-east side of East Falkland Island. The weather was poor as we navigated through the 200-metre-wide narrow gap into the sheltered waters where the docks of Stanley are located, but the approach in from Blanco Bay compensated by providing great views of the beautiful white sand beaches of Yorke Bay edging into crystal clear water on the south of the bay, just north of the airport. As soon as we had moored alongside the jetty at Stanley, I headed ashore to have a wander around the place. It was great to be back on land again. Stanley is the main town and the capital of the Islands, populated by about two thousand people, and the locals I met while having a stroll around were very friendly. When I explained what ship I had alighted from, they were keen to have a chat. Interestingly, it was when the people I spoke with realised I was a civilian working with BAS, and not a squaddie, that I seemed to receive a warmer welcome. It became apparent during the short conversations I had with a variety of people that, although they were hugely appreciative of being liberated eight years before, in recent years soldiers had been causing a few alcohol-induced problems in town, resulting in the Army imposing a ban on soldiers from using the few bars located in Stanley. After just fifteen minutes of walking on the road that fronts the town and follows the line of the bay, passing the beautiful terracotta and stone building of Christ Church Cathedral, I found myself on the western outskirts of town at the War Memorial, built in remembrance of those who had lost their lives here less than a decade previously. It was very saddening looking at the plaques on the wall bearing the names of those who died, some of them such young men, their lives ended much too prematurely in a conflict so far from their home shores.

After collecting some mail that was awaiting me at the Post Office in the town centre, I headed back to the ship to get changed into some walking gear and head up Mount Tumbledown, which lay just a few miles west of Stanley. Seeing the memorial had left quite an impression on me and I wanted to go and see first-hand the site of one of the final battles during the war; the ferocious fighting on Tumbledown (and its neighbouring peaks) ultimately led the British forces into Stanley to regain control of the Islands. Although I was keen to read my mail from home, the weather was unusually good for the Falklands, so it might be my only chance to head into the hills in decent conditions. I recall standing in my cabin with the mail in my hand having something of a dilemma about whether to read it now or not. What cinched it and had me putting on my walking boots was that I had not been out walking in the hills for some time and my body, and mind, desperately craved it. So, feeling slightly guilty, I headed back out, grabbing on the way a few snacks from the local shop in town to take in my rucksack for the trek to Tumbledown.

Within about an hour-and-a-half of brisk walking, I found myself on the craggy and wild summit of Mount Tumbledown. The journey up had been quite eerie, having to avoid areas of land that were fenced off with 'Warning – Land Mines' notices. Once I moved away from the faint path I had been following, I came across dozens of empty shell cases, used ammunition belt clips, the odd bit of discarded clothing, lots of empty ammunition boxes and even an old mobile field kitchen. Tumbledown was one of seven strategic hills which lie within about five miles of Stanley that had to be taken by British forces in the latter stages of the three-week conflict in order for them to be able to approach the Island's capital. The battle on the ground where I was stood was deemed a success at the time by the British military and media due to its strategic position above Stanley. I had read and heard that this battle was particularly ferocious as the British forces comprising of Scots Guards, supported by Royal Marines and Gurkhas, had met strong resistance from the well-trained Argentinian Marines who were firmly dug in on Tumbledown.

This battle was regarded by many as probably the fiercest of the war. During their night-time assault, the Guards had been pinned down in the freezing dark for hours by concentrated gunfire from the Argentinians. They battled it out through the night, and with dawn passing, the combined efforts of the three Guards Companies eventually overpowered the strong Argentinian resistance, with reports of fighting with fixed bayonets. Ten British and thirty Argentinian men died on this hill and more than 150 men were wounded; in the aftermath of the battle, medals for courage and bravery were awarded to troops from both sides by their respective governments. As I sat on a rock in the pleasant sunshine soaking up the environment around me, I could scarcely imagine the horrors that occurred here all through that night in the bitter cold of a Falkland's winter; it was difficult for me to contemplate such carnage, loss and suffering as a 'success'. However, I felt an enormous amount of respect for the men who had died up here and for those who fought alongside them on such an exposed and harsh rocky terrain. From where I sat, I could easily see the other hills and areas of raised ground whose names became quite familiar to those taking an interest in the conflict at the time: Wireless Ridge,

Mounts Harriet and Longdon, Two Sisters Ridge and Sapper Hill were all visible from my perch; all places which also saw fierce fighting between assaulting British troops and determined Argentinian defenders, likewise resulting in much loss of life. My walk back down off the battle-scarred mountain found me in a sombre mood. Normally, a walk in such a beautiful and wild natural environment on a calm sunny day would leave me feeling uplifted, but the mental images of what occurred on this hill had negated any sense of exhilaration. As I was just entering town, I stopped again to look at the War Memorial; eyeing through the names of the soldiers and sailors on the plaques in place on the curved stone wall, I could see that some of those who died were as young as seventeen; young men not even into adulthood sacrificing their lives on this remote island in the South Atlantic. A wave of emotion seemed to engulf me and my eyes filled with tears as I read through the names of those who had perished and thought of how many other lives would ultimately have been affected by the sacrifice these men had made.

That evening I had gone with a couple of guys from the ship to a local bar near the quayside. By some strange coincidence, while we were relaxing and reflecting on the journey down so far and talking about the events on the Falklands eight years before, one of the veterans who had been badly injured during the conflict came into the bar for a few drinks. It was a chap called Simon Weston, a Welsh Guardsman who was aboard the Sir Galahad when it was bombed and set on fire by Argentinian Skyhawk jets in Bluff Cove. He suffered terrible burn injuries in the attack, particularly on his face, head and hands; 22 of his 30-man platoon were killed in the attack. As I stood beside him at the bar, he initially thought I was a squaddie who was breaching the Army ban of socialising in Stanley, but after brief introductions, we sat down together and had an interesting chat; he asked about my forthcoming work down in Antarctica and we chatted about his journey. Simon was in the Falklands making a TV documentary about events during the time of the war and his recovery since. He struck me as an incredibly brave man with a warm, friendly personality who had fought hard to continue with life the best he could after receiving such terrible injuries; since the war he has done some incredible charity work and just recently had been awarded a CBE. After an hour or so, one of Simon's TV crew came in to collect him and I left the bar at the same time. While we were saying our goodbyes outside, there were two young squaddies standing by a Land Rover Jeep parked at the local store. They made some disparaging comments about Simon's appearance, but he just asked me to ignore them as he gets it all the time; I obliged his request, but as he was walking away in the opposite direction from these two buffoons, I couldn't stop myself approaching them and giving them some sound and honest advice.

We remained in Stanley for another two days awaiting the arrival of a few personnel who were coming in by plane, and I used the time to soak up as many sights on the island as possible. Although the walk onto Tumbledown had been something of a bleak experience due to the terrible events there, other places on the island offered incredible beauty. Rookers Bay, which lies a short distance east of Stanley, and Surf Bay just half a mile up the coast towards the airport, have to be some of the most beautiful beaches I have ever seen; pure white sand leading into crystal clear waters with dunes and tussock grass as a backdrop. A couple of years before I headed out to Antarctica, I had been on a bit of a global walkabout and visited the beautiful Tahitian Islands in the South Pacific; the beaches there were incredible, particularly those on the less developed island of Moorea. Those here on East Falkland were easily as stunning; however, the water was bitterly cold so a dip was out of the question, and there were a few sections that still displayed the 'Warning – Land Mine' signs; 'treading carefully' had a very literal meaning here.

The day before we set sail from Stanley, I managed to get myself into two bits of bother. In the morning, I borrowed Joe's mountain bike which he had put on the ship prior to leaving England. Joe was a geologist I had become friendly with while on the *Biscoe*; he was also something of an adventurer and had brought along his mountain bike just in case there were any opportunities to ride it. As I was out exploring the hillsides down towards Bluff Cove on the way to the military base at Mount Pleasant, it became apparent that there was some type of army exercise happening. I came across sections of soldiers while I was riding on and off road; one group attempted to stop me, but I peddled downhill away from them. As I looked back, I saw the irate looking section leader on his radio. When I hit the track at the bottom of the hill, there was another group of six soldiers waiting for me, and on approaching closer I could see a young Lieutenant with them. I stopped when requested and he asked me what I was doing riding on the hills when there was currently a military exercise occurring. I told him I was obviously enjoying my bike ride and as a civilian, was not part of the exercise; as he was advising me to stay off the hills, I couldn't stop myself from asking it the exercise was 'live firing' (I already knew it wasn't because the soldiers with him had 'blank firing' attachments on the end of their rifles). As he was responding with, "No, it's not, but…" I quickly cycled around them.

As I rode away, I smilingly said, "I'm not joining in thanks, enjoy your war games." When I looked over my shoulder, I saw the young officer talking furiously into his radio.

Later that evening as we were having dinner on the ship, the First Officer from the *Biscoe* called me out of the room. His opening comment as we stood outside the mess confirmed I had been reported by the army about my earlier mountain biking encounter, "Con, I've had a call from an Army Captain at Mount Pleasant. Were you out on a bike near Bluff Cove this morning?" Well, I thought it was funny.

I did not help my case for character redemption much by later on that evening being caught red-handed by the *Biscoe* Captain walking down the gangway off the ship with a five-gallon drum half full of petrol. It was the fifth of November, so a group of us had decided to collect lots of driftwood and build a bonfire on a secluded part of a beach just outside Stanley. We took some food and beers along to celebrate a piece of anarchic British history; however, the wood was not completely dry and wouldn't ignite very well, that's when I had my brilliant idea.

To the Captain's credit, after he chewed my ear for a while (he did appear extra exuberant in his chastisement, having also heard about my encounter with the Army Lieutenant earlier), I explained about the damp bonfire and the intended use of the petrol and he let me take the container off the ship, with the obligatory caveat of 'Be careful'. The petrol certainly did the trick.

South Georgia – Husvik Disused Whaling Station

We had left Port Stanley after collecting a small team of BAS marine biologists who wished to undertake some work on the spectacular and isolated island of South Georgia, which sits about 1,200 miles east of the Falkland Islands across the South Atlantic Ocean. The plan was to enter Stromness Bay on the north side of the island, anchor off the disused whaling/sealing station called Husvik, and take the biologists ashore to do their research. I had quickly put my hand up when the inbound Rothera Base commander, Pete, who had joined the ship in Stanley, came into the mess and asked for four volunteers to act as escorts for the scientists when they went ashore; the trip would not entail using any mountaineering skills, but the old whaling station was now home to an array of seals, including southern elephant seals, who could easily present their own weighty problems.

Besides Husvik, there are a number of disused whaling stations relatively close by; Grytviken, further south east down the coast in Cumberland East Bay, and Leith Harbour, approximately three miles north as the crow flies, which between 1909 and 1965 was one of the busiest whaling stations in the world, and at one point housed up to 500 men. Between Husvik and Leith, and just a stone's throw away (maybe with a very powerful catapult), lay Stromness whaling station. My one disappointment about the imminent trip ashore was that the biologists had not chosen Stromness for their research, as this was the location where Ernest Shackleton completed his epic 1916 journey from Elephant Island. Shackleton and five of his men sailed 1,280 kilometres across the ferocious Southern

Ocean in the lifeboat *James Caird*; navigator Frank Worsley using only a sextant to steer their way (in mostly bad weather) to land at King Haakon Bay on the rugged south coast of South Georgia, the opposite side of the island to where the Norwegian whaling stations lay.

Shackleton, Worsley and Tom Crean left three men sheltering under the lifeboat and then walked and climbed nearly 50 kilometres across the heavily glaciated central mountains of South Georgia (a traverse never done by humans before), arriving at Stromness whaling station to be met by the then station manager Peter Sorlle, the dishevelled trio on the brink of complete exhaustion. The sixteen-day voyage from Elephant Island to South Georgia could easily be ranked as one of the greatest boat journeys and navigational feats ever accomplished; and the whole trip as arguably one of the greatest journeys of human endurance and survival ever. Shackleton's trip in the *James Caird* was certainly not scheduled, his vessel, the *Endurance,* had been trapped and crushed in pack ice months earlier, this before his planned Trans-Antarctic expedition had even got underway, causing him and the crew to abandon the ship. They escaped onto the surrounding frozen sea, taking two lifeboats with them that would act as both shelter on the ice, and transport to get to safety. After camping on the frozen sea for two months, the ice eventually broke up, and with the two lifeboats full of men, they spent five harrowing days at sea until reaching the isolated and desolate Elephant Island, some 557 kilometres from where the *Endurance* had been lost in the destructive pack ice. It was from here that Shackleton and five of the crew made the incredible journey to South Georgia in the *James Caird*, leaving twenty-two men remaining in their bleak windswept environment, huddled under the scant protection of the second lifeboat. Despite all the misadventures, not a single man was lost; the crew on Elephant Island were eventually rescued by Shackleton four-and-a-half months later.

We went ashore in a 'Rigid Raider' craft that was lowered down using the ships crane. The weather was quite poor with horizontal sleet blowing in from the west, and the ship had anchored about a half mile from shore and out of danger of being blown onto any rocks. The Rigid Raider is a small landing craft made with a reinforced plastic hull which carries two powerful 140 horsepower outboard motors, and is often used by the Royal Marines; it can carry up to eight people. First Mate George was at the wheel and a moment after we hit the rough surface of the water, he got everyone in position and informed us, "Ye have tae hold on fuckin tight," as he pushed the throttle to full power. This was George's toy, and he certainly knew how to use it. We headed towards the shore at full speed, bouncing off the waves and avoiding the hazardous Bar Rocks. A couple of the scientist looked quite uncomfortable on this unscheduled white knuckle ride. As freezing cold sea spray blasted our faces and frosted our jackets as we held on tightly to whatever we could find, I felt sure that not even the Marines threw their crafts around like our Glaswegian boat handling ninja. The sight of the fast-approaching disused whaling station was made even more eerie and foreboding through the poor visibility; horizontal sleet blasted across it and a grey, cold blanket seemed to cling to the brown and rusty dilapidated buildings. George knew exactly when to reduce the throttle and the Raider came to a gentle halt on the sloping shingle beach. The landing place had in itself been a tricky choice, as much of the two hundred metres of beach that stretched across the bay in a half moon shape was occupied by huge southern elephant seals. There was an old jetty that came out into the bay from a central point of the whaling station, but its entry point onto the beach appeared to be completely blocked by seals. It was definitely not an option to disembark onto this, and then run the gauntlet around and between the enormous seals.

Myself and the new Rothera carpenter, Mike, jumped out onto the shingle beach carrying lines to secure the craft. While everyone climbed ashore, we were keeping one eye on the scientists and one on a group of southern elephant seals just twenty metres away. There was one huge bull surrounded by his harem of smaller female seals and he was looking a tad grumpy; maybe he saw the Rigid Raider as some kind of threat and he leaned up, arching his huge back and making loud spluttering and bellowing noises through the large proboscis at the front of his head. George shouted to us to untie the line we had just anchored to an upright thick wooden pillar; he knew enough about the island wildlife to understand that this fella, who was about fifteen feet long and probably weighed upwards of 3,000 kilogrammes, could easily bend the small boat if he took a serious dislike to it. We quickly untied and George skilfully reversed the boat back into the bay. He shouted to us to radio the ship from our hand-held sets when we were ready for a pick up. We gave him the thumbs up and then he spun the Raider around and blasted back out across the rough surface of the waves towards the *Biscoe*, whose shape we could only just make out in weather that was becoming quite blizzard-like. The Raider occasionally bounced up out of the water off the crest of big waves, causing the propeller to scream as it momentarily had no water to drive against; George loved his favourite toy.

The scientists had originally planned to take marine samples from two small lakes just a short distance inland, however, due to the weather conditions, all four decided to go to one site close by which really didn't entail the need for any escorts, so the two other climbers, Bruce and Asti, who had also volunteered to come ashore, joined us and headed over to the main base to have a little adventure through all the crumbling whaling station buildings (currently, we would be unable to do this due to the South Georgia government's ban on scientists and tourists from going within 200 metres of the base and its structures due to the buildings being unstable and dangerous). Mike and I split up from Bruce and Asti and we went back around the front of the buildings by the beach to have a closer look at the small colony of elephant seals, who didn't look the slightest bit bothered by the snow storm driving over their humungous bodies. But why should they be troubled by a summer snow storm with all that blubbery insulation?

It was quite easy to identify the bulls from the cows, as they are five to six times heavier and have the large proboscis. We walked dangerously close like a pair of naughty schoolboys playing a dare, but this didn't last for too long, as one of the bulls, which I had got to within ten feet of, turned away from all his girlfriends, reared up with his huge back arched and made a surprisingly quick dash directly towards me. I'm sure I was not any kind of threat to him and I most certainly didn't fancy any of his lady friends, so it was a bit of an unnecessary fuss really, but knowing how protective they are of the harem and with our visit coinciding with the mating season, I was expecting his behaviour and quickly dashed around the side of the building to avoid being squashed flat against the shingle, like a cartoon character run over by a steam roller. We left the bull to go and reacquaint himself with his girls and wandered through the buildings. This was quite an eerie experience and felt a little like I imagined an old town in the Klondike area up in the Yukon Territory of Canada might have been when the gold seams were mined dry and the small towns abandoned. The strong wind, sleet and snow rattled between the old iron and wood structures. Most of the buildings still had their roofs on but only a few had retained any glass in their windows, and most of the entrance doors had been blown off by the even harsher storms that winter brought.

Entering into one building, which by its contents was obviously the kitchen and mess, we found cups, plates and crockery on big old worn chunky wooden tables, which gave the impression that the men had just downed everything hurriedly when the ship came to extract them as the base ceased operations permanently in 1960. It really did feel like going through a time tunnel while wandering around, looking in cupboards seeing small tin or pot containers bearing labels and engravings written in Norwegian; my Norse was a little less than fluent to say the least, so if there was no content remaining in the containers, it was guess work, involving mostly using our noses to identify whatever used to be in there. As the storm worsened, we left the mess building to explore further, pulling our ventile jacket hoods tight. On entering into another ramshackle large barn-type structure, we came across the ironic sight of female elephant seals and some pups taking shelter from the blizzard outside; as well as hunting and processing whales on Husvik and the neighbouring stations, southern elephant seals were also killed and stripped of their blubber, which was boiled down to oil and sold for a similar price to whale oil; the ancestors of the seals we came across sheltering from the storm inside these buildings faced a very different fate indeed.

As Mike and I exited the building back into the ferocious winds that were being funnelled between the structures and which were carrying sleet and snow that bit at our exposed faces, we just made out a strange high-pitched crying type of sound only just audible through the noise of the wind. It was coming from around the corner of the building we had just left. When we went to investigate, we could immediately see the problem as we turned the corner. A young seal had managed to get itself stuck down some kind of square-shaped concrete drainage hole, which was about six feet square and four feet deep and appeared to be a type of inspection chamber for the drains. The pup was well and truly jammed; its cries of distress fortunately did not appear to be attracting any adult seals because, as Mike and I looked at each other, we didn't really need to have any discussion about at least giving it a try to get the chunky little bugger out; it would certainly perish if it was left in its current situation. Just as we started to look around for any ropes or straps, Bruce and Asti came into sight, they too had heard the cries of the seal. Four bodies were hopefully going to give little chubby a fighting chance, however, the seal was wedged in and looked to weigh a few hundred kilos at least. We eventually located some old straps and ropes and after much heaving grunting and avoidance of the pup's dangerous-looking snapping jaws, we hauled the noisy lump out onto the surface with a little cheer. Although it made no amends for the thousands of seals killed at Husvik, it felt like a moral victory. The pup, on the other hand, shuffled straight into the large shed where we had earlier seen the other cows, a very ungrateful child indeed, not even a salutary nod or wink of thanks!

Just as this happened, the radio in my jacket crackled into life and George informed me he was coming into shore to collect us; the scientists also had a radio and I suspect the weather was too bad to get any quality research done, so they had called it a day after only a few hours.

We all congregated on the beach about 50 metres from our drop-off point. An elephant bull and some cows had now moved into our original landing spot and we certainly weren't going to argue with them. George and the landing craft speedily approached through the soggy curtain ahead of us in the bay; he slowed and skilfully nudged the bow of the boat up to the steep shingle beach, keeping it ninety degrees to the shore with low power on the throttle as we all jumped on board at the front end and headed back to the *Biscoe*. Arriving back alongside the ship, it became quickly apparent that the sea was now much rougher than when we had departed hours earlier and our small boat was rising up against the steel hull of the ship on the swell of the sea, which fluctuated between six and ten feet. This was something of a problem; the way we attached the boat to the huge steel hook of the crane, which was lowered down on a steel cable, was to slip a large steel ring onto it. This steel ring had four chains attached to it, which in turn were attached to the four steel securing points at each corner of our craft. In calm water, this was a piece of cake; the Raider would come alongside and float gently against the ship, the crane would then span out over the side of the boat and lower the heavy hook down on its thick steel cable. Someone on the boat then lifted up the steel ring with the four chains attached (which was heavy), slot it onto the hook and the boat and its contents were lifted up out of the water and placed in the allocated place on the stern of the ship; as easy as shelling peas.

However, in big sea swells when the Raider was moving violently up and down the side of the ship, attaching this steel ring onto the bulky metal hook that was coming quickly down towards the boat, then speedily slipping out of reach as the Raider dropped away, was always a tad tricky and needed slick timing. It also entailed the real risk of injury; if you were unlucky enough to be the 'volunteer' in charge of attaching the steel ring, and the hook hit you, it could easily crack your skull or shatter a shoulder blade, or your hand could get trapped between the hook and the steel ring, which definitely wasn't recommended, especially if you were an aspiring pianist. Unfortunately for me on this occasion, as we manoeuvred into position and scraped up and down the side of the ship, all holding on tightly and nobody yet taking responsibility for the large steel ring with the chains that lay on the floor of our craft, the horizontal sleet and snow still lashing us from the west, I heard the dreaded shout through the wind and sleet in a familiar Glaswegian accent, "Con, get a held a that ring and get ready to hook it on" and, after a short pause, "And ye better put that hat on yer heed."

My fellow boat occupants looked at me with a sense of relief, and some with a wry smile, as they had escaped this unpleasant task – thanks, lads. I put on the hard plastic security hat, secured it tightly with the chin strap (I most certainly didn't want this coming off with about thirty kilos of steel flying past my noggin). I positioned myself in the centre of the boat, lifting the steel ring with the chains attached up to chest height while trying to brace my feet shoulder width apart to try and maintain some stability, which wasn't really working due to the heavy swell causing havoc with our craft. Mike and Bruce, who were sat hanging onto opposite sides of the boat, stabilised me to a certain extent by each grabbing a fistful of my jacket at waist height with one arm, and holding on the boat with their other arm, while George gingerly got us into place. He shouted up to the crew member who was leaning over the side to signal to the crane driver to lower the hook steadily down, then yelled at me to get ready, I still deliberately had the large steel ring and chains at chest height; it was heavy and I knew I would need to keep some strength back to lift it up over my head and slot it on the hook while maintaining some semblance of balance.

This was all slightly comedy-like. Even though George was utilising his entire seaman's skillset to keep the boat in place, we were now moving up and down by at least ten feet as well as banging against the hull of the ship and I was only just staying upright, mainly due to the guys hanging tightly onto my jacket. The first attempt was a disaster. The hook was stationary about fifteen feet above us, then just as George got us directly underneath it, a larger than usual swell came under our craft and we sped up to meet the hook. I had the steel ring above my head ready but I missed my target by a foot. The clunky metal hook smacked me on the helmet, then quite unnervingly slid down my back, fortunately missing my shoulders, before we swiftly and disconcertingly dropped away by about twenty feet, the hook sliding swiftly upwards against my back, our stomachs feeling like we were on a fairground ride (at least we didn't have to pay). The expected shout of "Fer fuck's sake, man!" headed in my direction. As the craft dropped back down on the swell, my only thoughts were; *I'm so glad I have this helmet on* and *I'm so glad that hook didn't catch the back of my jacket (or my helmet!) on our way down and leave me dangling from it like a drunken circus clown.* I can only imagine the tirade of Glaswegian abuse that would have induced. The second time I nailed it. George's timing was faultless, our craft rose up on a big swell right in line with the hook and – of huge importance to me – to the perfect height; in the fraction of a second we had at the top of the swell, I hooked the ring on, the swell dropped away but we and the boat remained airborne. The crane lifted us quickly on board and, with a sense of relief, we disembarked onto the *Biscoe* to head back to our bunks to get cleaned up. As George passed me on the deck, I got a gentle pat on the shoulder and a wink – praise indeed.

Drake Passage

After leaving Husvik, we sailed back across to Port Stanley to collect more supplies and prepare for the next leg of the journey. For a few days prior to our departure from the Falklands and heading further south towards Antarctica, some of the crew had been warning me of the potential perils that awaited us in crossing the infamous Drake Passage, the 800 kilometre stretch of deep sea separating the Pacific and Atlantic Oceans and bridging the gap between Cape Horn on the southern tip of South America, and the northern point of the Antarctic Peninsula in the Southern Ocean. No land mass breaks up this deep sea passage and it has one of the strongest currents in the world, with an estimated flow rate between 1,000 and 1,500 cubic metres per second; it had also earned the reputation of having some of the roughest seas on the planet – more fun to look forward to.

We threw our anchor lines off at the jetty in Port Stanley at mid-morning and slowly edged out into the open sea. It had been a great experience seeing the Falklands and the friendliness of the islanders left a lasting impression on me. Once we had left the sanctuary of East Falkland Island, we began heading south towards the Antarctic Peninsula. For a few hundred kilometres, we would have the mainland of South America to the far west presenting some protection, at least until Cape Horn signalled the end of the land mass and the beginning of Drake Passage, where the Atlantic and Pacific Oceans converged. We had been listening out for weather reports from the crew and the First Officer, and things were sounding quite ominous; storm force winds which on this stretch of sea meant only one thing: huge swells and massive waves – yippee.

As predicted, once we were parallel to the south-eastern tip of South America hundreds of kilometres to our west, with just the small isolated Argentinian island of Isla de los Estados between us, the sea began to change and we could feel the boat starting to slowly and methodically rise and fall. It was mid-afternoon and the majority of the field staff and some of the crew were on the decks, mostly at the bow looking out at a brooding sea ahead of us. We had encountered patchy sunshine since leaving the Falklands, but now it felt like mother nature was looking down on us and saying, "Don't think you lot are going to be that lucky, there's a reason this section of sea has got a fearsome reputation." The ocean ahead looked black, with white water blowing off the crests of strengthening waves in an ever-increasing wind, the sky now overcast and wild-looking. Once we were beyond the South American continent, the seabed would drop away swiftly down to the deep sea Yaghan Basin, nearly 4,000 metres below us; the next piece of land, approximately 800 kilometres ahead of us, would be Elephant Island, where Shackleton famously departed from on his epic 1,280 kilometre journey to South

Georgia, and then the South Shetland Island group off the northern tip of the Antarctic Peninsula.

Gathering on the deck facing this ominous-looking sea ahead, I spoke briefly with First Officer Paul who had joined us, asking about what lay in store ahead. His response about what sea state we should expect was frank and pragmatic; he smiled, maybe a little nervously, "I would get as much food down you now as you can, because the sea is likely to get quite 'tricky' over the next day or so, eating food and keeping it down may be a problem." – he wasn't wrong. Anyone who has experienced unusually rough seas on a ship of medium size will fully understand the difficulties of eating while down below decks, especially in a mess room with no windows, so one has no sense of where the horizon is; soup is definitely not the most popular or wisest of dishes to attempt to consume. The bowls and crockery may well have rubber bases to secure them, and the table may have small lips around the edges to stop things sliding off; however, when you have thirty-metre waves hitting the ship at the bow, and it is rolling at more than 30 degrees from side to side, the contents of your plate (or bowl, if you wrongly thought you were a smarty pants) do not remain where they should be and swiftly exit your chosen receptacle as the mess floor becomes a slippery and hazardous place for those brave enough even to contemplate eating; yes, soup was definitely off the menu.

Nearly all of us became badly seasick; once the waves were in excess of 15 metres, the ship was rising up and down and also rolling significantly from waves that were hitting us from the side. It became difficult to hold off nausea and unpleasantness. The Captain was attempting to hit the waves head-on to try and keep the movement to just up and down and reduce side to side movement, but the sea was so chaotic that the ship was beginning to feel like a cork in the ocean, moving in all directions. George had warned us earlier to avoid the decks as it was now dusk and the waves were starting to break over the bow, heaps of violent sea spray accelerating down the length of the ship. Losing one's footing and going overboard into this sea was not something one was likely to survive. I recall a safety briefing we had been given by the First Officer and George just before we left Port Stanley; one of the scientists had asked what the drill was if he or anyone were to fall overboard into the icy Southern Ocean. George calmly replied, "Swim fae the bottom as fast as ye fuckin can." Trying to do anything in the worsening sea was troublesome; moving through the corridors below decks would see you banging off the walls like a pin ball. All our bunks were now equipped with straps at two points that would go across your body in line with the chest and thighs, and these needed to be fastened securely once you were lying down or you would be quickly and unceremoniously thrown out onto the floor, which was quite painful if you were in the upper of the two bunks.

About ten hours into the crossing saw the waves hitting their peak. We were now in 'storm force' sea conditions and it was pitch black outside, the majority of the crew were strapped into their bunks suffering from seasickness, as were nearly all of us field staff. The Captain was up on the bridge with the First Officer and George, managing the ship as best they could in the appalling sea conditions. As I was strapped into my top bunk, listening to poor Mike moaning with seasickness below me, I was just about managing to keep the seasickness at bay; I had suffered badly with it earlier in the trip, but for some reason at the

62

time it had not really taken hold of me, which was a surprise. In these hectic surroundings, it appeared one really can get 'sea legs'. Everything in our cabin had been locked away, and as I listened to the contents of the drawers and cupboards shifting and moving around, I was contemplating whether there was anything I could do to occupy myself and take my mind off things, I felt sure the seasickness would engulf me if I remained in the bunk staring at the ceiling. Just at that moment, my cabin door opened and the smiling face of Joe appeared. He had all his outdoor gear on and announced, "Get your gear on and come up on deck, it's crazy out there."

"Anything's better than being strapped in here," was my instant response, so up I got and donned all my gear.

Mike muttered, "Don't bloody kill yourselves," as the door closed behind me.

Joe and I had hit it off early on during the trip; he was a qualified geologist, but was also a keen mountaineer and mountain biker who had travelled to mountain ranges all over the world; he told me he had embarked on geology as it would guarantee travelling to wild places. He was one of those, in my view, quite rare people who was academically very smart, but also possessed great common sense (although First Mate George might challenge the notion that such a person exists). We shared a love of wild adventure, so it was no surprise I accepted his invitation to take a look outside, even though we had been advised to ride the storm out in our cabins. Once we went through the external door onto the side deck, the ferocity of the storm really hit me; through the darkness of the night, we could just make out huge black waves slowly and menacingly looming up at the side of the ship with white spray blasting off the top of them. The ship was pitching forward and rolling from side to side in a howling wind, sea spray blasting us from the front and side as we hung on tightly to the ship's external railings; the waves looked to be higher than the bridge of the ship. Joe was beside me shouting something, but I couldn't hear him through the noise of the squalling wind, I beckoned him back inside and we both pulled the door open and crashed into the safety of the corridor, laughing as we pulled the door shut behind us, keeping the storm outside. "Let's grab some harnesses and slings and get up onto the monkey deck above the bridge, that should beat any fairground ride," Joe said mischievously, his face red from the driving sea spray, and regardless of my initial incredulous look, that's exactly what we did.

Both Joe and I had basic climbing gear that we had brought with us; I was unsure what route I might be taking home after my field season, so I packed a harness, basic rack and slings in case I ended up climbing somewhere on the return trip. We each went back to our cabins to get our harnesses, slings and a few karabiners and agreed to meet back out on the side deck with our gear on and secured. The monkey deck was directly above the bridge, consisting of about twenty square metres, with steel poles at waist height at each corner joined together in a square perimeter by two lots of tight steel cables at knee and waist height. It was generally out of bounds, but while we passed through the tropics, Joe and I had both previously sneaked up the ladder at the rear of the bridge onto the deck to catch some vitamin D, so we knew that we could use slings to tie ourselves securely onto the cables. However, in this violent storm it was surely going to be interesting. We were also aware that if the Captain, Paul or George discovered what we were doing, it was highly likely they would not be overly impressed; they had more than enough on their plate trying to handle the ship in these outrageous conditions.

Looking up towards the monkey deck through the rain and sea spray, we realised we could approach from the stern of the ship and climb the ladder at the rear of the bridge and then onto the deck above it. With the near-deafening noise of the wind and rain, it was unlikely we would be heard by the guys inside the sanctuary of the bridge. After much giggling, getting blown around and about ten minutes of slipping and sliding, while at the same time ensuring we didn't get blown over the side into a sea that would definitely provide an earlier than planned demise, we found ourselves stealthily climbing up the ladder and dragging ourselves onto the floor of the monkey deck. As we lay spread-eagled side by side being blasted by wind and spray, we looked at each other with smiles, faces that I recall also had a tinge of apprehension because the ship was now pitching violently forward, while rolling from side to side at an angle of about thirty degrees. Now we were up here, I thought maybe we had bitten off a little bit too much of this chewy adventure. Had we each been alone up on the deck, wisdom may have taken the lead and we probably would have climbed back down the ladder, having fleetingly seen the enormous black waves and turbulent sea all around us. But as is often the case in such situations, our combined machismo and bravado was pushing us to go a little further, which we obviously then did.

First, we took our slings and karabiners and clipped ourselves onto the front and back steel cable rails, then huddled beside each other and secured our harnesses together and attached the slings onto the outside cables on our left and right. This was all made more difficult by the violent movement of the ship, so we started out kneeling, making sure not to make too much noise on the monkey deck floor and risk being heard by those below us in the bridge. Then, slowly, we stood up as we got rid of any slack from the four connecting sides of the deck, until we were upright in a tight and reasonably stable position. Then we held on tightly and enjoyed one of the most amazing and outrageous rides one could ever imagine, muffling our screams, laughs and cries of delight on nature's greatest ever roller coaster. Looking into the blackness ahead was quite difficult; we had decided not to wear goggles as they would make things too dark. However, the sea spray and driving rain was making it tricky to keep our eyes open, so all we got were fleeting glimpses of the chaotic storm around us.

What we did glimpse was quite surreal, the huge black waves ahead of us seemed like dark, threatening hills topped by fierce white shards of spray. Either side, it was the same sight, the ship's bow pitching up high over the crest of each wave and then, once over the top, sliding down into the trough before the next massive swell drove it up again. All of this was while we were also being hit by waves from the side and, as exhilarating and exciting as this craziness was for us, if we were honest with ourselves, it was actually also quite terrifying. Unfortunately, our fun and games were cut short as our shuffling boots on the monkey deck floor had been heard in the bridge below us; we saw a strong torch beam coming from behind us at the top of the ladder. We turned and, through the driving rain and spray, saw the animated and furious-looking face of the First Officer Paul, who was mouthing words at us which we could not hear above the din of the storm, but by his expression, we guessed that he strongly wished us to come down from our wild perch. We untied ourselves from our secure position and put the gear back onto our harnesses, holding on tightly to everything in the darkness as it would be blown away quickly if we didn't, and made our way to the top of the ladder, shuffling on our knees so as not to get knocked over. Paul was waiting at the bottom of the ladder, also hanging on tightly as the ship pitched and rolled violently. He beckoned us towards him and put his face close to ours so we would be able to hear the kind words I knew were about to emit from him above the squalling wind and rain. He had always seemed a calm chap and I don't think I had ever heard him swear… "YOU PAIR OF BRAINLESS FUCKING IDIOTS!" blasted out loudly from his scowling face, which we both heard very clearly over the din, and then off he went back around towards the bridge.

Joe and I giggled to each other like naughty schoolboys, "I hope he doesn't snitch on us to the Captain and George, we will be in the shit!"

Lemaire Channel and Faraday Base

Travelling down the western side of the Antarctic Peninsula provided us all with views of one of the most spectacular coastlines I have ever seen, and I would often pinch myself as I gazed upon such a breath-taking landscape; it really did feel other-worldly. All down the coast, huge glaciers carved and cut their way through valleys, separating dramatic mountain ranges that presented jagged ridges angling down towards the sea. As we cruised down through the calm clear waters of this beautiful coastline, many of us had been talking on the ship about a place called Lemaire Channel, and whether or not we would be travelling through it. We had already travelled through Gerlache Strait, which had spectacular scenery of glacier-clad mountains edging steeply into the clear waters of a narrow deep channel; however, Lemaire Channel was supposed to be even more dramatic, the channel it passed through considerably narrower than the Gerlache Strait. The Lemaire is a narrow sea channel that cuts between Kiev Peninsula on the Antarctic mainland and Booth Island. At about 11 km long and just over a kilometre-and-a-half wide at its narrowest point, it is surrounded by cliffs and glaciers. The channel is regarded by many as one of the most beautiful sea passages in Antarctica, and possibly the world, but it is only passable in reasonable weather and with minimal sea ice. As we were approaching from the north we heard via 'rumour control' that the weather gods were looking favourably upon us and we were going to head through the channel; this was an unexpected and welcome surprise as further back up the coast we had encountered some unusually late sea ice for the time of the year.

The ship approached the entrance of the channel from the north and at quite a sedate pace. All of the scientists, support staff and non-working crew had gathered on the decks to gaze at the surrounding crevasse-strewn mountains as we slowly entered into this spectacular natural wonderland. I was at the front end of the ship, leaning on the rail above the bow and felt quite breathless looking all around. I had my SLR camera with me, but it was one of those situations when one didn't want to get too involved with photography as it might detract from the experience; but on the flip side, I really wanted to capture at least a few images of the amazing surroundings.

The glaciers that were wedged in between the mountains and hanging off huge rock ledges seemed to be defying nature and gravity as they clung on to the rock situated below them at ridiculous angles; at their leading edge, huge sections of ice the size of office blocks looked ready to crack off and drop into the sea below them. As the glaciers reached back and upwards into the distance, they were perforated and ripped apart by menacing looking crevasse fields. I'm sure the Captain and his colleagues on the bridge were keeping a close eye on things. Undoubtedly, they too were enjoying the spectacular surroundings, but as the ship was only a couple of hundred metres from the base of the cliffs and glaciers, should any huge chunk of glacier break off, the resultant tsunami-like wave would prove very interesting indeed. The majority of the mountains and glaciers around us had not yet had humans set foot upon them, which gave an extra sense of awe to the place. I was also aware that in just a few weeks' time, it was highly likely I would be travelling on dangerous crevasse-ridden glaciers just like these; this flash-forward brought me back to earth with a bit of a bump from the dreamlike state such surroundings always seemed to induce in me.

Faraday Research Station is situated on Galindez Island, an island just under a kilometre long that lies immediately east of Winter Island in the Wilhelm Archipelago (however, it changed hands from Britain to Ukraine in 1996 and renamed Vernadsky Research Base). It had been manned throughout the winter by a skeleton crew who maintained the base and prepared it for the following summer's scientific staff to arrive and undertake their research (which because of its location, was predominantly into marine biology, bird life, and flora and fauna). We were not scheduled to stop there as it was not directly on route to our destination; however, Pete, the inbound Rothera Base commander, called Bruce and I into his room in the *Biscoe* to ask for some support with a problem that had developed on the base that he had only just become aware of. The bases that are staffed by skeleton teams throughout the cold and dark winter months communicate with the BAS headquarters at Cambridge via satellite radio links, with generally two separate radio reports scheduled for each day. Pete informed us that Cambridge HQ had not heard from Faraday for nearly a week and neither had anyone else; that was up until this morning when the resident base doctor somehow got a radio message to our passing ship stating that the base's Glaswegian radio operator had gone berserk, smashed up all the radio transmitting equipment, armed himself with a huge 'Rambo' like hunting knife and was threatening to kill all the staff. It sounded like a visit was definitely in order; although Bruce and I did jokingly highlight the fact to Pete that we were not really employed as security officers or 'bouncers', me teasing him that just because I was from a tough estate in the north of England, that didn't necessarily equate to my being keen to disarm a potentially armed and dangerous Scotsman.

As the incoming Rothera Base commander, Pete, had the 'power of magistrate' within the British Antarctic Territories, the plan was to go ashore in one of the Raiders under the thin pretext of dropping off fresh produce, 'arrest' the radio operator, bring him back to the ship and then somehow get him back to the Falklands and onto the UK. Bruce and I had a quick one-to-one conference in my cabin and agreed to put numerous layers on to help prevent a knife going through our clothing should it get a bit messy when the guy was confronted by Pete and ourselves, and maybe try to stab us. We also put thick industrial gloves on should there be any unplanned pruning action. It all ended up in tears.

We went ashore to be met at the jetty by the radio operator riding a skidoo and pulling a sledge. It was easy to identify him as the skidoos are normally red in colour, but the one he was sat upon had been painted in the green and white stripes of Glasgow Celtic football club. It was apparent to see by his edgy behaviour that he suspected that dropping off fresh food was not the real reason we were there. Pete jumped on the back of the skidoo, while Bruce and I sat on some bags of potatoes on the sledge as we headed the short distance over a small snowy rise to arrive at the base. As we travelled towards the base, I felt acutely aware that this was not the most favourable of circumstances for my first landing in Antarctica; however, I remained philosophical, telling myself this situation was just a little grit in the oyster, and would hopefully be resolved without too much fuss. Once inside, Pete quickly gathered the half-dozen staff in the small lounge area while Bruce and I kept a close eye on 'Scottish Rambo' to try and gauge his possible reactions to what he probably knew Pete was about to say.

One very striking aspect of the situation was the tired and gaunt faces of the guys as they sat in the lounge chairs. They looked very demoralised, yet also showing a collective sense of relief that we were now here; their ordeal over the past week had obviously been emotionally traumatic and had clearly taken its toll on them. As Pete was telling all present the real reason we had called at the base, 'Rambo' had slowly moved himself behind the small bar, placing himself beside bottles and glasses which could easily be used as weapons. Simultaneously, Bruce and I got into position at either end of the bar to block any move to escape, and tackle and disarm him should he be up for a grand finale; things were certainly getting a bit tense. The guys that were sat down appeared to have one eye on Pete, and one eye on 'Jim Bowie'. Everyone was looking very unsure of what further crazy actions might follow as Pete quickly came to the crunch point of his brief narrative. Bruce and I were also very aware that we did not know if he had the hunting knife hidden inside his jacket. Pete's voice was now directed at Rambo and he informed him that unfortunately the radio operator's time at the base had come to an end, Rambo's chest rose, he glanced at both Bruce and me. For a moment, I thought he was looking intent on going for one last stand, but then, fortunately for all concerned, he chose the wise option, his shoulders slumped as he let out a sigh and became tearful and deflated; drama over.

Some choice final 'saving face' macho comments were directed at Bruce and I as we escorted him back to his room, confiscated the hunting knife (which was quite an impressive piece of workmanship, I have to say), helped him pack his belongings and then back to the ship we went. Prior to our leaving the base and returning to the ship, I left Bruce outside with the ex-radio operator and went back into the lounge to collect Pete and say bye to the guys inside; the change in the atmosphere in the room was quite perceptible, the smiling, happy and thankful faces a sharp contrast to those just twenty minutes before. They had gone through a few tough days indeed; it transpired that the base doctor managed to get access to a field radio that he was familiar with using, and as he was aware that the *Biscoe* was due to be heading past, sent out a hopeful radio call. To spend nearly six months on a small Antarctic base with just a few other men is going to present many psychological tests, especially through the constant darkness of the mid-winter months; keeping harmonious relationships is essential to maintaining group morale and supporting people's emotional and mental health. In such a unique environment, what normally might be described as mercurial or capricious behaviour can soon escalate into serious behavioural problems if left unaddressed. The results, as we witnessed, can be quite damaging and traumatic for all those involved. I am unsure what happened to the radio operator, other than that he transferred to another ship and headed back north.

We eventually continued our journey south towards Rothera, soaking up the wonderful mountain and glacier vistas that presented themselves as we cruised down the west coast of the Antarctic Peninsula. The sea was calm and crystal clear the morning after the unscheduled visit to Faraday, I had just finished breakfast and had nipped out onto the deck, and was standing on the bow soaking up the amazing view, wrapped up tight in my winter gear, a beautiful blue sky above. As I gazed around in contented silence, I was rewarded with one of the most beautiful sights I had seen since leaving England; just to my left a pod of orcas (killer whales) came cruising past the ship just fifty metres or so off the port bow, the dramatic backdrop of glaciers and mountains behind them making the sight even more intense. I had seen so much amazing wildlife in the seas and oceans since leaving Grimsby, but this was something truly special. Most people will spend a lifetime having never seen these awesome creatures, and here I was witnessing a whole pod. I felt hugely privileged. These stately, beautiful animals are at the top of the aquatic food chain and I counted about eight adults and two calves as they glided majestically past on their annual journey south.

The sea was so clear it was easy to see their powerful black and white bodies surge through the water, their distinctive large dorsal fins slicing through the tranquil surface. Stood there, I realised my camera was back in my cabin, but no way was I leaving the deck; the images would have to be etched in my brain, rather than on film. The silence was broken by a quiet "Wow" to my left; two other guys had come onto the deck and all three of us were so engrossed and mesmerised by what we had just seen that none of us had noticed the presence of each other.

Our progress south came to something of an unexpected halt as we approached the ten-mile gap between Renaud and Larrouy Islands; the sea ice was firmly blocking our way. The following couple of days were spent trying to navigate east around Renaud Island and more sea ice in order to get to Adelaide Island, on whose south-west side Rothera lay, but our destination was still more than 200 kilometres away, and our efforts met with little success. Antarctica had erected its first major hurdle.

Damoy Hut, Wiencke Island

Following our failed attempts to get through the sea ice south of Faraday and head on down to Rothera Base at Adelaide Island, a Twin Otter had flown up from the base to check the area around our location to see if the ice was breaking up, or if there were any open patches of sea within our vicinity that we could try and head for. Unfortunately, the pilots reported back that the sea ice looked quite solid for many miles to the south. After spending most of the day waiting around to see if the wind and current would shift the ice, the Captain and Pete made the decision to retrace our route and head north to a place called Damoy Hut on Wiencke Island, part of the Palmer Archipelago. Damoy is situated in a beautiful sheltered bay on the north west of the island, looking across to the dramatic mountains and glaciers of Anvers Island.

There is an old 'summer only' research hut situated there which is occasionally used by visiting scientists, at the rear of which is an elevated plateau with a reasonably flat area about eighty metres wide and three hundred metres long, sloping slightly downhill to sheer ice cliffs that drop vertically down to the sea about 50 metres below. The plan was to unload all the Rothera kit from the ship onto the island, move it by skidoo to the plateau, where we would then mark out and flatten a makeshift ski-way on the narrow plateau for the planes to land and ferry us all and the kit down to Rothera. As with all plans in Antarctica, one has always got to have an 'adopt and adapt' approach and be prepared to formulate contingency plans at short notice; once again, mother nature was definitely calling the shots. The other thing I was not so sure about was how keen the pilots would be on using such a limited runway, especially with the sudden drop into the sea at the far end. As expected, when we got news of the change of plan, everyone engaged with things enthusiastically, it just seemed to be the nature of all those on board to get stuck into tasks without hesitation. One positive aspect of our situation was that the *Biscoe* was now anchored in a bay that was really calm with only a few ripples on the surface; loading cargo down from the boat with the crane into the Rigid Raider and ferrying it ashore was a walk in the park compared to the chaos I had experienced back at Husvik when trying to hook up the craft while alongside the *Biscoe* in those big swells. As the ship was approaching the entrance to the bay, I was stood at the bow when I noticed a small sailing yacht anchored within the bay at the west side, this was a strange sight indeed in these waters. Having not sighted another vessel for many days, seeing a small yacht in such a remote location was highly unusual and I feared the worst as it sat motionless in the water. My fears were unfounded; the noise of our approaching large vessel and the slight wave it generated towards the yacht brought the craft to life and a chap appeared on the deck. He was about two hundred metres away, so we couldn't really make out his facial features but he waved towards the ship and did not appear to be in any kind of distress at all. I, for one, was certainly intrigued as to who this could be.

The *Biscoe* anchored in the bay about a hundred metres from the landing point where Damoy Hut was situated. It was a one room building and could sleep up to eight people on basic wooden bunks; I was very quick to volunteer as one of the shore party that would start unloading all the relevant kit from the *Biscoe* and also move into Damoy Hut. It had been an amazing experience on the ship and I could have stayed there for a couple more days until everything was unloaded for the aircraft to ferry to Rothera; however, the next part of the journey beckoned. Over the next two days, we offloaded all the equipment and provisions that were to be transported by Twin Otter from the makeshift ski-way we were to make up on the narrow plateau above the hut, down to Rothera Base, some 400 kilometres further south. It turned out to be great fun getting everything ashore; the weather was really favourable, sunny and only a few degrees below freezing with hardly any wind. The bay was lovely and calm, so there were no shattered skulls in the Raider as kit was lowered down on the crane. There were also two old skidoos that had been stored under tarpaulins at the rear of the hut through the winter months so, using a Nansen sledge brought ashore from the ship, we ferried all the boxes and equipment to a designated storage area just by the hut. The sledges are named after Fridtjof Nansen, the Norwegian scientist, explorer and humanitarian, their four-metre length can carry just over 450 kilogrammes in weight and they have been used in the polar regions since Nansen's expeditions in the 1890s; their strong, flexible, lashed wood construction produces a sled which is effective at cushioning shocks and which flows relatively smoothly over uneven surfaces.

At the end of the first day, we noticed the chap from the yacht we had seen in the bay had moved his boat much closer to shore and was now anchored just twenty metres from a rocky outcrop near the hut. He rowed ashore in his small inflatable dinghy and, as we were the first people he had seen in over seven months, he was understandably excited and giddy as we greeted him with handshakes and smiles. I invited him into the hut for a cup of tea which he enthusiastically agreed to and, as we sat on the old rickety stools for a chat, he introduced himself as Amyr from Brazil. He had a weather-beaten face, sparkly eyes and a permanent grin, probably caused by his being overjoyed at his first human interaction for such a long time. I was really interested to find out his story, but had only just got talking when Bruce came into the hut to tell me I was needed outside, I quickly finished my cuppa and gave my apologies to Amyr as he followed me out of the hut door. When we were saying our goodbyes, he invited Bruce and I to come across to his yacht later for some food and a proper conversation, we gladly agreed.

While Bruce and I sat on the yacht eating some delicious food that had been designed by a specialist Brazilian company specifically for his trip, Amyr Klink shared with us the story of how he had ended up here in Dorian Bay. He had spent all his adult life getting involved in adventures, mostly sailing the oceans. However, about six years previously he set himself the challenge of rowing single-handed across the Atlantic Ocean in his self-built boat 'I.A.T.' This journey, from Namibia on the west coast of Africa to the east coast of his home country of Brazil had never been undertaken before, but after many epic adventures and near misses, he successfully completed the 3,700-mile trip in 100 days. His safe arrival home really captured the heart of the Brazilian nation and Amyr was encouraged to pen his story of the trip. The book, *Cem Dias entre o Céu e o Mar* (100 Days Between Sea and Sky) went on to become a best seller and hugely popular in Brazil, and was included in the school national curriculum; Amyr used the proceeds to personally design and construct the yacht *Paratii,* inside which we were now sitting. He told us he had been on the *Paratii* for nearly a year, arriving in this part of Antarctica at the end of the last Austral summer, when he deliberately decided to spend the winter months alone here in the secluded and sheltered Dorian Bay, allowing his boat to be set fast by sea ice for nearly six months. Now the weather had warmed and the sea ice melted, his plan was to set sail again soon and explore Antarctica further, then sail north to the Arctic via the west coast of South and North America; I later read in his book *Paratii entre Dois Pólos* (Between Two Poles) that at the end of this trip; he had been afloat for 642 days in total, and sailed approximately 27,000 miles; what an exceptional guy.

Amyr's English was excellent (and far better than our Portuguese) and he had us quite enthralled talking about his ocean adventures; he seemed a very modest guy and I don't think he realised that what he was telling us in his matter-of-fact way, was indeed quite special. The *Paratii* was an example of design excellence; he had built it for lone sailing and it had an elevated seat that was covered by a Perspex dome to allow him to sail at night in a semi-horizontal position so he could look to the heavens and navigate by the stars in good weather. He told us that as much as he liked his electronic navigation systems, what he really enjoyed, and preferred to use, were traditional methods. To keep him active during the winter months when the yacht had become bound solid by the sea ice, he had been using a 'sail board' out on the ice. This was a small windsurfing board that he had adapted back in Brazil to use on sea ice by securing some steel runners (a long version of what you see on ice skates) to the base of the board, with a small mast and sail the same as one would use for windsurfing. While he was telling us about the fun he had whizzing around the perfect icy surface of the bay on dark days and nights lit only by the stars and the moon, my only disappointment was that the bay's sea ice was now melted. I had been a keen windsurfer in the past and Amyr's 'ice surfer' sounded like fantastic fun. He also had some ski-mountaineering boots and a good pair of skis which he had used to walk up and ski down some of the nearby slopes through the dark winter months (wearing a head torch for 'safety'). We didn't ask the obvious question about the consequences of getting injured or falling down a crevasse on his own, hundreds of miles from any help; he was one of those individuals who definitely marched to his own drumbeat. Amyr had even saved a couple of bottles of lovely Chilean red wine for his first encounter with other people after his isolated winter. He hadn't expected a BAS ship to visit the area and thought the first humans he might see would be in the New Year when he might come across a tourist ship further north; meeting some fellow adventurers was a real bonus for him and we certainly didn't present too much of an argument when he offered to crack open the wine.

A couple of hours later as Bruce and I, a tad tipsy, were climbing down into the small inflatable dinghy to head back to the hut, Amyr tried to give us both the ice surfer and his expensive skis, as he told us he would not be using them again. His hospitality and generosity had already touched us, so we both politely declined the offer of his gifts, gingerly rowed the short distance back to the rocks, making sure we did not fall in (which most definitely would have happened had we accepted his bulky gifts). As we climbed out of the dinghy, we waved our thanks to Amyr as he pulled the inflatable dinghy we had just disembarked from back to his yacht on a piece of long chord that was attached to the ship.

By the end of the next day, just about everything that needed to be unloaded from the hut was stored in quite significant piles adjacent to the hut. The next task was to drive the two skidoos up onto the elevated plateau and use them to flatten out and make a 'runway' in the snow. Once again, I jumped at the chance to do this; riding the skidoos was quite novel to me and they were great fun to drive around, I had been a keen motorcyclist when I was younger, although these machines did not present the same easy handling as a big bike, it was a new and enjoyable experiencing blasting through the snow on them. They had sturdy 500cc two-stroke engines that could get them going reasonably fast when the skidoo wasn't fully loaded, but it did take a little bit of practice to get them turning correctly, especially in deeper snow. Bruce was the other volunteer who joined me up on the plateau, which was at an elevation of thirty metres or so, at the top of a slight gradient 200 metres to the rear of the hut. Alongside was Oz, the inbound deputy base commander, who had taken responsibility for overseeing the loading of the aircraft. We all knew that the task ahead was going to be interesting; the de Havilland Twin Otters that were coming up to ferry all the equipment and personnel down to Rothera Base have an empty weight of approximately 3,000 kilogrammes (with all the passenger seats and paraphernalia removed) and a maximum take-off weight of 5,670 kilogrammes.

This meant that every box, crate, carton and person would have to be accurately weighed before loading into the aircraft prior to it taking off. Our first task was to use the skidoos to make a decent runway for the aircraft. This was simple enough as Bruce and I raced up and down the plateau like gardeners on ride along lawn mowers grooming a snow-covered football field. The air temperature was well below freezing, which meant that once we had driven up and down the snow a couple of times, the surface was reasonably firm; this would make take-offs much easier for the pilots as there would be no deep snow clinging onto the skis as the plane hurtled down towards the abrupt termination of our makeshift runway at the ice cliff. Once we had the runway completed, we went back down to the hut to ferry up the first load with both skidoos, each one dragging a 'Nansen' sledge loaded with gear.

Oz had been liaising by radio with the pilot of the first aircraft who was about an hour away from Damoy; we had made the runway as identifiable as possible by placing empty black fuel drums at fifty-metre intervals on either side of the snow we had flattened out, and the weather was calm and sunny so the landing should not present any major problems. What all three of us up on the plateau were a little concerned about was the aircraft taking off on a relatively short runway while fully loaded, with no margin for error; overshooting the runway would have potentially dire consequences. While we were waiting, we had weighed everything using industrial scales, written the calculations down for the pilot to see; this included two nervous-looking passengers, John and Andy, who had walked up to join us, each carrying a small bag of personal belongings (and a perceptible anxious persona); they had earlier been volunteered by Pete to be the guinea pigs on the inaugural flight from the new Damoy 'airstrip'. We could see and hear the aircraft approaching from a few miles out; the two Pratt & Whitney PT6A-27 turboprop engines had a distinctive sound, and the red colour of the aircraft made it stand out against a bright blue sky.

The aircraft's pilot was a guy called Neil. It was his first season with BAS but we had already heard that he was a great flyer who didn't shy away from a challenge; the plane dropped down to a few hundred feet from sea level as he grew closer to the plateau. He looked confident as he touched the skis down nice and gently on the snow surface then put the brakes and reverse thrust on as he hurtled up the slope towards where we were, turning around in a tight circle to come to a halt perfectly at the spot where we had all the equipment stacked. We watched Neil climb out of his seat and walk back down inside the aircraft to jump out of the rear door with a big smile and an enthusiastic, "Hello chaps, what's on the menu today?" Flying with him was

Dave, the current mechanic from Rothera, who had acted as co-pilot for the trip up. I took an instant liking to the pair of them due to their beaming smiles and happy demeanour; I also think Dave was smiling because, other than the pilots and his fellow wintering base colleagues at the base, we were the first people he had seen following the long winter months at Rothera.

Oz and Neil went through all the calculations as we stood by chatting, but I was also listening in to what Neil's attitude was towards the task ahead, I was quite impressed with his approach as he enthusiastically just said to Oz, "No worries, I'm happy with all that, let's get the show on the road!" They were certainly accurate about him having a 'can do' attitude.

What he did do, as Bruce and I were loading up with Dave, was to walk with Oz down towards the end of the runway we had marked out (Bruce and I had also checked the area closer to the cliff edge to see if there were any apparent crevasses, but it looked clear). Neil then estimated the distance from where the plateau ended at the ice cliffs, back up to a point on the runway that would allow a long enough stopping distance should the pilots need to abort the take-off. They took a red spray paint can and Neil marked out a line running at a right angle across the white runway. This would be the point of no return; i.e. the last point that the pilot could apply the brakes and stop on the snow before dropping off the cliffs into the sea. As they arrived back at the aircraft, Neil smilingly referred to this point as, "The red line of doom."

Once all the equipment was loaded securely into the aircraft, Neil and Dave climbed in and scrambled over all the kit to get through the narrow gap at the front of the fuselage and take their seats in the cockpit. The two 'volunteers' then climbed up the steps and looked for a comfortable spot atop the cargo; the inside of all the BAS Twin Otters are stripped bare to accommodate field equipment, consequently there is no seating, so one has to create it from whatever kit is lying around; forget about safety belts or harnesses.

As I went to close the door, I looked at John and Andy sat in their makeshift seats on packing cases and gave them a jovial smile and a "Good luck, lads" wish.

"Cheers," John replied, but with a sarcastic smile. Andy was just looking at the floor and didn't respond. Bruce, Oz and I then walked up to the side of the aircraft alongside where Neil was seated; as we stood just beyond the wingtips, he opened his window slightly and we gave him the thumbs up that the aircraft was secure.

With a huge smile and a "Yeehaw!" which we could just make out over the noise of the two idling propellers, he responded with his own thumbs up and we could see his arm reach up and thrust the power levers forward onto full throttle. The propellers screamed into life and the aircraft slowly edged forward, their action blasted the surface snow violently behind it as it picked up speed and hurtled down the ski-way away from us. As we squatted down on the snow, shielding our faces from the driving spindrift, something told me that Neil had no intention of easing off and hitting the brakes at the 'red line of doom'. As the snow from the propellers' draft eased off a little, Oz, Bruce and I stood up and watched silently while the aircraft bounced and careered down our runway; we could see he was going for a first-time take-off because we could easily make out the noise of the engines, unrelenting at full throttle. Neil tore over the red line in the snow a few hundred yards from us and I think my heart stopped for a second as the aircraft dropped off the lip of the ice cliff and momentarily went out of sight, the engine noise now also muffled due to the ice cliff being between it and us, until suddenly it re-appeared, climbing safely away from the sea surface.

There was a simultaneous trio of audible sighs and gasps of relief from where we stood as we caught sight of the plane climbing up from the sea, not to mention a couple of "Crazy fucker" comments; I can only imagine what it must have been like for the two guys in the back who would have undoubtedly been looking forward from where they were sat inside of the aircraft, out through the gap between Neil and Dave through the cockpit window as the plane was speeding off the end of the runway. It was daunting to realise that this was something I would be experiencing tomorrow.

The rest of the day continued with three other aircraft arriving to load up and experience our unique runway. Some pilots were more apprehensive than others; none had a similar approach to Neil, who came back for another load, smiling and chatting enthusiastically. One chap insisted on painstakingly going through all our calculations before accepting the aircraft was the correct weight for take-off, which was fair enough, I suppose, but he did appear a tad twitchy about the whole situation. As he hurtled down the runway on his first take-off attempt, the three of us took bets on what might happen as the aircraft approached the 'red line of doom'; my prediction of a 'bail-out' was perfectly timed as we heard the roar of the engines being put into reverse just before crossing the line. The pilot taxied back up, turned the plane around, and against our diplomatic advice, he insisted on taking a few boxes out; this happened a second time and then a third, until finally the throttle remained on full power as he went over the line and then the ice cliff, unnervingly for all (particularly the occupants) dropping out of sight, then reappeared rising up from the sea. I would have really liked to see the faces of his three passengers, although they stayed quiet enough during the two unloading kerfuffles, they had looked distinctly anxious when we closed the doors for the third attempt.

My time eventually came. Fortunately, there was only about 700 kilogrammes of cargo to be loaded onto the aircraft, plus me, Bruce and Oz, so we were well below the maximum take-off weight. Another great bonus was that as we saw the incoming Twin Otter approach and land, we realised it was Neil who was sat in the cockpit; we were all reassured that there would be no hesitation crossing his 'red line of doom'.

The *Biscoe* was waiting in the bay until the last aircraft had successfully taken off, we had secured Damoy Hut and said our farewells to Amyr, who had rowed ashore in his dinghy. He was planning to set off the following day and left us with a firm handshake and a huge smile; he was quite a unique character. We closed the cabin doors and made ourselves as comfy as possible on the boxes and cargo; I was about halfway down the aircraft and picked a spot on the left-hand side in order to look out of the window onto the coastal mountains and glaciers. I saw Neil through the gap in the cabin thrust the throttles fully forward with his right hand. The engines revved into full power and we careered down the runway, the ground racing past as I looked out of the window. I saw the red line flash past below us and then we were airborne, well before the ice cliffs. Bruce, Oz and I looked at each other in the cabin as we climbed steadily, all sporting a wry smile; it had been an interesting two days.

Photographs

Lemaire Channel

Elephant Seal, Husvik

Paratii, Damoy

Adelie Penguins Damoy

Twin Otter on makeshift runway at Damoy

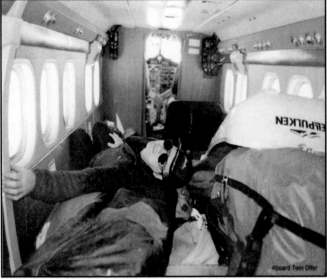
Aboard Twin Otter

5. Rothera Research Station

Due to my arriving on the last aircraft from Damoy, there was not a great deal of equipment left to ferry from the ski runway on the large glacier known as the Wormald Ice Piedmont, down to Rothera Base. The trip from Damoy had rewarded me with incredible scenery as I sat atop a large crate, my face pressed against the fuselage window, eyes wide in awe at the spectacular coastal mountains down to the east, leading up to the huge white glaciated plateaus which stretched into the far distance. The aircraft made an excellent landing up on the ice runway, which was about a hundred metres above Rothera Station's elevation, fortunately there was a large 'Sno-Cat' tractor waiting for us so we had a relatively luxurious journey, travelling the three miles down to Rothera inside a warm and cosy cabin.

I had seen Rothera Base from above as we flew over it prior to landing, so I had a general idea of its size and location. There had been twenty-two guys 'over-wintering' there; however, once all the summer staff arrived this number would rise to nearly one hundred people. The chap who drove us in on the Sno-Cat was Steve, a smiling Mancunian with a dry sense of humour who I took an instant liking to. It was his second summer on the station working as the base electrician, having spent the winter months maintaining everything electrical there. On the journey down to the base on the glacier, we passed below a spectacular 'saw tooth' series of cliffs called 'Reptile Ridge'. This dramatic ridge, with its numerous jagged peaks, eventually petered out as it reached the ice cliffs and, after following the well-worn snow tracks beneath it, we turned left to follow the route down a three-hundred-metre-long slope which led to the research station. This comprised of three main buildings and various smaller outer buildings, and was built on a large, relatively flat, rocky outcrop, probably covering about eight acres in size. The base was kept in good condition and the buildings looked reasonably modern. The central building was the largest, it was a two-storey structure which housed science labs on the ground floor, with the accommodation, dining room, kitchen and small bar on the upper floor; the control/radio room was also in an elevated position on this floor, allowing an excellent vantage point out across the base. This building also had a basement area which comprised of separate bays where food was stored, plus non-combustible equipment in other sections. The second largest building was the equipment store which lay just fifty metres to the west of the main building, all the field gear was kept here, it also housed the generator. One striking aspect of the buildings was their sturdy construction, this was a mixture of prefabricated panels, timber and steel; the entrance door of the main building was extra thick, with a two-door system, the second door about two metres inside the first, this was to protect the interior from the harsh conditions that the Antarctic winter would present.

Rothera Base was a hive of activity when we arrived in the mid-afternoon; introductions to both the wintering staff and new arrivals was done 'on the hoof' as everyone mucked in to get all the equipment and supplies to their appropriate location. Once all of this had been stored away, we put our personal kit into the small rooms in the accommodation section. These were reasonably comfortable, fairly small and cosy with a double wardrobe and a chest of drawers, the two-foot square triple glazed window looking out onto the front area of the base; I was sharing with Mike, who had travelled down with me on the *Biscoe*, so there was no requirement for any 'getting to know each other' sessions.

Arriving on the base gave me a new sense of excitement and a feeling that the real work for which I had applied for was now starting. The journey down had proved to be an amazing adventure in its own right; however, now I was keen to get into the day to day activity on the base and prepare for some field work. One thing I had noticed when we disembarked from the Twin Otter up on the glacier, was that the temperature down here was colder than at Damoy a few hundred miles further north, although saying that, it was still only about minus 15C which is not overly cold for the Antarctic; I felt sure there would be colder times ahead. What became quickly apparent after a couple of days spent getting familiar with station layout and the field equipment was that everyone was required to get involved with all the required tasks around the base, regardless of their actual job title; there was certainly no room for egos and prima donnas were soon brought down to earth. This meant that, other than the base commander and his deputy who were both great and never came across as authoritarian, there was no real sense of hierarchy, and I thought this arrangement created a community spirit with people mucking in whenever asked. However, one of the least popular or enjoyable jobs to be allocated on a rota basis was referred to as 'gash day'; this entailed supporting the chef in the preparation of all meals, setting out tables throughout the course of the day, washing up the dishes of nearly a hundred people after each meal, getting rid of all the waste and then cleaning the kitchen and dining room at the end of the day. Seeing one's name on the 'gash' rota caused the occasional quiet grumble, causing some staff to mutter, "I didn't come down here to clean a bloody kitchen."

'Gash' is an old Royal Navy term describing rubbish and was one of many terms used around the base and in the field; a term that was particular to Rothera and BAS which I was not overly fond of was 'jingly janglys'. This was used to describe the combined equipment one has attached to one's harness when out in the field – karabiners, slings, figure of eight devices, ascenders and jumars, etc – and was born from the noise the kit made when hanging off your climbing harness; interestingly none of the staff with a mountaineering background used it (including myself... largely because it sounded like something children in a blooming nursery might say!)

There was one aspect of base life in which nearly everyone tried to get involved to some degree or other during their time at Rothera; the base Huskies. These dogs had been introduced in the 1960s and were originally used as 'mushing' teams to transport scientists, field assistants and sledges out into the mountains and glaciers to undertake the research projects. Since the advent of the Skidoo motorised toboggans though, the dogs had become redundant. Even so, they remained on the base and were now used for recreation and played a significant role in maintaining positive moral, particularly for those staff that remained at the base through the winter months. The dogs were beautiful animals, much bigger than the Huskies one sees in Canada and Alaska, which generally have leaner physiques; the Rothera dogs had evolved through the very harsh climate on the Antarctic base and so their physiques had developed to cope with their environment, their bulky bodies resembling that of a large Rottweiler in stature and size.

The dogs were fed food which was often frozen due to its being left outside on pallets, which did not deter them in any way at feeding time; their jaw strength was so impressive that they would enthusiastically crunch through the food at feeding time, regardless of it often being in a frozen state. The sixteen or so dogs lived outside most of the time, hence their having evolved with much thicker coats. They were all in great shape due to base staff taking them out of an evening to run them on the snow, which they appeared to be born to do, as they absolutely loved it. They were kept tethered out on a steel cable about eighty metres away from the base, just next to a bay, each a little out of biting distance from the next dog; although they were very gentle with humans when being handled, they would certainly have a rumble and tear into each other from time to time, occasionally requiring the base doctor to adopt his vet's persona to stitch the odd bite wound. At evening feeding time, I would take great pleasure in going out to feed them with one of the guys who had tended to them through the winter and so knew them well; after they had eaten and calmed down, we would sit and slowly interrupt the quiet by making howling noises, cupping our hands to our mouths, leaning back and doing our best imitation of a wolf. Within a minute, the whole pack would be sitting back with their heads pointed to the sky enthusiastically joining in with us. The raucous clamour which this created, of a wolf-like choir at its best, never failed to make the hairs on the back of my neck stand on end; a transcendent experience indeed.

One particular task on the base that some people loved, and others loathed, was the role of co-pilot. This was in name only, as the de Havilland Twin Otter aircraft that is used to deploy teams into the field is a twin turbine plane that has two seats in the cockpit; for safety reasons the pilot had to have someone sitting in the other seat, regardless of their lack of flying qualifications. Should there have been an airborne emergency, I'm not so sure a cook, carpenter or mountaineer would understand the complex-looking control panel in front of them, but we would certainly have given it a try! Each morning, the pilots would come into the base canteen and ask for volunteers to co-pilot; the flights were generally to go further south into the mountains to build fuel caches for the season ahead, or to deploy and support field parties during the season. Those sat having breakfast who did not like flying would not look up when they heard the request for volunteers, their gazes remaining firmly focused down onto their toast or cornflakes to avoid eye contact with the pilots, like children being asked by a teacher, "So who drew the silly picture of me on the blackboard?"

Like others who loved these mini adventures into the field, I would shout out "Yes!" and then stuff the toast hurriedly in my mouth, getting up from my chair so as not to miss out on one of the seats; each to their own, I guess, but I knew how beautiful the scenery was while out flying, regardless of the nerve endings getting a little frayed during the scary take-off and landings on snow. My co-piloting duties were mostly flying south to drop fuel caches, stores and equipment at Fossil Bluff transit station on Alexander

Island, about 400 kilometres away, which entailed flying over breath-taking scenery on the way down.

Prior to leaving the base for my trip onto the Dyer Plateau, I was fortunate enough to bag a co-pilot seat for a short trip further south down the Antarctic Peninsula to drop off a part that was required by a field party to repair a damaged track on one of their skidoos. Although it was a relatively short round trip of about two hundred and fifty kilometres, I was immediately hooked on this very novel role. Approaching the glacier where the two-man team were camped was a fantastic and exciting experience; their camp lay towards the end of a remote valley, surrounded by spectacular dark, jagged peaks, some with blueish white hanging glaciers on their flanks, a clear blue sky above giving a beautiful contrast to the vista below. The pilot, Andy, flew over their tent at speed when we initially flew into the valley, this was to let them know we had arrived, but also appeared to be a bit of fun as we had descended low and hurtled over the site and 'buzzed' them at only 20 metres or so above the tent. Andy then turned the aircraft around in a tight arc, headed back down the valley, before coming back up the slightly sloping glacier, demonstrating fine judgement in descending and landing on this surface because the approach in showed us there was a lot of heavy crevassing only a few hundred metres from their site. Following a quick chat with the two guys, taking off from the glacier was equally, if not more, exhilarating, the Twin Otter charging down the glacier, bouncing on the hard, icy surface, the cliffs around us racing past my peripheral vision, before lifting off and climbing into the cloudless sky, with the dangerous-looking crevasse field directly below us, probably just a hundred metres from where we had lifted off.

6. The Field Diary

The Dyer Plateau

The bulk of my season was spent working on the Dyer Plateau. This area of Antarctica was first explored on land and photographed from the air by the US Antarctic Service (USAS) from 1939–41. It was named after J. Glenn Dyer, a surveyor with the then United States General Land Office, Department of the Interior. He was leader of the USAS surface party that sledged from Fleming Glacier southeast across the plateau to the Welch Mountains. While working on the Plateau, I kept a diary, the following field diary comprises of the entries made each evening or the following day (in italics), followed by a retrospective analysis after having time to reflect on events.

Tuesday 27th November: Rothera Base

8:00 am The Dyer Plateau was going to be an interesting challenge, it is at an elevation of more than 6000 feet, and similar in size to Wales, and Asti and I were going to be the only people there, the ice below us ranged in depth from 1000 to 3000 feet. The glaciology team, who worked there the previous season to extract the ice cores, had reported experiencing some ferocious storms and still air temperatures below minus 30C; they had also reported it to be an amazing place in good weather, a white desert with the tips of coastal mountain peaks barely revealing themselves in the far distance – bring it on!

1:00 pm *Asti and I loaded the plane with all the gear, there's so much kit, and we can't miss a thing, as well as the basic survival gear of tent, sleeping kit, food and fuel, etc., there's all the skidoo and sledging gear – and a bit of scientific kit! We are both giddy and keen to get going, just hoping for decent weather both at Rothera and on the Dyer – bit of a waiting game really.*

The planning for the trip to the Dyer Plateau had taken a few days, all the gear had to be checked and re-checked – then checked again. Asti and I had painstakingly gone through all the kit and felt confident nothing was amiss; it was his second season with BAS so I was hoping to learn a few tips from him. He was from the Scottish Highlands, and a true outdoorsman whose life was dedicated to the mountains, he was quiet and friendly with strong features, a weathered complexion topped by a wild mop of dark hair and I felt sure we would get along fine. I try to have a calm and philosophical outlook on life, and in the short time I had known Asti; he always seemed of a similar disposition, time would tell. As well as the clothing, food, tent gear, sledges, radios, medical kit and scientific equipment, we used 'Skidoos' to travel on the glacier, all the potential spares and fuel calculations we needed for these motorised toboggans also had to be accurate. Good planning was essential; once the aircraft lands on the glacier after a two-hour flight from Rothera, and you and all your kit are unloaded onto the ice, it is definitely 'un-cool' to state,

"Hmm, I think I forgot to load the bloody food boxes." And don't even think about saying, "Did you load my battery powered curling tongs?"

Today, we had been heavily reliant on good weather even to get started. Not only did we need good conditions at Rothera, we also needed to have decent weather hundreds of miles south at the Dyer Plateau. Although the satellites can give reasonable indications of the weather, we had no idea if the visibility or the contrast on the surface snow would be good enough for us to make a landing. The proposed landing area had the extra danger of the hazardous two-metre long glacier poles that were positioned half a kilometre apart by last year's glaciology team over quite a large area. These are virtually invisible against the snow due to their light silver colour – they cannot be dark coloured, as that will attract heat and cause the surface snow around them to melt, giving false data regarding snow accumulation ('ablation' is the appropriate term to use, a learned glaciologist colleague informed me).

If we had weather problems at the glaciology site on the Dyer Plateau and we couldn't land, then we could 'lie-up' at Fossil Bluff transit station until things improved. Even with good weather, I did not share the pilot's optimism about finding, from the air, the single two-metre long bamboo pole with a black flag atop that was the only marker of the underground chamber housing the ice cores – in an area the size of a small country, although we had the grid reference, it still felt quite ambitious! The remote transit station at Fossil Bluff on nearby Alexander Island was manned throughout the summer; it acts as a fuel cache for planes to re-fuel and then carry on to drop teams on deep-field research programmes.

10:30 pm *Good weather at both ends, excited about flying down, nearly 24-hour daylight now so we have plenty of time and decent light to get there – base commander made the decision to fly tomorrow, a bit of an anti-climax but 'c'est la vie'.*

We eventually received confirmation late in the evening that the weather was clear both at Rothera and Fossil Bluff transit station, and possibly at the Dyer Plateau. The guys at Fossil Bluff on Alexander Island gave a reasonable weather report from their position, but this is more than 250 kilometres south-west of our proposed landing site on the Dyer Plateau so was not a cast-iron guarantee of good conditions, but it was the best and only weather report we had available. Asti and I were looking forward to getting our teeth into this project; earlier we had spent a couple of hours eagerly loading all the equipment into the Twin Otter; these twin-propeller aircrafts are the workhorse of Antarctica, the pilots flying them were wilderness experts and had a wide variety of experiences between them. Our pilot was to be Murray, a hardy New Zealander who had flown in wild environments all over the world.

The base commander decided we should fly out first thing the next day, which I thought a strange decision, as we were ready to go and the weather could easily change again; however, I kept quiet and got a good night's sleep on the base for the postponed trip the following day. I remember feeling a degree of anxiety before falling asleep; the Dyer Plateau is very remote and isolated. I was also hoping I would get along with Asti; he is a cool guy but quite reserved; however, we were planning to be there for four to five weeks and it has a reputation for bad weather.

I knew it could be quite a psychological test if we were to become tent-bound for a few days, or even weeks.

This 'isolation' element of working in Antarctica is one that people may not be fully prepared for. Although all of the field assistants had mountaineering experience, and the majority of us would have spent periods of time stormbound in tents (some more time than others), this unique experience of being confined within a small space while horrendous weather relentlessly batters the walls of the tent, nearly always keeping the occupants from sleeping, takes some getting used to. Maintaining group harmony under these conditions requires a certain degree of emotional discipline; an ordinarily trivial mistake such as putting sugar into someone's tea who doesn't take it can be surprisingly amplified when in cramped spaces for days on end: "Just like I said yesterday, and the day before, NO FUCKING SUGAR!"

The psychology of isolation, particularly in cold environments, is an interesting topic and I'm sure there is a lot of scope for academic research on the subject; however, to undertake an authentic field study of significant duration, in somewhere extreme like a remote part of Antarctica, would likely cause the researching scientists as many problems as the participants they were studying. I can imagine the potential newspaper headline if such an intensive study were undertaken and things went a little wobbly: "A psychology scientist was sectioned under the Mental Health Act and returned to Britain last week after being extracted from a remote Antarctic mountain range at the halfway point of a three-month deep field research experiment which was studying the effects of isolation; one of the mountaineers who was a case study for the research team was overheard speaking about the incident, 'The professor just walked out of his tent naked one morning into the snow, saying he was going to watch the new Bond film at the Bradford Odeon and was really looking forward to some popcorn while viewing the spy-centred blockbuster; he didn't look very well, and not that warm judging by his frosty demeanour, mind you, it was minus 24C at the time.' The professor's university was unavailable for comment." Joking aside, there were many scientists going out into the field who had never even been camping; I suspect this leads to a few rude awakenings.

Wednesday 28th November: Rothera/Dyer Plateau/Fossil Bluff

1:00 am Currently sat on a rock looking out across the Sound, can't be a long entry as it's quite cold and the fingers are already packing in, about minus 15C, I reckon. We eventually got underway at lunchtime and flew down towards the Dyer, spectacular scenery across the Marguerite Bay and the coastal mountains, George VI Ice Shelf looking chaotic as it hits the bay. We headed up onto the Dyer and spent a while trying to locate THE FLAG, flying low at stall speed, the weather turned a bit crap and finding the location really is like a 'needle in many haystacks' – mission aborted. Decided to head across to Fossil Bluff, landed on a very hard and icy runway, bounced a lot but fortunately in a straight line! – awesome pilot. While heading to the hut on skidoos, we were buzzed by Neil in another plane at about 20ft, nearly knocked our blooming heads off at full speed – that's one crazy pilot. I cooked a curry in the hut – with dehydrated meat granules, always an interesting challenge! Great to see the other guys who are heading out into the field, decided to sleep out in the caboose – fantastic view across the Sound to the Batterbee Mountains – somewhere up there is our landing site, hopefully get there tomorrow, mixed feelings of excitement and adventure, but some trepidation creeping in – relax, it will be great!

Asti and I had breakfast in the relative luxury of Rothera's canteen; this would be our last decent cooked breakfast for a while, so we both over indulged. The base was its usual hive of activity with scientists and staff busying themselves for the season ahead. We had time to have one last look at the gear inside the Twin Otter before we jumped on board with our 'P-bags', these oversize stuff sacks contain one's sleeping bag and survival kit, and field staff never go anywhere without it!

It was 1:00 pm when the plane eventually took off from the ski-way on the glacier above Rothera. As we climbed steadily up to about 3,000 metres, I settled back and laid on top of all the gear for the two-hour trip south. We left the safety of Rothera Base and headed out over an iceberg strewn sea known as Marguerite Bay. The inside of the cabin was stripped bare to accommodate the field gear, including two eight-feet 'Nansen' sledges and two skidoos, so we tried to get as comfy as possible on top of all the kit (ensuring a window seat of course!) Staring out of the aircraft window provided me with an incredible view, a beautiful blue sky which met a distant pure white landscape peppered with dark, protruding jagged rock, and then led closer to spectacular mountain ranges with huge crevasse-laden glaciers slowly edging into the bay below us.

I felt quite emotional viewing the amazing scenery all around, and the images that flooded my brain induced a wonderful feeling of euphoria, a sensation that has often overcome me when I have seen natural landscapes, and I am sure I am not alone. I remember being in Yosemite National Park for the first time with Rob Scott, an old college pal from Edinburgh, as we undertook a rock-climbing road trip along with a few other friends; Rob was equally passionate about the mountains; he had been to Yosemite several times and was always enthusing about the place. As we arrived late in the evening, it was dark and I couldn't see much except the tree-strewn valley floor and the dark-looking Merced River meandering through the centre of the valley. Early the next morning, we awoke from our VW campervan, which we had parked overnight in a layby just off the narrow tarmac road that looped around the valley floor (strictly speaking, against Yosemite's camping 'rules'). After a quick coffee made on a small camping stove, Rob insisted on us walking out into the 'meadow' in the middle of the valley just as the morning sunlight began to cut diagonally through the tops of the tall California black oak trees and the ponderosa pines in shafts of misty light. With my eyes looking only at the grassy floor as we walked (as instructed by Rob), he said, "This is the only way to see Yosemite for the first time."

Then, when we reached the central point, away from the view obscuring trees we stopped and Rob quietly instructed me, "Ok mate, look up." I did as I was told, then looked up some more, to see the enormous eastern rock walls of light granite called Cathedral Rocks that reached up into the sky. The euphoria was rising inside me as Rob added calmly, "Now turn around." I did so slowly, catching my breath as I gazed in a kind of shocked state at one of the most amazing rock faces on the planet; the gigantic granite monolith of 'El Capitan', which rose almost vertically a thousand metres into the crisp morning sky. My mind was filled with such a wondrous feeling, and after the momentary stunned silence, I just felt myself laugh out loud, almost maniacally as elation overcame me. I felt unable to say anything remotely profound, or anything that could reflect how I was feeling and I recall the only words I eventually spoke were, "Holy shit".

"Thought you would appreciate that view, buddy," smiled Rob, who had a grin on his face like a Cheshire Cat that had just gulped down a pint of cream. It was only then I noticed that about a dozen other people had arrived in the meadow and were viewing the same things in the early morning light, all looking up in awe, some also swearing at the outrageous beauty of it, others shaking their heads in disbelief; these were kindred spirits indeed.

Now I was sat in a small aircraft some 16,000 kilometres further south with another such amazing view in front of me, once again feeling uplifted at such breath-taking landscapes; I genuinely felt privileged and humbled to be in such a place. Below us, the sea suddenly met the glacier of the King George VI Ice Shelf which occupies much of King George VI Sound. The glacier is a floating ice shelf wedged between Palmerland on the Antarctica Peninsula on the east, and Alexander Island on the west. Its depth varies from 100–400 metres and it is approximately 40 kilometres across at the snout and 350 kilometres long, with the deep sea channel running below. Huge football-field-size tabular icebergs and giant seracs were slowly carving off into the sea at the snout of the glacier (unknown to me at this point, we would have to make an emergency crossing of this glacier in a few weeks' time – thankfully further south and away from the glacial chaos below). After one-and-a-half hours in this awe-inspiring landscape, the plane banked away from the glacier below, and with the transit station of Fossil Bluff still further south, we began heading east up over the coastal mountains towards the plateau. It was time to start working!

Asti and I squeezed through the gap between the cabin and the cockpit and surveyed the ground below, also in the cockpit was Dave who had flown with us from Rothera as 'co-pilot'; he was actually a mechanic, but every flight had to have a second person in the cockpit for safety reasons. I was to do this on numerous occasions while at the base; some of the more enthusiastic pilots would give intensive flying lessons and I amassed about 40 hours flying time, graduating to a point where I could take control of the aircraft just after it left the snow on take-off, and just before it touched down on landing – the tricky bits indeed! (this could never be officially logged as I was not registered to fly an aircraft). As we levelled out with the mountains dropping away behind us, a white desert extended in front of us as far as the eye could see until finally it met the light blue sky and protruding mountain peaks on the distant horizon – the Dyer Plateau!

Once we were above the grid reference where the ice core depot was reputedly buried, Murray began flying at stall speed in a grid pattern about 150 metres above the surface of the snow. Asti and I went back into the cabin and took our places looking out of the windows on opposite sides of the aircraft. We scanned in every direction, peering at the white blanket below us, vainly trying to catch sight of the small black flag which topped the two-metre bamboo cane; my earlier cynicism about the success of this search seemed to be being realised. The weather was starting to close in; the plateau is about 1800 metres above sea level and cloud was beginning to form. After another 20 minutes of zig-zagging around without success, Murray, Asti and I decided to abort the trip and head over to Fossil Bluff transit station and drop us off there; we would fly back tomorrow when the weather would hopefully have improved - 'like a needle in a haystack' seemed a very apt analogy at this point, not a great start to the project. I felt a little emotionally deflated at not achieving the first part of our goal; my excitement levels had obviously been quite high at the prospect of landing up on the desolate Dyer Plateau. But strangely, I also felt slightly relieved. I puzzled for a while over these polarised feelings and concluded that the anxiety about what awaited us on the Dyer must have been strong enough to induce some 'flight' emotion.

We flew back over the mountains, down across the 30 kilometre wide frozen sea channel towards Fossil Bluff and negotiated our landing on the makeshift glacier runway that was marked out with empty black 45-gallon fuel drums. The plane came to a halt at the edge of the glacier near Fossil Bluff hut after a very rough and bouncy landing due to the snow surface being very hard and a strong cross-wind. Witnessing the pilots keep the plane under control when landing with skis on hard snow always commanded my respect – rather them than me! As we were approaching the 'runway', I imagined the presence of an effeminate cabin crew member, the ones you often find on 'bucket airways', voicing an alternative script through a squeaky microphone to passengers just prior to landing: "Okay ladies and gentlemen, can you please return to your seats, ensure your seatbelt is fastened… Oh, you haven't got either, your tray table is stowed away, hmmm… oh dear, and any baggage is placed under you, well we have that at least!… Oh, and one more point I need to raise, we are landing on a rock-hard glacier, on skis in a strong cross-wind, and you are likely to bounce around like a ball in a pinball machine, so please use the sick bags, and maybe prepare to soil your underwear. Thank you very much. Please enjoy your stay at Fossil Bluff and do fly with us again".

We unpacked essentials from the plane for the overnight stay and Murray radioed Rothera, who agreed that he and the aircraft could stay with us for the night and make a further attempt at the Dyer tomorrow.

Asti and I helped tether the plane down to the glacier surface using six-foot long snow-stakes; the previous season a pilot and field team had been a bit relaxed and decided not to tether their plane down one evening due to the settled weather at the time. However, (isn't it funny that a 'however' preceded by positives, is invariably followed by negatives and vice versa, e.g. thank you for your excellent job application; however, unfortunately on this occasion, etc, etc) a 'Katabatic' wind picked up during the night and with ferocious gusts tipped the plane upside down before the guys could lash it down with snow anchors. Consequently, it had to be taken apart and boxed up for a flight home – a very expensive 'oops' (at today's prices, a new Twin Otter costs in the region of £4.5 million), but a lesson learned the hard way. 'Katabatic' winds can be extreme in force as the build-up of high density cold air over elevated ice sheets is pulled downwards with enormous gravitational energy through glacial valleys and towards the coast, propelling the winds up to speeds in excess of 300 kmh. There have been occasions when tents have been shredded by ice particles contained in these winds; also instances when they have been blown completely away. This is why the pyramid tents that field parties use do not have sewn-in ground sheets, if we got caught in such a storm, we had to get inside our survival bags with our climbing harnesses on and tether ourselves to snow and ice stakes in case the tent 'goes west', then construct a snow shelter, or abseil down into a crevasse until the storm blew through – not an appealing prospect as some of them have lasted weeks.

As we were driving the skidoos from the landing zone on the glacier to where the Fossil Bluff hut was located, at the base of the mountains about 300 metres away, a second Twin Otter plane that had just dropped off aviation fuel and taken off again, circled back around and 'buzzed us'. There was no sophisticated air traffic control as such in Antarctica, once the planes are out of visual site of Rothera Base, how they fly is entirely up to the pilot. The pastime of 'buzzing' field parties on the ground was a common one among the pilots; there was an unwritten agreement between field staff that we never reported it as it was fun to witness, but obviously very dangerous, especially as the pilots seemed keen to earn the 'closest to the ground' title.

I had previously been 'co-pilot' in an aircraft when the pilot decided to 'buzz' a field party in a glacial valley we had flown into to drop some equipment off for them. Travelling at full throttle twenty metres above the snow can be very exhilarating (and some might say, quite terrifying!) The pilot that buzzed us today was Neil who I had already met while we were up at Damoy, he was previously a commercial 747 airline pilot, but also a stunt pilot and he flew particularly low to the ground (many staff thought he was a little bit crazy, even for an Antarctic wilderness pilot). This evening he was about ten metres from the surface of the glacier as he approached us at full speed, we could even momentarily see his wild smiling face through the cockpit glass as the plane roared towards us; the heavy landing skis were about three metres from our heads as we ducked down and were nearly knocked off the skidoos from the blast of air as he shot directly over us at about 200 kmh in a big red flash – great fun!

Back in the hut, there were two other field parties, along with two additional staff who kept this transit station running through the summer months. Fossil Bluff is a single room hut (with an outside chemical loo); there is bunk space on the walls for about six people (this on a first come-first served basis, so we were on the floor). The hut is built half on the bottom of a rock slope and half on a wooden platform. Its location is spectacular; to the east lies the frozen sea channel in the Sound and the coastal mountains leading up to the Dyer, and directly behind us to the west, and a short walk away, the steeply rising mountains and glaciers of Alexander Island.

I cooked us all a curry (a very basic one with the available ingredients, I have to say, but it's amazing what can be conjured up with meat granules, tinned tomatoes, dried onions and curry powder) and had a good catch up with the other guys who were also waiting for better weather to be dropped at their designated working areas. The mixture of scientists, field assistants and support staff led to great dinner conversation; it was predominantly a male environment save for one female glaciologist who, thankfully, impacted positively on the gender imbalance. People were in great spirits and hugely enthused about the pending field trips, I felt so privileged to be working down here in such an amazing environment; the hardships that undoubtedly awaited us were easily compensated for by the amazing landscapes and natural beauty that surrounded us. There was an emergency shelter called a 'caboose' just next to the base hut which I decided to sleep in rather than on the hut floor, the predicted snoring and curry-induced farts from seven other people would undoubtedly have had an adverse effect on a good night's sleep if I slept inside the hut! The caboose was like a giant-sized coffin, it was built in case the hut was ever destroyed in a fire and would provide emergency shelter – it was a snug fit for one, and I would imagine very 'cosy' indeed for two.

Prior to getting into the caboose and my sleeping bag, I sat for five minutes on a rock soaking up the view. It was about 1:00 am and we still had good daylight; the sun would not set again here until early March next year, it just sat low on the horizon, but the temperature was a 'refreshing' minus 15C. Directly behind me stood the mountains of Alexander Island, and the view in front of me was spectacular. The immense white/blue flat glacier of King George VI Sound stretched about 30 kilometres across the valley to the coastal Batterbee Mountains on the Antarctic Peninsula, the huge Ryder Glacier to the north and McArthur Glacier directly opposite, both with stunning ice falls and enormous crevasse fields as they slowly inched down towards the Sound; beyond them, the stubborn Dyer Plateau.

From where I sat, it was about 2,800 kilometres to the South Pole, at this time there were probably only a few people between me and the staff at Amundsen-Scott Research Station at the Pole itself; some at the US Siple Station on the Ellsworth Land glacier, and maybe some commercial expeditions in the Sentinel Range, attempting to climb Vinson Massif, at 4,892 metres, the continent's highest peak (its first ascent being as late as 1963). The only other people that would be between me and the Pole before winter set in would be a handful of BAS colleagues on field trips. In this remote landscape, my senses were mixed; a feeling of extreme isolation, trepidation, adventure and excitement, and admittedly, an element of anxiety, possibly bordering on fear. I spent a short time analysing why I would be feeling any kind of fear at all, I had been so looking forward to this great adventure for weeks and months before, so I did feel a little puzzled why this was happening; maybe it was the very remoteness of the Dyer Plateau. Was I feeling a little out of my depth? Should a lad from a council estate in Leeds be down here at all? Was I unsure of Asti's abilities in bad weather and conditions? All these questions flashed into my mind, but the doubts didn't linger too long and after 'having a word with myself', I eventually drifted off to sleep in my tomb-like sleeping compartment feeling reasonably confident about the days and weeks ahead.

Thursday 29th November: Fossil Bluff

8:00 am Awoke to a poor weather forecast, I squeezed out of the 'very cosy' caboose (a bit like an oversized coffin really) things looked quite bright across the Sound, but the Batterbee Mountains and the Dyer were cloaked in grey cloud – no flying at the moment. Up and packed all the gear, skidoos and sledges, etc all ready to go the runway, told by Dave that the earliest we could consider flying is 1:00 pm. Dave's role had changed from co-pilot to Fossil Bluff radio operator and 'proprietor' for a few weeks – a much sought-after job by Rothera support staff. Asti asked me if I wanted to go out cross-country skiing on the glacier, I left him to it and headed up the hill behind the hut, a long hard, slog up the scree slope, climbed about 2000 ft to the ridge top, more spectacular views west across Alexander Island, and east across the Sound to the coastal mountains, the crevasse fields are breath-taking. Ran back down the scree to discover no flying to the Dyer today. More crazy low passes from Neil who has dropped another field party off, two field parties went out doing crevasse rescue with their scientists, however, one was called back and gets the nod they can fly south to their work area (lucky buggers) – I waved them off (surprisingly alone). Dave 'the radio man' cooked us all a decent spaghetti Bolognese, a mechanic by trade but loves getting out in the mountains and will stay 'holding the fort' at Fossil Bluff as long as he can, he's a very dry and funny guy, often quoting his life mantra of "never play your joker too early". Headed out with Asti at 7:00 pm to do another big walk behind the hut, loads of exposed scrambling and a great bit of exercise, back at 11:00 pm but bed at 3:00 am, a bit tipsy as Dave had managed to get some beer flown in from Rothera – the sneaky devil!

The weather over the Dyer Plateau had a reputation for being very changeable and quite unpredictable. We were not far above sea level at Fossil Bluff, and the Dyer sat at about 2,000 metres above us; consequently, it presented differing weather conditions. Although Asti gave me the option of heading out on a cross-country skiing trip, I diplomatically informed him that I had already decided on going for a walk up one of the local peaks. Knowing that we were due to spend twenty-four hours a day with only each other's company for a month or so, I was conscious of keeping our relationship harmonious, but I also needed some 'me' time. Also, and a little selfishly, I guess, as a keen landscape and wilderness photographer, I was keen to get up high and take some photographs of the view across the Sound to the coastal mountains and beyond.

It took me a couple of hours to get up a loose scree slope onto the ridge; for anyone familiar with walking up small loose scree, it's definitely 'one step forward, two steps back'; however, the hard exercise felt really refreshing and once on the top I was rewarded with a spectacular view. To the west across the Sound lay the vast array of mountains and glaciers, to the east the outstanding vista of Alexander Island, its rocky peaks and pristine glaciers shimmering in the bright sunlight.

I had an exhilarating 'scree-run' back down to the hut; the leg-aching and frustrating walk up had been relegated to a distant memory as the loose scree cushioned my long strides and occasional leaps down. Running down such a scree slope can be quite dangerous, each leap allows you to land in the loose scree which drops away with the momentum of body weight; however, if there is a solid boulder hidden amongst the small scree, a shattered lower leg was easily a potential outcome. I was also very conscious of the chastisement I might receive from any geologists looking up from the hut, as they rightly frowned upon such activity due to the environmental damage continual scree running can cause to a slope. On this occasion though, I let my childlike excitement overcome any such qualms as I hurtled down the slope, compromising my normal ecological awareness – and my defensive excuse if challenged was that I didn't want to be late for the radio schedule.

Later that day, one of the field parties at the hut was fortunate enough to get decent weather to the south, enabling them to get underway. I helped them load all their kit onto the plane and waved them off. Surprisingly, I did this alone; I was unsure if everyone else was busy; perhaps there was some tension between field parties I had not noticed, or people just couldn't be bothered, which was even more unusual, as by nature the people down here were definitely of a 'can do' mentality. The wisest decision was not to mention it and be glad that I at least had waved the guys off.

Dave our co-pilot/mechanic/radio operator and now newly appointed Fossil Bluff 'manager' was relishing his new role and threw together a rather pleasant spaghetti dish. I hit it off with him on our first meeting back at Rothera; he was a slightly built, prematurely balding guy in his early thirties from north London, mild mannered and friendly, with a dry sense of humour and sharp wit; I also enjoyed his pseudo-philosophical musings, particularly the one about playing the joker early (which no one ever really understood, not even him I imagine!). Dave would stay at Fossil Bluff as long as he could, rather than be back at base on oily mechanical duties. After dinner, Asti and I decided to head out for another trek up the local peaks, mainly to walk the food off (of which we had both consumed too much). I guess we were also mutually aware we would be living off ration packs for a month or so, and savoured the luxury of a 'spag-bol', which was most definitely not on our rations menu. The walk was great and very strenuous; we kept to the scree and rock ridge so didn't need to rope up and as usual we were rewarded with fantastic views on reaching the top. I will never be nonchalant or blasé about such amazing scenery, once again, I felt like I should pinch myself at being so fortunate to be able to look upon such spectacular mountain scenery.

The mountains have been an inspiration to me since the first time I discovered them, but that didn't happen until my late teens after I had started playing rugby, when a teammate told me about the fantastic scenery, and more importantly to me at the time, the great fitness levels you can achieve by walking up hills carrying a rucksack. I had started playing rugby to channel my energy away from getting involved in negative stuff around the estate I grew up in, and specifically to try and stop getting into street brawls. One incident that occurred at my debut game did make my theory about utilising rugby to divert me away from negative stuff seem a tad ironic. The club I joined was Burley Rugby Union Club in Leeds; they played at a reasonable level, had four teams, but also a bit of a reputation for being a 'no nonsense' side.

I was unaware of this prior to my first game; during the second half I was in my delegated position on the right wing, that being a position often allocated to new players to test them out (so that if you were absolutely rubbish it would not have too much of a negative impact on the game). I had managed to have a few runs with the ball without messing up and made some solid tackles on my opposite number, so was reasonably pleased with my debut performance so far. About twenty minutes into the second half, a big fight erupted amongst the forwards after a scrum broke up in the middle of the pitch; the ref was frantically trying to bring things to a halt; the incessant shrill of his overworked whistle didn't appear to be having the desired effect. As I was wondering what to do next, the centre beside me said, "C'mon mate, it's like the Three Musketeers 'ere, one in, all in." And so, with a reluctant sigh, I had to join in the fray. In the end, the fight turned into a full scale brawl, resulting in the referee abandoning the match. As was the norm in rugby, both sides shook hands as they walked off, regardless of the fact that only minutes earlier they had been knocking lumps out of each other; all I could think of as I strolled off the pitch, shaking hands and joking with my opposite number, who moments before I had been wrestling with on the floor, was that I had taken up rugby to stop getting involved in fights. One of the older players in my team who I had confided in about the reason for my taking up rugby, must have sensed my mood and was quick to reassure me that this was not a common thing. This, thankfully, turned out to be true, and full team brawls were indeed a rare event, even at my old club.

At the time of my mountain discovery, I was also involved in amateur boxing at St Patricks Club in Leeds (another 'positive diversion!') and something of a fitness fanatic, training at least twice a day and always keen to push myself even further; one of the lads there also liked hillwalking, and so this, combined with the remarks of my rugby colleague, had made me ponder on getting involved in the mountains in some way. The first weekend I had free I headed up to the Yorkshire Dales and had a wander up Ingleborough, one of the Three Peaks, stupidly putting a few rocks in my old battered rucksack to make things a bit tougher. It soon became very apparent after walking uphill for half an hour at a fast pace, that hillwalking was more than tough enough without the added weight (however, the rocks obviously stayed in the rucksack until I returned to my car which was parked just outside Ingleton village, yes, what an idiot!). The Three Peaks is a challenging Dales walk of about twenty-four miles that many people undertake each year, the other peaks are Whernside and Pen-y-gent. Although the highest peak of Whernside is only 736 metres, the route can often be extremely boggy in places if undertaken in bad weather; I have fond memories of being up to my waist in soggy clinging peat mud when one year I ran the route and thought I was clever taking a slight short cut on a notorious section below Pen-y-gent. With two more peaks to go and no change of clothing, this was not one of my most enjoyable days in the hills.

From that point on, I fell in love with the mountains and never looked back, eventually making the decision to give up my weekend rugby playing, which I really loved and knew I would miss, to concentrate on getting into the mountains to walk and climb; at the time I was also in a relationship with a wonderful girl called Jean and we discovered a mutual love of the mountains together. My mates on the estate did think it was funny when I told them I was heading off to the Lake District for the weekend to go walking rather than into the pubs of Leeds city centre. Another inspiration to get into the hills was advice from my elder brother, Ed, who has been a huge positive influence in my life generally. He joined the Navy aged 17, and I vividly recall all the family tearfully waving him off when he jumped into a taxi to take him to the train station to head south. He had heard in letters from my parents that I had got into mountaineering and would write to me with lots of encouragement to progress with this, as he knew it was such a positive and rewarding pastime, and one which would keep me out of trouble. It was he who also really got me into serious fitness training; after going through his basic Navy training and completing a few years touring the world, he successfully applied to get into the Field Gun Crew and spent many years involved with them; an incredibly fit and tenacious bunch of guys indeed. When he came home on leave, we would be out doing circuit training on the field in front of our terraced house, or sprint training in the steep steps that went onto an inner city dual carriageway flyover, or up the concrete slopes from the subways, both places overlooked by blocks of high rise flats and maisonettes. When my younger brother Damian was old enough, he also joined in.

The locals definitely thought something was wrong with the Curtis brothers; this was not expected behaviour for inner-city youths. Our sprint training in all weathers in the graffiti-strewn subways was in sharp contrast to the antics of some of the younger local youths, who were often down there drinking cider, or the more desperate ones sniffing glue. When I was younger, I would also get up to mischief in the same subways we were now doing sprints and circuit training in. One positive aspect of our being there was that the local population knew they wouldn't be hassled by anyone in the subways if we were around; it certainly wasn't in the best interests of anyone unsavoury to bother older residents using the subways if we were in the vicinity doing sprints and circuit training. We also enjoyed going out and having a few beers together, but he would always insist that we exercise hard prior to socialising, "You have to earn those cold beers, bruv, and they'll taste much better after a good workout." A philosophy I still try and live by today. My late brother Ed was short in size at five feet seven, but huge in stature; a true gent, always smiling and looking for the good in people, and definitely someone who you would want by your side if you got in a scrape. He was such an inspiration and a great role model for both of us (except for the occasion when he and I ended up explaining ourselves to a custody sergeant following an altercation we had with some guys while out having a few beers in the city centre, and then afterwards more worryingly, having to face our mam and dad). Damian and I always wanted Ed to be proud of us, as we were of him; so as well as rugby and the mountains, we became involved in triathlons, mountain

120

marathons, and a heap of other adventure sports. He was also my inspiration to travel globally and experience different cultures.

Arriving back at the hut from our trek at about 11:00 pm, we witnessed Neil indulging in more aerobatics. Although we all collectively held our breaths (and ducked our heads) as he passed the hut with only feet to spare, I had to admit it was a very impressive flying skill indeed – as he headed off north to Rothera, the question of whether he would last the season remained a constant one. As we went inside the hut, we were welcomed by Dave offering us a couple of cold beers, which we were more than delighted about, and very surprised to receive. Alcohol is not normally abundant at Fossil Bluff, for the obvious reason that people needed to be clear headed in such a wild and dangerous environment. Back at the base, people can put in an order for cases of beer and bottles of spirit by radio to a member of staff on one of the research ships, who can then purchase it for them at the Falklands on their way down. Field staff generally don't consume it (well, not in large quantities) until they have returned from their field trips, or at the end of the season. However... Dave had somehow managed to get a few cases of beer and some wine dropped off by Neil (maybe his earlier antics were a pre-celebration 'fly-by?'). Due to the weather forecast not being predicted as favourable for the following day, we all decided to have ourselves a little party and drank and sang into the early hours. Feeling a little the worse for wear, I retired to my sleeping bag at about 3:00 am on the hut floor with my fleece as a pillow. As I fell into a deep slumber from the hard exercise, and quite a few beers, I believe Dave was still having a tipple and amusing people with his anecdotes.

Friday 30th November

6:10 am I woke up to hear Dave running and stumbling around the hut with his finger on his lips whispering, "Shh!" eagerly to those just waking up – he was supposed to be on a 6:00 am radio sched with Rothera which he missed due to him getting a bit hammered until 3:30 am – he's trying to give the weather report, everyone giggling in their bunks at his half-drunk ramblings, very funny indeed, but bizarrely he seemed to make sense?! Still no flights to the Dyer, its high elevation is producing some poor weather, went for a wander on the glacier while the other field parties are 'fine-tuning' their gear. Back in the hut and cooked another curry (lamb flavour meat granules – what a delight!) bed at 10:00 pm but reading Tom Sharpe's 'Riotous Assembly' until 1:30 am – others telling me to stop laughing so loud.

The morning wakeup call of 'desperate' Dave's ramblings were hilarious, I think he had already had a warning back at Rothera about some unruly behaviour and didn't want anything to jeopardise his current duties of looking after Fossil Bluff. The radio schedules were justly seen as an important and key element of the field operations, Dave had been tasked to give an accurate and up to date 6:00 am weather report for Fossil Bluff, in order for the base commander to decide on whether or not to authorise flights there from Rothera. Dave had been awoken by the radio's persistent and rhythmic recital of "Rothera to Fossil Bluff, Rothera to Fossil Bluff" (which immediately made me mentally recall the iconic radio transmission of *Broadsword to Danny Boy* from the classic film *Where Eagles Dare*). These required weather updates were fairly robust and heavy in content: wind speed, surface contrast, cloud cover, type of cloud, height of cloud, wind direction, etc. As you can imagine, this was not something you would expect a half-drunk mechanic from Camden Town to be able to blag his way through. Dave had not even glanced outside the window to see what conditions were currently like; he looked intent instead on 'winging' his way through a weather update as he approached the radio. Those of us who were watching this slow-motion comedy were silently gesticulating to him, "No!" and mouthing, "Look outside first!" To our utter half-awake amazement, he appeared to successfully do it! However, it transpired he just read out last night's weather report which was written on a piece of paper by the radio; and, fortunately for him, it was quite accurate as the weather had not changed a great deal.

Stubborn was definitely becoming a name attributable to the Dyer; once again the cloud was swathing both it and the upper reaches of the coastal mountains and there was no flying. As both Asti and I were sporting a bit of a hangover, we decided against any vertical lung-busting travel and headed out instead on the flat, more welcoming glacier. We roped up just to get used to walking as an 'alpine pair' again. Although our planned trip would not probably entail much footwork and would be predominantly skidoo and sledge travel, we both knew that down in this part of the world, one had to be ready for any eventuality, we therefore thought it would be a good idea to rope up and re-acquaint ourselves in using this very traditional method of travelling on glaciers by foot

Saturday 1st December

10:00 am Bit of a lie in due to me overhearing the weather on the radio sched with Rothera who informed Dave there is no flying today. After some breakfast (which was a luxurious porridge) Asti and I headed on a long trip on the Eros glacier, me in ski-mountaineering boots and Asti in cross-country gear, out for six hours. Fantastic exercise, some nerve-cracking noises as we went over crevasses, the snow also seemed to occasionally slump a few inches at times when we weren't on crevasse bridges, the slump was a few square metres, we were not sure what it was so in true Antarctic spirit, just picked up the speed and hoped for the best! More field parties arrived, mental Neil buzzing people on skidoos again, as good a pilot as he is, it's only a matter of time! Fossil Bluff is becoming more like a main base than a transit station, eight for dinner. Mail from Blighty, lovely letter from Sandra, does get me wondering what am I doing here, I'm sure she understands, letter from Damian, very funny, Viz from my ex Jean, and letters from Annabelle and Gail. Great to receive mail, everyone collects up their mail, then seems to go into a cocoon and a silence descends the room, each having their own thoughts, I guess. Got myself designated as duty chef, again, good blooming job I enjoy it, however, Asti tipped a tin of red kidney beans into a beef curry just prior to me serving, with a warm Highland comment of "There ya go, Con, ya can cook chilli as well, man." Fair point, really. Face feeling really burnt as I go to sleep – factor 50 not working hard enough in the depleted ozone – have to be careful.

When Dave delivered the weather forecast at 6:00 am it was pretty poor and so clear that there was no chance again of getting up to the Dyer, so I decided to make the most of it and have an extended snooze. I also had the pleasure of a wonderful sweet porridge breakfast that Asti had prepared; what sounds like a very ordinary way to start the day back home was surely a luxury down here!

Both Asti and I were keen to keep our fitness levels up to a good standard, so prepared ourselves for a cross-country ski trip up the Eros Glacier. Cross-country skiing is a great form of aerobic fitness training. I had read somewhere that Lasse Viren, the double Olympic Gold winning Finnish middle distance runner, often used this as his out of season fitness training in preparation for the summer athletics season; as Asti and I cranked it up to a sprightly pace, my legs, heart and lungs understood why. During the long slog, we had more than a few anxious moments when the ground we were on seemed to slump, this was an entirely novel experience for both of us; the hard surface snow felt like it dropped for a couple of inches from the pressure of the skis, not just the area I was stood on, but a section of at least two metres across. There did not seem any apparent signs of crevasses (dips, open slots, different coloured surfaces etc.) Consequently, we were slightly perplexed and a little unnerved at times. We poked around with our ski-poles and couldn't feel any open 'space' under the surface, which would be an indication that the ground may give way; after a brief chat, we shrugged our shoulders and cracked on. The next 'slumps' we felt were ignored, but as we speeded up each time, we did hold our breaths in unison. We were roped and well-versed in crevasse escape, so it wouldn't be a major problem if either of us dropped through anything, in fact, it would be ideal on-site refresher training for us both!

After a circular trip of about 18 miles, we arrived back at the Hut to find more field parties had arrived, and also saw a Twin Otter flying like a distressed bird charging predators hungry for its young; this had to be Neil. A couple of the less experienced scientists had been visibly shaken by Neil whizzing over their heads as they approached the Hut. One of them voiced a strong view that the pilot obviously had mental health problems and questioned whether he really should be in charge of a large air plane, never mind being responsible for transporting human cargo; we diplomatically advised him to live with it; I guess we all really enjoyed Neil's antics.

We arrived in the Hut to find most of the current residents had received some mail, kindly dropped off by Neil. A lovely letter from Sandra had me questioning the validity of my presence here; she wrote such kind, sincere and loving words, and always reassured me that she understood why I was down here. However, this was then balanced by her telling me how much she missed me. Once again, I pushed my longing for her to the back of my mind; it was the only thing to do as I needed to be focused on the tasks ahead of us. It was also good to hear from my ex-girlfriend, Jean, who sent me the highly amusing (and very childish I guess) *Viz* comic. We had been together for many years and had travelled extensively culminating in a winter season on the South Island of New Zealand; we had parted company in Christchurch about 18 months ago when I returned to Scotland to complete a year-long outdoor education course in Edinburgh. Our mutual love of mountains and outdoor adventures had bonded us well, however, a 19,000-kilometre gap did not prove healthy for the survival of the relationship. Fortunately, we remain friends, and I retain the utmost respect for the incredible woman that she is. Letters from my brother Damian, sister Gail and an old friend Annabelle from the summer camp in the States were also wonderful to receive, each of them full of a variety of news from back home. An eerie silence descended on the Hut as everyone withdrew into their own world and digested their mail. Although everybody appeared happy to get mail, you could see people's faces hiding other emotions; regardless of the fact that working in the Antarctic tests one's mental strength and requires resilience and inner toughness, we are only human after all and missing loved ones is perfectly understandable.

Once again I volunteered as duty chef. I have always been enthusiastic about cooking, preferring eastern dishes with interesting spices and flavours to traditional English food; even with very limited ingredients I managed to put together an edible meal for the group. Amusingly on this occasion, Asti tipped a tin of kidney beans into the pot just prior to serving, transforming my beef curry into a chilli. Both Asti's face and mine were quite burnt from having been out on the glacier; even with many applications of factor 50 sun cream, one still got burnt. The depleted ozone layer over the Antarctic summer raised the risks so we had to be very aware; prevention rather than cure was the order of the day.

Sunday 2nd December

7:00 am Up early to unload two aircraft, again more low passes by Neil, he even had the other pilot joining in, got photo proof this time, hope it comes out, a few beers from them will guarantee secrecy! Murray flies back to

Rothera with empty fuel drums, I would rather Neil not try and fly us in, that may result in very early retirement, however, I suppose if anyone can land in marginal conditions, it's him!

11:00 am *Chatted with Pete, the base commander at Rothera, he thinks the weather may allow us to get dropped within 60 km of the depot and we can drive in – that should be fun. Light dinner of crackers and cheese (which had a 'best before' date of 1986, but having lived outside below freezing for 4 years, it was fine).*

10:00 pm *Went on a solo climb up onto a ridge at the back of the hut, headwall was a bit tense, front pointing while breaking through the cornice, a nice 1500 ft slide if it went wrong, nimble foot work and plenty of snow down my neck brings success (and relief). Once off the ridge, a fantastic scree run nearly all the way back to the hut, three hours up, twenty minutes down.*

Both Asti and I were up early as we heard an aircraft landing and were keen to be active; unfortunately, it was Neil at the sharp end of the cockpit. Once we had assisted him in unloading the fuel drums, he hastily took off, banked around and did an extremely low pass. Murray had also been notified to return to Rothera and took off behind Neil, followed his flight path and then passed directly over the hut with about five metres to spare; it seemed the flying shenanigans and airborne lunacy are contagious! Murray was now returning to Rothera, resulting in the distinct chance that Neil might fly us up to the Dyer; although this was an unsettling prospect, if anyone could land us there, it was Neil. Many people had commented disparagingly on his crazy flying, but there were also plenty of admirers of his extreme piloting skills (including myself) who had praised his ability to land in extreme conditions, with limited space, and on dubious surfaces.

Much of the day was spent around the hut and checking our equipment. I spoke with Pete, the Rothera Base commander, who thought that the best plan was to fly us to a glacier near a place called Auriga Nunatak, and then drive up overland with the skidoos and sledges to the Dyer to find the depot. The weather high up on the Dyer looked to be unsettled indefinitely; if we could be landed at a lower elevation about 60 kilometres west and make our way up to the depot; we had a better chance of getting the project started. Asti and I agreed that this was the most positive plan; we had been at Fossil Bluff for too long now and wanted to get working. However, the prospect of driving from Auriga up to the Dyer, very likely in poor conditions, was an interesting challenge, and one which we were both quite relishing, but with a certain amount of anxiety.

With my sense of adventure now enthused and alight, I headed off to do a solo climb up the headwall of one of the glaciers behind the Hut. Asti was testing the gear and in particular making sure the skidoos were all set to go. He did question my idea of solo climbing, but we kept it quiet as others in the Hut would have undoubtedly tried to dissuade me. As far as anyone knew, the glacier headwall I had seen earlier in the week had not been climbed before, so I felt urged to give it a whirl.

As a climber working in Antarctica, one occasionally gets the chance to put up a sneaky 'new route'; my climbing skills were average which limited the opportunity to get 'first ascents' in the more popular ranges of the world. So when the chance arose down here, it was difficult not to take it. However, this had to be kept 'hush-hush, as if word got back to base, I would be getting chastised; science, not a personal climbing goal, was the reason we were here. (For any of my former climbing partners who may read this, I'm sure they will note my modest climbing self-appraisal as 'average'). I remember climbing on a tough rock route in northern California with my close friend Andy Tugby from Camden Town; I was struggling in the blazing sunshine on my lead pitch on a beautiful granite rock face protruding skyward from the surrounding forest, doing plenty of huffing and puffing. We always had great banter together; I fondly recall his supportive and hugely respectful words of, "C'mon you big Yorkshire pudding, you're climbing like a drunk donkey," as I grunted and sweated up the vertical rock face in the glorious sun – happy days.

The approach walk up the glacier to the headwall was reasonably straightforward; there were lots of small open crevasses only a foot or so wide that could be easily stepped or jumped across. The glacier then progressively steepened more and more, and I ended up 'front pointing' on my crampons and placing ice axes until the face became near vertical for the last twenty metres or so, which I wasn't really expecting when I had viewed it from below. Front pointing results in the majority of one's weight being taken on the two protruding spikes of each crampon, which are strapped securely to the base of one's heavy-duty mountaineering boots. Each of these points are about two centimetres in length and shaped like a narrow, horizontal shark teeth, two pointed steel teeth peeking out from below the toe of each boot. Consequently, they were under enormous pressure, as were my calf muscles, it was vital not to let the points drop to an angle where they may come out of the ice. Standing on the front points with a good 400 metre 'drop and slide' below me if things went askew had me twitching for a moment or three, until I broke through the final summit cornice. I would definitely describe the route as 'interesting'.

After an apprehensive bit of tunnelling and some ginger footwork, I eventually climbed through the cornice onto the ridge and breathed a sigh of relief, my pride (and body) intact and heaps of snow in about every part of my inner clothing. I also felt quite thankful that the ridge was well out of view from the Hut and no-one could have seen my floundering over the summit ridge through binoculars, and then welcomed me with a sarcastic, "That looked fun" on my return; I was not so sure that such hubristic soloing at this juncture was such a marvellous idea after all! I had experienced a very similar situation back in England when I was out walking in the Lake District with my younger brother Damian, his partner Louise and a couple of other friends. We planned on having a scramble up the classic 'Sharp Edge' on Blencathra, a beautiful mountain just a few miles east of Keswick. As we were approaching Scales Tarn, which lay just below the start point of the classic scramble, we discovered there was a heap of late winter snow around and most of the group didn't have crampons with them. On approaching the base of the Edge, we found it was plastered with wind-blown snow, and so to attempt it without crampons and being roped up would have been a tad reckless. However, as we were coming down from the base of the ridge I looked across at the face rising up steeply towards the main summit, and it looked to be in great condition.

Feeling the need for a challenge and being slightly disappointed that we had not gone up Sharp Edge, I decided to give that a whirl on my own as I had crampons and axes with me. Damian and the group were on a well-defined path back down into the valley, so I set off to the base of the face for some solo fun (as one can imagine, the group were a little concerned about this, but I reassured them I would be fine and see them soon enough down at the bar). An hour later, I found myself tunnelling through a surprisingly wide cornice on a face equally vertical to the one I now found myself on, the point of my crampons shaking from a brief bout of 'disco leg' as I only just managed to keep them in contact with some hard ice. With a substantial drop below me should I lose my footing with the crampons, I dragged myself onto the ridge, feet kicking forward frantically to gain some purchase and both axes struggling to bite onto the frozen rock summit plateau. Thankfully due to the weather being a tad nasty on Blencathra summit, there was no one about to see my thrashing through the cornice. Right now as I floundered onto this spectacular ridge thousands of kilometres south of the Lake District, I concluded that there are some situations in which we don't learn by our mistakes.

Here on this isolated Antarctic summit I was feeling elated, not just from the endorphins released during the hard physical exertions, but from the vista that surrounded me, and also the sense of achievement of being the very first person to climb this route to the summit. Once I was off the top of the semi-circular ridge, it was a short walk to the top of the scree run back to the Hut, the descent taking a fraction of the time of the ascent. My leg muscles had been placed under immense pressure when front pointing on the headwall, the long strides and bounds down the scree were once again exhilarating, and also loosened up my stiff legs.

Monday 3rd December

9:00 am More flights in bringing two further field parties, one field party has a break in the weather and heads to their work area, the Dyer once again shrouded in cloud – will we ever get up there?! Given that we may be getting dropped on a glacier and travelling into the Dyer, Asti and I went out to do some pulley work on a nearby crevasse to refresh us both, which I certainly needed! Will compile an airletter to Sandra this evening; once we eventually get up onto the Dyer Plateau, we probably won't see another aircraft until the New Year. Eleven for dinner tonight, great company with lots of laughter, all but the two guys looking after FB are heading out into dangerous territory very soon, we all need to laugh out the anxieties, I think.

It was becoming slightly frustrating sitting things out at Fossil Bluff while the Dyer remained shrouded in poor weather, but as with all things Antarctic, nature is always in charge and determines what happens with us mere mortals. Patience is an attribute one needs to learn very quickly down here if one wants to retain inner harmony. Asti suggested we go and do some crevasse rescue work to refresh ourselves; it was unlikely we would encounter any crevassing up on the Dyer Plateau as the glacier up there hardly moved and therefore should not have any fractures in the ice, but my philosophy has always been, 'If possible, it is always better to have something and not need it, than to need something and not have it.' Having finely tuned crevasse rescue techniques was definitely a requirement; who knew what the future might hold... (Where I grew up back in England, some of my younger and somewhat

133

'wilder' acquaintances might well have applied that same 'Better to have it and not need it...' philosophy about having a machete or a baseball bat when venturing onto other turf). We had fun and games with our pulleys and 'jumars' trying to get things running smoothly as we each took turns dangling down a ten-metre-deep crevasse; the jumar is an ascending device which is attached to one's harness with a sling and then clipped and locked onto the rope, it has a cam which allows the device to slide freely up the rope, then provides a firm grip on the rope when pulled on in the opposite direction. A novel part of the pulley system was that we used one of the skidoos as our anchor point. Mountaineers will be familiar with using snow bollards or two ice axes in a 'T' shape as an anchor; there were slightly different practices down here, and a 230 kilogrammes stationary skidoo makes a stable enough anchor, and certainly can provide better support than some of those I have seen certain friends of mine make while in the mountains, from which I certainly wouldn't be overly keen to abseil (I won't mention any names). Both Asti and I had fits of giggles while doing this rescue training, him more so than me, I think, as I seemed to be scratching my head as we tried to remember exactly how to set up the pulley system; it is a reasonably simple arrangement in theory, but as with most 'technical' rope work, if you don't practice it regularly, it's easy to forget. I was just glad there were no scientists out on the glacier watching as Asti shouted abuse up at me from the freezing cold depths to encourage me to sort things out as he dangled down the crevasse, his harness squashing the family jewels.

Dinner was great with us all packed in tightly around the table or eating sat on a bunk due to the relatively cramped space inside the hut, everyone sharing their stories and hopes for the field season ahead. All the field parties were going into isolated areas and would be travelling on dangerous glaciers that had crevasses that are hundreds, and sometimes thousands, of feet deep. This was a constant threat to all BAS staff doing mobile research in the glaciated mountain regions. But the work was also extremely exciting, rewarding those who undertook this perilous pursuit of scientific advancement with the privilege of encountering some of the most beautiful, pristine and spectacular landscapes on the planet, often as the first humans to travel to certain areas. I didn't manage to get the airletter completed as I stayed up chatting around the dinner table; there was such a broad range of backgrounds and personalities gathered here for a common purpose, to be out in the mountains supporting the advancement of science, yet each individual probably had their own unique back story and extra reason beyond science that spurred them on to be in this very special environment. One thing I had noticed, both here at Fossil Bluff and back at Rothera, is that nobody really boasted or became a bit self-indulgent about their previous mountaineering or outdoor adventures; humbleness, modesty and humility are things I view as great qualities in people and it seemed abundant amongst those that had chosen to be down here. It is also worth noting that if anyone did start shaking their tail feathers and adopting a 'Jonny big spuds' persona, they would soon be brought down to earth with some healthy banter.

Tuesday 4th December

6:00 am No flights today other than Murray returning with a plane full of aviation fuel drums, the Dyer remains cloaked in grey cloud. Everyone out doing activities today, Dave and Steve, the other FB minder, went for a walk up a local glacier, I advised them to stick to the rock ridge and skirt the glacier (none of them have much mountaineering experience), they stuck to a route on the glacier and Dave ended up to his armpits down a crevasse, un-roped with legs dangling into the unknown – I told him so!

10:00 pm Went out late with ski-mountaineering gear to skin up a local slope and then ski down – had a few runs but the up was very strenuous, back down at 2:00 am, still daylight, have to be disciplined about keeping my body clock straight.

Today found us still at Fossil Bluff. I spent the day reading and also composing the airletter to Sandra that I meant to do last night; it was a fairly brief letter telling her about my current situation and the anticipation of hanging around here until the real work began. I also told her I was missing her; this was very true and the feeling was certainly amplified just kicking my heels until the fun and games on the Dyer could commence. Once I was up on the Dyer, I wouldn't have too much time to dwell on things back home, I think this is probably the case for all relationships when one half goes off on some adventure; the person remaining at home remains in their normal day to day environment, and so is likely to feel the separation more than the one off doing the gallivanting. The main event of the day was seeing Dave come back into the hut, looking very flustered and covered in snow, swearing and cursing about him nearly being killed.

I looked up from writing my letter with a wry smile on my face, about to enquire as to what had happened to him, but the words, "What happened to you, smiler?" didn't have time to pass my lips.

He saw me about to chip in and quickly cut me off with, "Don't say a word, smart arse". Sometimes people set off in the mountains to do things and one can make an educated guess as to the potential of anything going wrong, mostly by looking at what they are wearing and carrying, and adding that to knowledge of their mountain experience. As Dave and two others headed out that morning to walk up the glacier, I had estimated the chance of an accident at about 50:50; they had limited equipment with them, none had significant mountaineering experience and by the sound of their conversation, it appeared they intended walking on the glacier. Looking at his traumatised demeanour, I thought it not prudent to remind him of my earlier parting words of advice about their roping up and staying on the ridge; it was something Dave did really not want to hear right now. Luckily, his unscheduled drop into the crevasse resulted in no physical injuries, but his nerves looked a tad frayed and maybe a change of underwear was required. I eventually got him laughing about it; I have had similar experiences and when you drop through a crevasse bridge unexpectedly, it happens quicker than you can blink and can be very frightening. Fortunately the bridge he fell through had deep enough surrounding snow that didn't give way and he was left dangling from his armpits while Steve laid down beside him and offered him a hand to pull himself out.

'Do as I say, not as I do' could have been directed at me later on that day as I contradicted all my own advice about unnecessary risk-taking by going out on my own to do a bit of ski-mountaineering. In my defence, I had checked the slope I intended going out on from the ridge above it and it looked safe enough; also, when travelling on skis on the glacier, you are far safer than on foot due to the more even weight distribution provided by the skis (depending on the width of crevasses and stability of their snow bridges, of course). Fortunately, there were no dramas and I ending up staying on the mountain for much longer than planned, walking up the glacier with skins on the base of the skis for uphill travel was great exercise. Then the exhilaration of blasting down the slope after taking the skins off and clipping the heels of the boots into the bindings gave a real rush of adrenaline; skiing in such an environment was so far removed from what one experiences in ski resorts, with the ugliness of the ski lifts and tows scarring the mountainside, not to mention the huge crowds that can often be found in the popular European resorts at the height of the winter season; being alone here in this beautiful pristine environment felt incredibly special. I could have carried on all through the night, such was the beauty of the surroundings and the uniqueness of the skiing, but like a hungry schoolboy loathe to leave the evening football kick around with his mates when he hears his parent calling him, I reluctantly skied all the way down to the hut and made a very late supper of boil in the bag rice, with a soy sauce drizzle to give it some flavour.

Wednesday 5th to Thursday 6th December: Fossil Bluff and Dyer Plateau

We got the word that we would be heading towards the Dyer at 10:00 am, to be dropped at a place called Auriga Nunatak, about 60 km west of the buried depot. Gear packed into the plane, with me nearly piercing the skin of the plane driving the 'doo up the steel ramp too quickly as one of the supports started slipping! Murray dropped us at Auriga in reasonable weather, lots of crevasses about, he did a fantastic job finding a decent landing site, had to test the surface once or twice, which was a tad 'twitchy'! Comedian Dave had bagged co-pilot for the trip, he waved us off shouting from the plane window, "Have fun fellas, and no kissing in the tent when the storms hit!" – funny guy. Camped quickly after a short drive to a sheltered area at the NE tip of Auriga and roped up for a walk up a 1000 ftnunatak to view the land to the east, looks feasible, need to be aware of crevasses, these monsters will be hundreds of feet deep up here. Back down for grub and the radio schedule. As the weather was so good (and having spent six days at FB), we decided to have a go at getting onto the Dyer tonight, broke camp quickly, making sure to leave nothing behind and set off at midnight.

We had a compass bearing to the depot and took turns doing 'lead skidoo' for 10 km at a time, intense concentration levels as I scanned the ground ahead. As we gained height, the ground began to flatten, but the weather began to turn again, we don't expect any major crevassing up on the plateau but the surface contrast was fading; however, we decided to complete the remaining 30 km distance set on the skidoos, very, very slowly. Arrived at what we think is the correct site at 7:00 am in very shitty weather – bad visibility, strong wind and about minus 25C hands very cold and numb, especially the 'throttle' thumb, body really stiff from kneeling on the skidoo all the way. Set up camp, which was fun in the weather, brief burst of sunlight, and no flag to be seen, in my sleeping bag at 9:00 am (Thurs) completely exhausted – what an incredible journey, and a very 'interesting' 24 hours, I contained a giggle earlier hearing Asti in the tent losing his sense of humour having to blow up his single airbed for the second time in a day, "Am no blowing up this fucking airbed any fucking more, it's givin me a bad fucking headache, which I dinna need right now!"

I couldn't resist shouting through the tent wall, "Give mine a go when you're done, mate." – easily predictable response!

A busy day and night indeed. We received the news to go at about 10:00 am; Murray had returned from Rothera and would fly us and the gear up to the top of the Bertram Glacier and land to the east of Auriga Nunatak. The only maps we had were the United States Geological Survey (USGS) 1:500,000 taken from satellite images which only showed the mountain ranges and areas of heavy crevassing; we would have to make low passes of potential landing areas to find good ground. We packed all the kit into the Twin Otter as quickly as we could; this included two skidoos and two Nansen sledges. The standard way of getting the skidoos up the steel ramps and through the side doors of the aircraft is to use a pulley that is situated inside the plane on the opposite side of the doors, and winch them up slowly on a steel cable. However, the more confident field staff would drive them up gently, ensuring that they stopped before the ski at the front of the skidoo went through the skin of the aircraft fuselage on the opposite side. As you can imagine, this was a very anxious time for the pilots as they watched us drive the skidoos up; as I was driving mine, one of the steel ramps began to move so I accelerated before the ramp came away from the doorway; I slammed the brakes on inside the entrance as the front ski stopped just an inch from the inside of the fuselage. Murray was pulling his hair and cursing under his breath, but hey-ho, it was safely in.

The short flight up was a delight, with more stunning scenery all around us. We flew across the Sound, up the crevasse-strewn Ryder Glacier, over the top of the Pegasus Mountain range with the amazing Bertram Glacier extending twenty miles to the west, then by Aldebaran Rocks until we could see Auriga in the middle distance with the Dyer Plateau beyond. The stark contrast of huge white glaciers, sometimes perforated with crevasses that revealed blue walls within their depths and the dark colours of the surrounding rocky peaks was a breath-taking sight. The ground to the south of Auriga looked very dangerous as it dropped to join the top of the Bertram Glacier; towering seracs frozen at ridiculous angles with huge crevasses lacerating the ground for a few miles behind.

After flying low and as slowly as possible around Auriga, Capella Rocks and Perseus Crags to view the ground below, we eventually landed on a reasonably flat part of the glacier about five kilometres east of Auriga. It had taken a while finding what looked like good surface and after a few 'touch and gos', Murray did a fantastic job of landing on unfamiliar ground; touching down and hammering across an unknown snow surface was always unnerving, as crevasses can sometimes be completely hidden; dropping into one in a fully loaded Twin Otter at high speed was a nightmarish prospect for all field staff. 'Touch and go' is a common thing for winter wilderness pilots to do; the pilots partially land on the snow surface with only a certain amount of the plane's weight on the skis, testing out the condition of the ground as they travel along the surface. It is very impressive to witness, but always a little anxiety-inducing when inside the aircraft! Causing much less stress for Murray, we unloaded all the kit quickly from the aircraft onto the glacier; driving the skidoos down the ramp onto the snow had considerably less serious ramifications should I mess it up. Dave had bagged the co-pilot seat and waved us off cheerily as they taxied down the glacier. Just prior to the engines revving up, he found great amusement in shouting out of the cabin window, teasing us about time spent tent-bound together; he was always joking about it being unhealthy for men to spend too much time in a tent together – I guess it meant the comedian was going to miss us. We waved them off as they climbed safely away off the glacier and headed back to Fossil Bluff.

Asti and I lashed all the equipment securely to the sledges, roped up the skidoos into a convoy, and drove the short distance to a sheltered spot by Auriga, looking out for crevasses on the approach. We didn't want to be in the middle of the glacier in case a storm picked up as the location where we had landed appeared to be in a bit of a wind tunnel. Once at Auriga, we quickly made camp. There is something of a fine art to putting a 'pyramid' tent up and we had it off to a tee. Once everything was secure, we roped up to go and climb about two hundred metres up a nunatak just east of the Auriga group, in order to view the ground to the east towards the Dyer Plateau, our proposed direction to the Depot. The walk to the base of the peak entailed weaving through some crevasses and hopping across a few; the climb was mostly scrambling, but it had a pitch that would be graded as 'diff' back home. The crevasses we hopped across were only a metre in distance at the widest point, although jumping across these very deep cracks can be a little unnerving, the sides were solid with hardly any overhanging snow and we had enough combined experience to do this without any discussion; I'm sure the inexperienced might find hopping across these slots a tad anxiety-inducing. Once at the top, we had a good vantage point of the glacier to the east. The ground looked reasonably safe with limited crevassing, but we both knew we would need intense concentration levels in the lead skidoo as the glaciers up here were between 300 and 1,000 metres deep; dropping through a snow bridge into such a deep crevasse was not an appealing proposition.

After arriving back down at camp, we had the 7:00 pm radio schedule with Rothera Base and a small amount of food, some boiled rice and a couple of bland biscuits – going back to eating ration packs was not great after the reasonable food at Fossil Bluff. The weather remained clear, so during dinner we decided to break camp, pack all the gear and head for the grid reference of the depot. Although we were both fairly tired, the weather was always the deciding factor in decision-making down here, and it was certainly 'good to go'. It was a positive sign that we both easily made the decision to go for the Plateau; making camp and securing all the kit easily took between an hour and two, depending on the weather. We had only just made camp earlier, but neither of us hesitated during the discussion about packing everything away and pushing to the Plateau; we were kindred spirits, I guess.

Both Asti and I were acutely aware that we needed to be very focused during this leg of the trip. We decided the best way to remain alert would be to take turns driving the lead skidoo for ten kilometres at a time. The skidoos and sledges are all roped together as a 'full unit' to provide safety should anything drop through a crevasse; there are no emergency services down in Antarctica. The lead skidoo is attached to the front of the first sledge by a thick rope about seven metres long, the back of the first sledge attached to the front of the second skidoo, which then has a similar length of rope connecting from the back of the skidoo to the second sledge at the rear of the convoy (the absence of a second sledge was called a 'half unit'). On undulating ground that has downhill sections, one has to put chain 'brakes' on the runners of the back sledge, as there is nothing behind to prevent the sledge's forward momentum; the steel chains on the underside of the runners slow it down should the convoy have to stop abruptly. The sledges can weigh about 200 kilogrammes fully loaded, so you didn't really want it crashing into the back of the rear skidoo at high speed. However, as we would be travelling uphill to the Dyer (we hoped), we didn't need to put brakes on the rear sledge. We broke camp quickly; making sure the site was completely clear and set off on our compass bearing at midnight (still in good daylight in the Antarctic summer) in search of the depot.

I took the first ten-kilometre leg on the lead skidoo, travelling on unknown ground on very deep glaciers is always a little unnerving, I was only going at a speed of about ten kilometres an hour due to my having to closely scan the ground ahead for crevasses. Asti had the task of keeping the ropes between us at the right tension; just as in walking as an alpine pair, the ropes cannot be too taut or too slack. Although being the second skidoo driver removes the pressure and responsibility of leading and surveying the ground ahead, Asti still had to keep one eye on me, and one eye on the ropes. There are standard hand signals that the second skidoo driver has to look out for from the lead driver; arm moving slowly up and down means 'slow down', up in the air and stationary means 'stop', and gesturing vigorously forward with a pointed finger in a frenzied manner roughly translates as, 'fast as fuck, we're going over a snow bridge!'

The skidoos have speedometers which show the speed and distance in kilometres, as I signalled to slowly pull up to swap our positions, the ten kilometres seemed to me stretched for a lot further, which I imagine was due to the concentration levels required in the lead skidoo. Just after stopping for the first time, we gingerly swapped positions, being sure to attach our climbing harnesses to the ropes as we walked between skidoos and held onto the sledge as we passed that in the middle of the two sledges. I knew of staff who had not clipped into the ropes on unknown ground and had gone through small hidden crevasse bridges as they stepped from their skidoos, intent on walking back to swap positions (even so, later on during our time on the plateau, we became somewhat blasé, and often didn't clip in). We safely swapped positions and Asti drove the next ten kilometres without incident; however, halfway through my next leg, after swapping over positions once again, the weather began closing in and a strong wind picked up the surface snow, drastically reducing the visibility around us.

I signalled to Asti with the 'stop' sign, and after a brief but loud discussion (because of the noise of the wind), we both agreed, "Bugger it, let's crack on." We didn't want to set up camp again for the second time today with only 30 kilometres to go to the depot. As we had gained height, the ground had begun to level out, the visibility was deteriorating due to the surface snow now being blown around, and a grey sky was reducing the good light we needed to travel, but we guessed we were up on the plateau and the chances of encountering any major crevassing were remote, so we pressed on. Unfortunately, the conditions really slowed our progress to a jogging pace, the visibility in front had reduced to about 10 metres, but we didn't feel we were being over cautious going so slow, as really we should have stopped and camped. We knew we were stretching our luck driving in such poor visibility on a relatively unknown deep glacier, but as the saying goes, "Fortune favours the brave." (Hopefully not, "A deep crevasse welcomes the foolhardy!")

The remainder of the journey was exhausting; physically, mentally and psychologically. The concentration levels required had been intense due to the need to be extra-vigilant about scanning the ground ahead, the visibility and the surface contrast were very poor, and so it was very mentally taxing driving slowly into the unknown while trying to maintain a constant bearing on the built-in skidoo compass. Poor surface contrast in whiteout conditions is difficult to explain to the uninitiated, skiers will understand this strange feeling if they have been on a surface in poor weather and bad contrast, and don't know which way they are moving until they see some kind of marker. To try and explain further, here's an example; at one point I was looking back over my shoulder and spotted something on the ground, I signalled Asti to stop and I stared at a small shape that I could not identify which was off at a 90-degree angle from the first sledge, it looked to be about twenty metres away, but my brain seemed to be processing the situation differently and I began thinking it was something quite a distance away from us. After looking for a few minutes with both the naked eye and through my goggles, I climbed off the skidoo, clipped into the rope and began walking back towards the first sledge, I suddenly stopped. In the grey/white flat light, I started to believe the shape was actually an old hut or some other small structure that looked to be in the distance down a slight slope, *How can I see so far in this light, and there should be no old structures in this area?* The more I gazed through squinted eyes the more I became confused about what this could be; *Oh shit, we have ended on the top of a ridge,* was my conclusion.

Asti came slowly forward from his skidoo, and after staring at the shape, began to agree, "What the hell's that down there?!" After a brief discussion, we decided that maybe one of us needed to rope up and go and have a look. I walked very cautiously for about six paces, surprisingly to us both not downhill as we expected to happen, until I stood on the 'hut'. It turned out to be a small square piece of cardboard about two inches square that had blown off one of the food boxes – our brains were certainly being muddled in this light!

Without any features whatsoever to aim for in the grey/white blanket ahead, it was tricky keeping a straight line, especially while using the skidoo's built-in compass; the only thing we could do was look back at our tracks regularly and make sure they were as straight as possible. However, we could not see very far back due to the terrible visibility, but cracked on regardless. It took about five hours of driving until we reached what we thought was the right grid reference at around 7:00 am. The skidoo has a 'thumb throttle' on the right hand side of the handle bars; I had been holding this down just about constantly, save for the occasional pee stop, and now I had lost most feeling in it, as well as in the rest of my hands. My back also felt like it was frozen rigid, as to gain slightly more elevation to better scan the ground ahead, I had been kneeling up on the skidoo seat rather than sitting (which is the common position for field staff). I felt as rigid as a board as I stepped off the skidoo and slowly straightened my body with an "Uurgh".

The weather had truly closed in, the wind was now blowing the surface snow high into the air, reducing visibility to just a few metres, and the temperature had fallen steadily due to our greater elevation. Luckily Asti and I were well-versed in 'storm-pitching' and had the tent up reasonably swiftly; while I was lashing down the sledges and skidoos, I could hear Asti muttering and cursing inside the tent as he blew up his single airbed that acts as the base insulator. The airbeds were too cumbersome to be stored on the sledges if left inflated, so one had to deflate and stow them when breaking camp; it was definitely agreed to be the 'worst bit of making camp' amongst field parties, due to how time-consuming it was, and the inevitable headache it induced. Blowing his up again for the second time today, bearing in mind how tired we both were, was testing Asti's sense of humour; we did have a foot pump, but in true British adventurer style, it didn't work. I was giggling outside the tent listening to his grunting and swearing, and couldn't help teasing him by requesting that he also blow mine up when he had finished his, his response through the double skinned tent wall was unprintable, and I felt quite sure the airbed would not fit up where he suggested.

Just prior to getting back into the tent, there was a very brief break in the weather, and for a moment we could see the pristine white glacier all around for a few hundred metres; it was flat in all directions but alas, there was no sign of the flag marking the depot. Hopefully, we weren't too far away and should find it once the weather improved. Before I crawled into my sleeping bag, I slowly re-warmed my hands by the cooking stove in the relative warmth of the tent. The pain of the blood regaining status in my hands after the frostnip I had in most fingers, was 'something else' – once experienced, never forgotten! It had been an interesting twenty-four hours and a very tiring journey; as I lay in the sanctuary of the sleeping bag, with the wind still battering the walls of the tent, I drifted into the most wonderful sleep, the sort that only real physical and mental exhaustion can bring.

Thursday 6th December: Dyer Plateau

6:00 pm Woke from the greatest sleep ever, weather still really bad outside, checked all the gear, everything is secured, visibility down to five metres, reading and more sleep. Finding it hard to write this bloody diary, fingers and hands are very cold.

Regardless of the noise created by the howling strong wind battering the external skin of the heavy cotton tent, the driving surface snow often sounding like someone throwing handfuls of tiny stones against the outside of the tent, and the intense cold, I had managed to have a great sleep; entirely, I'm sure, due to the exhausted state I was in this morning as I got into my sleeping bag. Asti had also succeeded in snoozing through the storm and we both had rice and cooked meat granules for breakfast/dinner. Unfortunately, the bad weather was still raging outside, and other than going out to check the gear and use the toilet, we would have to wait for improvements before we could go in search of the depot. The tent was also beginning to get buried which meant a move of location if the storm continued – if only by 10 metres! We spent the rest of the evening eating and reading; the temperature had now dropped significantly due to our elevation and once the stove was turned off, the temperature inside the tent, quickly matched that outside. At minus 26C, it was difficult to do anything that required any dexterity as one's fingers and hands would get bitterly cold quickly if the gloves were removed, I tried to read a book for a while, but turning the pages wearing two pairs of gloves caused me much frustrated chuckling, so after twenty minutes I gave it up and pulled the hoods of the sleeping bag in close around my head.

Friday 7th December

6:00 am Not much movement today other than getting out of the sleeping bag to have a pee (in the pee bottle in the tent). Sleeping and reading in the sanctuary of the tent as the wind howls outside, blowing snow hard against the tent outer, these 'Pyramid' tents have been the mainstay of BAS for decades; they certainly can take a battering. We are about 6500 ft above sea level now so the temperature is far colder than at FB.

7:30 pm Radio schedule with Rothera, poor communications so couldn't hear them, Dave cut in from FB, telling us about the steak and red wine he was enjoying in the hut, such a blooming comedian. Weather bad all day, it's hard to sleep when it's this cold; have got two layers on, a down jacket, two gloves and two hats in the best Rab bag in the world - on a sheepskin rug, two mats and a single airbed, but once that stove's off – holy schamoley, the temperature plummets within minutes; as Asti calmly and eloquently tells me, "Aye Con, it's fuckin freezing alright," the thermometer in the tent showing minus 29C.

"You Highlanders are getting soft," I quipped. "If you were Glaswegian, you'd sleep outside."

Life in the tent had been particularly uncomfortable due to the extreme cold as mother nature appeared to be bearing her sharpest teeth outside. I spent the night shivering uncontrollably, Asti and I were both watching each other for the tell-tale signs of hypothermia (mumbling, stumbling, grumbling and fumbling was the old traditional army rhyme) and each of us kept an eye on our own body's extremities for frostbite, or frostnip. I had the most up-to-date and technical clothing (and many layers) and the best sleeping bag and insulation equipment available; however, I still felt in harsh physical pain due to the extreme cold; only those who have experienced extreme still air temperatures may have a true understanding of the 'pain' of cold weather, how it bites at exposed skin and clutches one's whole body in its icy grip. Trying to stay warm becomes the focus of everything one does, ensuring no skin is exposed to the elements; however, inside this deep freezer of a tent, regardless of our modern equipment, within ten minutes of the stove being extinguished I never felt warm, just slightly less cold at times. When I reflect on the hardship of the early Polar explorers such as Shackleton, Amundsen, Wild, Nansen, Crean, Bruce, and Scott, with their basic clothing and equipment, I genuinely feel humbled; however, this didn't detract from how blooming cold it was inside that tent! Asti never complained once and I had the utmost respect for his resilience and physical endurance in such an environment; he was a 'hard Highlander'.

I often reflect on the terms 'hard' or 'tough', which can be viewed differently dependent on one's background and life experiences. Having lived life as a teenager on a tough inner-city council estate, and also experienced extreme conditions in the mountain ranges around the world, I have witnessed a variety of interpretations and perceptions of what being 'tough' means to different people.

Life on a council estate invariably saw such terms attributed to guys (and sometimes girls!) who could handle themselves in a street fight or bar brawl. Kudos and 'respect' from peers was quite often achieved by gaining a reputation for standing one's ground and being able to fight well. However, within the mountaineering community the ability to cope and perform well with extreme cold and harsh conditions in the mountains, is generally regarded as the true definition of being 'tough'; yet such people may never have had a 'fight' in their lives (however… I do know of one or two who meet both requirements!). There is also another type of 'toughness/hardness' I have come across. I worked for a couple of years with Irish contractors laying water mains. We were paid per metre of pipe laid, so worked pretty much flat out all day with just a couple of short breaks. In the depth of winters, these guys from County Mayo and Connemara would stay out in the harshest of weathers in their work suit (a suit for work, and a suit for the weekend). Sometimes on a severe winter's day, they were covered by a blanket of snow, grafting away but never complaining. After work some of them would often go to the local pub and dry out by the fire with a few pints of beer before heading home to bacon, mash and cabbage, time with the family, and then do it all again tomorrow; a special breed of men indeed.

I try not to be influenced by traditional notions of 'class structures', which I find divisive. All the same, I have found that the differing background and upbringing of individuals does have an effect on their attitudes as to what makes someone 'hard' or 'tough'. I have close friends who have attended exclusive private schools and progressed to prestigious universities, where peers may well have seen the term 'hard' attributed to someone who could row a boat ferociously, or strike the ball well in full gallop on a polo field. Anyway, stereotyping and pigeonholing is never fair or productive; so in conclusion, Asti was as 'tough as old boots'.

Although my in-tent conversations with Asti were never immensely lengthy, and probably wouldn't have won either of us a place as the president of a debating society, they did range through incredibly diverse topics; from music, climbing and religion, to girlfriends, the mountains, politics, philosophy, family and more beyond. We even somehow came to discuss Nazi war criminals in hiding in South America, still being sought out and prosecuted fifty years after the Second World War, and whether or not the passage of time diminishes the horrific nature of those terrible mass murders; we agreed unanimously during that discussion; the perpetrators, regardless of their age, needed to be brought to justice for those heinous crimes.

Asti was from the Highlands of Scotland, me having Irish parents provided us with something of a tenuous Celtic link. We were also similar in that we each were fortunate to have had a close, stable, happy family unit. Neither of us had experienced any kind of family dysfunction and we didn't personally witness any of the social ills that were commonplace in the local community in which I grew up, such as domestic violence, unemployment and alcohol abuse. However, our experience as teenagers was very dissimilar; while Asti enjoyed his spare time discovering the forests, walking on the hills and fishing in the local streams and lochs, I was out on the council estate with the 'crazy gang', climbing up the sides of inner city tower blocks (un-roped, of course) and making small explosive devices with gunpowder removed from fireworks. Asti was in hysterics (and I believe a little shocked) as I recalled how the gang would use almost anything in the area as target practice for our low powered air rifles and air pistols ('but no women and children' was our misguidedly honourable standpoint). One day, a double-decker bus came slowly up our street on a driving lesson. It was like everyone's birthdays and Christmases had come at once, the driver and instructor must have thought they had been teleported to a war-zone. I recall the only disappointment was the lack of efficiency and speed of the re-loading skills.

Saturday 8th December

Still no break in the weather, major operation to go for a number two, which is probably the quickest poo of my life, minus 25C and a ferocious wind chill does not inspire one to hang around too long, don't bother bringing a glossy colour supplement to peruse.

Method

1 – Get dressed in all your outdoor gear.

2 – Place shovel in hand.

3 – Exit tent, with colleague fastening tent quickly behind you.

4 – Dig small pit in snow to correct size to accommodate one adult, use these snow blocks to make a windbreak.

5 – Place shovel VERY, VERY FIRMLY into snow between you and the windbreak.

6 – Swiftly lower bottom layers, hold shovel tightly and squat, ensure pants are not in the 'drop-zone'. Even more swiftly, poowipebumpulluppants, bury deposit with snow block.

NB: Do not, I REPEAT DO NOT, poo on clothing, stand back or fall onto own poo!

7 – Return to tent, without bringing in a ton of snow (or any poo).

What a relief it was despite the weather conditions, I had been saving up for three days, shame I couldn't have enjoyed the moment a little longer!

Poor communications with Rothera remain, also still struggling to sleep in the intense cold. This has to be the most inhospitable place I have ever been, the bizarre thing is that it is only wind stopping us moving, it doesn't really snow up here, the wind picks up the surface snow and blows it around twenty feet into the air, causing really poor visibility. Made yet another curry for Asti and I, shame he hasn't got any more kidney beans to alter it to chilli again as he did at Fossil Bluff!

To say we have been cooped up in the tent for a few days, we are getting along fine; I guess we are both pretty laid back and don't convert crises into dramas easily. Thinking about Sandra in-between reading, and coping with the blooming intense cold.

The weather remained horrendous outside the tent. However, when nature calls and one needs to do a 'number two', then there is little option other than to get dressed like a 'Michelin man' and venture into the storm. Although we used a pee bottle in the tent, which does take some getting used to, and requires good balance, there was not the option of a 'poo bottle'. As described above, the technique required to make things as least unpleasant as possible (it was never going to be exactly pleasant) was a finely tuned method and had to be completed as quickly as possible. It wasn't beneficial to one's sexual health to leave the 'bits and pieces' dangling in a 40 mph wind; with the still air at minus 25C, which gave a wind chill temperature of about minus 50C. Flesh tends to freeze rather quickly in such an environment, and I, for one, was quite attached to my tackle, and didn't relish the prospect of a frostbitten todger – hence the need for swift action.

As indicated, the firm and solid placement of the shovel was an essential element in the process; it was the only thing to hang onto as you were squatting facing the snow blocks you had just quickly cut and placed for scant protection against the howling wind and the 'sandblasting' snow. Failure of a robust shovel placement had dire consequences. Falling back into fresh poo, with no washing facilities, was not conducive to retaining in-tent harmony with your companion, especially when the stove heated the tent up and the pong from the soiled boots circulated – NO, firm shovel placement was THE key to Antarctic tent happiness!

It's worth mentioning that washing was generally a luxury that field parties rarely had the chance to enjoy; fresh water was a precious commodity, and involved both time and energy in melting snow to get it. The water we melted was used for drinking and cooking, and a small amount saved to brush our teeth, leaving none to clean ourselves, I had taken a tip from the base doctor and packed some wet wipes to clean 'down below' so as to remain reasonable hygienic, and also snow-washed my face each morning (Russian style) if the weather wasn't too unpleasant.

We were having problems with radio communications with Rothera, the di-pole radio antenna, which had to be set up outside the tent to produce the best signal, kept freezing up which meant further forays into the storm to shake it clean, and sleeping was also remaining difficult in the extreme cold. Regardless of the harshness of our situation, Asti and I managed to maintain our sense of humour. In such wild environments, being able to do this and remain in harmony with your travelling companions are arguably some of the most important survival skills.

Sunday 9th December

7:00 am Decent weather, so up and out with the half unit to search for the flag, or at least one of the aluminium glacier poles. Headed west for about 9 km, saw nothing, visibility down to about 2 km but intermittent. The plateau is so flat, just a white desert, have to be careful not to get lost, our tracks can easily blow over and then we'd be well buggered if we lost our bearing back to the tent, the half unit survival tent is definitely not too cosy! Came back in our tracks for about 5 km then headed north for 3 km, Asti then spotted a flag about 1 km north east – ya fookin hoo! Turns out the flag was not THE FLAG, but one some joker had put on the top of a glacier pole last season, we checked the number on the pole and it put our tent about 6 km south of the depot. Both well chuffed at finding it after only a few hours, back to the tent, plotted a route to the depot and found it on a bearing of 352 degrees. Drove back to the tent (tracks still showing) and cooked some food, packed all the gear (which we are getting quite slick at!) and set up camp at the depot; a great relief to be here at last, we were a bit unsure of our position, eventually in my sleeping bag at

1:30 am (Mon). Had a strange dream about Sandra, she had hooked up with another guy and was making soft porn films – very bizarre – tent fever – not sure how Freud would interpret that dream?!

Awaking to reasonable weather and seeing a partially sunny sky overhead was a relief after being cooped up in the tent. It was still very cold, but as we were up on a 2,000 metre high Antarctic plateau, I guess this was just a given. Asti and I set up a 'half unit' and he took the lead skidoo position as we headed west to where we thought the depot might be buried. It was such an eerie environment, there was hardly a breath of wind and intermittent cloud; looking in every direction as we drove along brought the same images back - a flat white landscape leading off into the far distance. Occasionally, the cloud would lift completely and then you could gain the odd glimpse of the top of the coastal mountain many miles away on the horizon; the clarity and visibility was amazing, there were certainly no pollutants in this neck of the woods to contaminate the view. After heading out west for about ten kilometres, we stopped and had a quick chat. Although there was no wind and there was not the chance of our tracks being blown over at present, we knew that could quickly change. From previous recent experience, we were acutely aware of the difficulties of accurate navigation up here in bad weather, so we decided to head back along the tracks we had made; finding our tent without using those we had come out on could prove tricky in 10-metre visibility. We traced our way back along the tracks towards camp until we estimated, using the skidoo readings, that we were five kilometres from the tent, and headed on a north bearing in search of the flag. After travelling only a kilometre north and still in great visibility, Asti let out a whoop; he had spotted the flag in the distance towards the north-east. A wave of satisfaction came over me at our find. We had spent all that time at Fossil Bluff waiting for decent weather to get here, then all the lie-up days in horrendous storms and excruciatingly cold conditions since our initial input at Auriga; now we had found the flag and could finally get started on the project; it was satisfying, rewarding and exciting knowing we could commence on the real work; there was also a distinct sense of relief that we had got this far unscathed. Although we both felt confident in eventually finding the depot, the weather was always going to be the dictator of how quickly this could occur; as in any mountain environment, mother nature is always the 'boss' when it comes to allowing one to achieve goals.

Later that evening while I was relaxing (or at least trying to in the extreme cold) that earlier thought had me pondering about those mountaineers and climbers who have used the term 'conquer' when speaking of a peak they have summited or a rock-face they have climbed; admittedly it's a term less commonly used in contemporary times. My own view, which is probably shared by many mountaineers, is that we never really 'conquer' a mountain; we just visit it for a brief period, when the mountain and the weather systems around it give us mere mortals a fleeting opportunity to stand on a summit. Although this may seem a somewhat philosophical view, I have always found the mountains to be very spiritual places; one can sit briefly on a summit and view a landscape untouched by humans, enjoying a panorama that has remained the same for hundreds of years, ignoring for a moment the many ways in which man's presence has changed things dramatically outside this environment, both positively (like advances in medicine) and negatively (such as the cultural 'curse of reality TV'). Anyway... what was clearly obvious on this trip was that the weather was going to be the deciding factor regarding our successful completion of this project.

Quite amusingly, it transpired that the flag we were overjoyed at finding, was not 'THE' flag, but one that some joker from last year's field party had placed on a glacier-pole; their distorted sense of humour was obviously a bid to throw the following years team off the scent; but alas, their plan was foiled as we worked out exactly where we were in relationship to the depot due to the poles' having individual numbers stamped on them. Relating the number on the pole to the diagram we had with us allowed us to easily work out where the depot was. We retraced our tracks back to camp, quickly packed all the gear onto the sledges and, after fuelling up on meat granules (cooked) and rice, drove as a full unit on a bearing for about six kilometres until we finally reached the depot at 11:00 pm. We had travelled at a moderate pace as we did not want to risk missing the real flag, the speedometers on the skidoo were reasonably accurate regarding distance travelled, but our navigation had to be spot on; if the weather suddenly changed it would be simple to miss it. We stopped once to reassure ourselves the compass bearings were accurate and double check we were on the right route, we also came across more glacier poles and checked their serial numbers against our diagram, these confirmed we were spot on and with about 150 metres to go from where we estimated the depot was, we saw a small dark shape ahead of us. There we found THE flag – two cheesy grins adorned our faces as we pulled up with a sense of achievement at this mini-victory. Auriga Nunatak was only 60 kilometres away from where we were now camped, yet it had taken four days to arrive at our goal, a journey which in good weather and on safe ground could be reduced to less than an hour on a modern snowmobile – the Antarctic weather had certainly showed us who was in charge.

While sleeping last night I had been having some strange and quite bizarre dreams about Sandra having a relationship with someone else and becoming involved in making pornographic films. Without having access to a psychologist, it was quite difficult to analyse this dream; I had read that dreams are often a metaphor of what's occurring in your waking life and there is a link to one's subconscious mind while dreaming – I would need some bloody help to find the metaphorical link in that dream to my current situation (if Asti had suddenly produced a camcorder while we were up there, we would have been in big trouble!)

Monday 10th December

7:30 am Up to fantastic weather, blue skies, good visibility and just a light breeze, our first sight of the Dyer proper, what an amazing vast flat landscape, we could just make out the top of the distant 3184 m Mount Jackson in the south west, which must be about 60 miles away, and 2680 m Mount Charity to the north in the Eternity Range – just the tops showing on the horizon. First main task was to get the buried ice cores to the surface, due to my experience with a shovel (and Asti's lack of it – it's a fine art indeed!), I got stuck in at 10:00 am and had the entrance to the underground depot accessible by 11:19 am – Asti timed me, he has never seen someone dig so fast – my time labouring with the Irish contractors was paying off! The chamber was well built, about 20m x 3m x 2m, and well shored up with timbers; about eight feet of snow had accumulated over the entrance in just a year. The weather turned while I was halfway down, which left me covered in spindrift that froze completely, back in the tent in the afternoon as the wind really picked up again, took a while thawing out all my frozen clothing. Spoke to Pete, the base commander at Rothera, during the 7:30 pm radios schedule, they may get an aircraft out next week to pick up the ice cores. Bit of reading until 1:00 am, hopefully get some decent weather tomorrow to get the ice cores to the surface.

The following morning, we awoke to the wonderful sight of cloudless blue skies above and hardly a breath of wind at ground level. This meant that there was no surface snow blowing around to hamper our work plans. Both Asti's and my spirits were visibly lifted, as we could now crack on with the project we had come down to the Dyer to complete; although it had already been a great adventure since flying down to Fossil Bluff from Rothera, it had taken nearly two weeks just to get to this starting point, and we felt professionally and morally obliged to get the job underway and successfully completed. Prior to getting some water on the boil for breakfast, I had a wander around our camp to view the unique landscape that surrounded us; it really was quite a surreal place. There was nowhere to get a proper vantage point so I stood on the seat of the skidoo to try and gain just a few more feet elevation, allowing me to gaze around this vast white desert. From high above, our camp must have looked like a speck of dust on this incredible and vast flat white landscape. On the distant horizon in the north east I could just make out the summits of a high mountain range on the Peninsula; this was the wonderfully named Eternity Range with its Mounts Faith and Hope just out of sight, and the nearest of the trio, Mount Charity at 2,680 metres, slightly more clearly visible than her two virtuous sister mountains due to her location at the southern end of this beautiful range of mountains that stretched north to south for about 45 kilometres. I estimated Mount Charity to be about 95 kilometres from our current location. We couldn't see the lower sections of the mountain due to the curvature of the earth, but such was the clarity of the air between our position and this peak that we could just about see its upper reaches; it was wonderful to be able to breathe such clear untainted air into my lungs.

Gazing down to the south west, I could only just make out the top of what I thought must be Mount Jackson. It was also a similar distance away, but the Dyer Plateau must have been rising between our locations because with a height of 3,184 metres (making it the highest mountain on the Peninsula), it should have been more visible than Mount Charity, yet I could barely make out its summit on the distant horizon. The mountain has a significant BAS connection; the first ascent was made by the pioneering Scottish mountaineer John Cunningham back in 1964, during the many years he spent working in Antarctica with BAS, during which he managed to get to the Welch Mountains where Mount Jackson is situated at the southern reaches of the Dyer Plateau. Stood on the skidoo soaking up this amazing landscape was really exhilarating but, alas, a beckoning breakfast and a long day ahead interrupted the moment; there was some work to be done. We decided our first task would be to bring the buried ice cores up to the surface. The aircraft could then land and collect them; once this was complete we could then commence the second part of the project; extending the large grid of aluminium glacier poles, while at the same time measuring the amount of surface snow that had accumulated around each one since they were placed into the glacier a year ago.

The ice cores were sealed in cardboard boxes, which were laid on pallets buried in an underground chamber; the entrance to this chamber was marked by THE black flag. I quickly volunteered to be the man on the shovel; there are certain digging techniques that can only be mastered by spending some time at the business end of a shovel, and I was not confident that Asti had experienced what I had in the digging department. I had certainly served my 'apprenticeships' with the boys from Mayo and Connemara while laying water mains in all conditions back in England; digging down into snow was a pleasure in comparison. After about an hour of quick excavation work going down nearly three metres to the entrance, I pulled away the two metre by one metre board made from thick plywood that sealed the entrance to reveal a very well-constructed chamber in which one could just about stand up; 2" x 2" timbers were used as vertical supports around the perimeter of the chamber with 4" x 2" timbers acting as horizontal roof supports and large 1" thick boards over the top as the roof; the construction had certainly withstood whatever horrendous weather the winter months had presented. However, when I had dug about halfway down to the entrance, the weather changed and the wind picked up, blowing all the surface snow around, while the wind chill brought the temperature right down. I carried on regardless and after we went inside to have a look and assess the task of raising the ice core boxes to the surface, we retreated out into the increasing storm. I resealed the chamber with the same plywood board that had been originally used, and we withdrew to the sanctuary of the tent, all my clothing now frozen stiff from the blowing surface snow. The rest of the day was spent eating and reading in the tent while the storm raged outside. The break in the weather was certainly short-lived; the Dyer was definitely going to be a challenge. During our brief evening radio schedule with Rothera, Pete advised us that he was hoping to get an aircraft out to us next week to collect the ice cores; hopefully we would have another spell of good weather, but it wasn't a major problem because at a push – and if we really had to – we could still dig out the boxes and bring them to the surface, regardless of what the weather was doing.

Tuesday 11th December

8:00 am Up to more reasonable weather, quite strange for the Dyer I had heard. I cleared the entrance to the ice core chamber (which had nearly filled up again with spindrift) and cut some steps to help get the ice cores up, they were all packed in large heavy duty cardboard boxes and quite heavy. After much huffing and puffing, and a bit more huffing, Asti and I got all the boxes to the surface (being careful not to damage the ice cores inside). All out for 7:00 pm then back in the tent for another curry (again). Radio schedule – Pete thinks weather permitting at both ends we can expect an aircraft tomorrow, he also couldn't believe we had the lot out already – Asti quips, "It's that mad navvy, Con!"

9:00 pm Out to lay down a line of ski-way markers in the snow for the possible flight tomorrow, then off to measure and extend some glacier poles, got seven done, back in the tent at 1:00 am for some hot orange and welcome sleep after a long day. Been having some good banter with Asti all day – the relief of being up here and working hard has lifted both our spirits.

The weather remained surprisingly good for the Dyer, with clear skies and hardly any wind. The cold we could endure (obviously, because we were from Scotland and the north of England), but strong wind was our main adversary in working on the Dyer; there is very little falling snow up there through the summer, but the wind picks up the surface snow and can produce the same effects as a blizzard, even when there were blue skies just 10 metres above our heads. Fortunately, the weather gods were looking favourably on us and we had all the heavy ice core boxes up to the surface after a long hard day of work. I also had the pleasure of re-digging out the chamber entrance, as yesterday evening's stormy weather had blown tons of snow back in overnight and completely undone all the work I had done yesterday. Asti initially gave it a whirl, but it is something of a fine art effectively digging out an appropriate entrance for our requirements, and with all due respect to Asti's enthusiasm and effort, I was certainly the one to do it quicker and make the chamber more accessible for our needs. I cut it in deep wide steps so we were not floundering when carrying out the robust boxes containing the heavy ice cores. The ice cores that had been drilled out by the collaborative US/BAS team of glaciologists last summer were to be analysed for the purpose of investigating climate change over previous centuries; they had drilled down to approximately 100 metres, which meant that some of the deeper cores were samples of snow that had fallen here nearly one thousand years ago. We were therefore very conscious of not damaging any of the boxes as we hauled them up from the depths of the chamber.

Finally, we had all of them up to the surface; each box was a little over one cubic metre and there were fifty of them in total. As we had to be relatively gentle with them so as not to damage the precious heavy solid ice cylindrical cores inside, the task took much longer than expected and we eventually flopped down in the tent for some much needed dinner at 7:00 pm. During the radio sched with Rothera that evening, Asti was singing my praises about my turbo-digging exploits; they sounded very pleased and surprised with the progress we had made in raising all the ice cores, adding that we might get a flight in tomorrow to return some of them to Rothera. We were not far off the flight path that some of the Twin Otters were using to stock fuel caches at Fossil Bluff, so it wasn't much of a diversion for an aircraft to come in and land to collect the cores. As the weather remained calm and sunny (but still very cold), Asti and I decided to make the most of it and begin working on the other element of our programme; as tired as we were from our day's efforts, our work ethic remained really positive and we both were fully aware that the good weather might not last. Prior to locating, measuring and extending seven of the glacier poles on the grid, we also used some green petrol cans to mark out a makeshift runway for the proposed aircraft landing tomorrow. The glacial poles were light silver in colour, which gave them an element of camouflage against surface snow; they were therefore not easy to spot from a distance, and even more difficult from the air. The green jerry cans would hopefully help the pilots navigate their landing safely without hitting any of the poles.

Asti and I had been getting along really well today. We were both very tired, but he never once complained about anything as we toiled away in the cold for more than 18 hours, joking and laughing as we heaved what seemed like a never ending convoy of ice core boxes up to the surface, with just a short break for dinner and the radio sched with Rothera. We had both taken it in turns to break off to go into the tent to melt snow on the stove in order to keep ourselves hydrated, which we probably didn't do enough of. Being so isolated up on the Dyer didn't really seem to be affecting us. We both knew we were out on a limb in this location but seemed to be coping well; I wasn't focused on anything other than the task in hand, and Asti appeared to be in good spirits and adopting the same approach. We had been so busy today and so tired when we sank into our sleeping bags at about 1:00 am that we didn't really have time to think about anything other than entering dream land and getting much needed sleep.

Wednesday 12th December

Hectic day, great weather so a lot done.

7:00 am Up to check all the gear and breakfast, biscuits, cheese, and tinned fruit – 5* luxury indeed.

9:00 am Radio schedule with Rothera, weather good here but not there, review later this morning. Dug out some old food boxes and skidoo fuel jerry cans, they were about six foot deep, lots of spindrift blowing around so difficult to see while digging.

11:00 am Rothera tells us there should be a plane landing about 6:00 pm. Asti and I out to do some more poles, managed to do the 18 we had planned and back for 6:00 pm for the flight coming in, gave a weather report to pass to the pilot. Unfortunately, it was Neil flying who completely ignored our runway markers (which were perfectly placed, into a headwind I might add), just after his skis touched, he missed one of the aluminium poles that he couldn't see by about ten feet, still going about 90 mph – that would have been fun had he hit it! As usual, Neil just chuckled when we pointed it out, his response of, "Your runway looked a bit boring," came as no surprise, if he and his aircraft finish the season in one piece, I will be astonished! Steve co-piloting.

Loaded up ten of the ice core boxes, then back out on the skidoos to do more of the glacier poles, also put some empty black fuel drums we nicked from the plane out on the ski-way, this to make our runway a bit more distinctive, this might deter any further rogue 'Neilesque' landings - and potential disasters!

11:00 pm Murray and the base plumber, Ray, in to collect 12 more ice cores, and they managed to use our ski-way – YEY! Only 28 to go. Plane took off about midnight, sleeping bag at 2:00 am My eyes have been sore all day, took my goggles off digging the food boxes out earlier in the spindrift – big mistake and I should know better. Thinking of Sandra as I try and snooze, eyes very painful and struggling to write.

More brilliant weather resulted in another long, productive and tiring day, including the arrival of two aircraft in to land to collect some of the boxed ice cores. I spoke to Rothera in the morning, although the weather up here on the Dyer was perfect, this was not the case further north at the base, where they were experiencing low cloud and poor visibility. However, the forecast was for improved conditions and we were told to expect at least one Twin Otter.

After spending much of the day driving the skidoos around the 'grid', extending the poles and measuring the snow accumulation against the base of each one, we returned to camp for a flight that was due in at 6:00 pm. Extending the poles was a straightforward task that took little time; they were made of strong aluminium, each two metres in length and about two centimetres in diameter with measurements engraved up the side; each length could be slotted into the other, as one does with tent poles. Fortunately, these had been stored in the chamber at the depot last season so we didn't have to bring them on the sledges. Although it was a simple enough task to slot one onto the top of the existing upright glacier pole, one had to be vigilant in never handling them without wearing gloves, as one's skin would stick to the freezing metal. We were both quite pleased that we had the foresight to lay out a makeshift runway with the green jerry cans; the pilots would obviously be thanking us and singing our praises for our initiative. The Twin Otter that approached had Neil in the hot seat; even though we could not see into the cockpit from where we were, once it veered away tightly and then loomed in to touch down nowhere near our expertly marked, airport-like runway, we both simultaneously exclaimed, "Neil".

As the plane touched down and thundered towards us through the glacier-pole 'minefield', Asti and I peered through the gaps between the gloved fingers of hands that were now held up to our faces, holding our breath and waiting for the inevitable crash that would now occur as the big red aircraft hurtled towards us. Its engines now screaming in reverse, the wing just missed one of the tall poles by just half a metre; the extended poles were easily at propeller height and the consequences of a propeller blade hitting one didn't bear thinking about. As the plane came to a halt and the engine's propellers slowed right down, Asti and I approached. Neil had clambered into the back and jumped out of the rear door into the snow – "What's up with you two, you look like you've seen a ghost!" he declared, beaming out of his perpetually jovial face. We mentioned the runway we had laid out for the pilots to allow them to avoid the aluminium poles, but he just replied in his normal cheerful manner. He was an incredibly talented pilot and we had every confidence in his ability to get places and land in testing conditions. However, if given a straightforward landing task away from the eyes of senior base personnel, he always seemed to enjoy pushing boundaries.

On one occasion when I was back at base and flying in the co-pilot seat with him, we were returning to Rothera from a fuel drop when Neil decided to land the plane on top of a huge flat tabular iceberg (approximately the size of six football fields) that had carved off a glacier and was floating in Marguerite Bay. He kept the plane going fast on its aluminium skis along the surface snow for about 150 metres, racing towards the edge of the ice cliff; as the rim of the sheer drop approached us very quickly, we suddenly fell off a cliff that was about 50 metres high; as we headed down towards the very cold-looking dark sea, my heart was in my mouth as I thought, *Shit, time to check out early.* Neil then applied full-throttle power and we slowly pulled up away from the beckoning sea surface. I can still recall him "Yee-hawing!" in my headphones as I slowly extracted my fingernails from the seat armrests.

This evening, Steve the Rothera electrician was accompanying Neil as co-pilot; it was great to see him again as, like Dave, he had a quick, dry sense of humour and we had good banter as we loaded up the ice core boxes into the Twin Otter, with Steve joking about my good fortune of working up in the 'tropical heat' of the Dyer Plateau. As they fired up the engines to take off, I gave the pair the thumbs up and shouted to Steve through the open cockpit side window to enjoy the flight back; he responded with a grimaced smile and crossed his fingers. Neil just shouted across "Tally-ho", and off the plane roared, this time respectfully down our fantastic runway, blowing snow back at us as we shielded our faces from the spindrift. The weather was still really settled, so after some food and the 7:00 pm radio schedule with Rothera, we headed out to complete some more pole extensions. During our chat with base, they had told us another flight would be coming in around 11:00 pm to collect a further batch of ice cores. I hoped that whoever landed would use our runway and not take out any poles.

We had taken some big cylindrical black 45-gallon empty fuel drums from Neil's aircraft when it had landed earlier and replaced the small green jerry cans with these much more distinctive markers; Murray, the hardy New Zealander who dropped us at Auriga Nunatak, paid due respect to our efforts and professional-looking runway, and landed perfectly on it. As we were loading up the ice core boxes onto the aircraft, I slowly began to feel an increasing discomfort in my eyes, I didn't mention it to Asti or Murray, or the base plumber, Ray, as we secured the boxes inside the aircraft. Once the plane had taxied and taken off, Asti and I retreated to the comfort of the tent and cooked up a bit of soup for a late supper, I finally told Asti that both my eyes were now feeling quite uncomfortable, and after a brief review of the day, I remembered taking my goggles off for about thirty minutes while I was digging out some buried food boxes and some ice core boxes that had been covered by blowing snow. It took me no time at all to realise that I was starting to suffer from the early onset of 'snow blindness'; what an idiot I was for removing those goggles.

Thursday 13th December

Writing this late due to being out of action from snow blindness from removing my goggles yesterday for thirty minutes, luckily the weather turned crap so wouldn't have worked today anyway – that would have felt really bad had it been a good day, my stupidity causing me to be tent-bound. Not experienced this before, last night and today it felt like someone throwing sand in my eyes and someone drilling into the back of my eyeball at the same time – blooming wonderful, was considering one of the morphine phials at one point, however, paracetamol, eyes covered and ice dabbed on them seemed to ease things, feeling a bit better now – having a pee was fun! Asti giving me updates throughout the day, I apologised for taking my goggles off but he understood and was very cool about it. The wind has been blowing at 30 mph, visibility 20 metres and still air temperature about minus 25C; that makes a wind-chill of about minus 40C and exposed skin getting frostbitten in just a few minutes – my snow blindness timed very nicely, I guess. Have been chatting a lot with Asti, we have been sharing our travelling experiences, and I've again been causing him more laughter reminiscing about all my teenage antics on the council estate. Also been thinking

about Sandra, missing her a lot, probably been feeling
sorry for myself and my poorly eyes! Extremely cold in the
tent tonight.

Exposing my eyes to the elements and the resulting snow blindness was frustrating and a little embarrassing, I had spent enough time in the mountains to be fully aware of the consequences of removing glasses or goggles in snowy conditions, especially down here with the depleted ozone layer.

Asti and I spent the day in the tent, passing many hours talking about our lives, upbringing and global travels; my teenage misdemeanours that caused Asti much amusement were in no way a reflection of a poor upbringing, quite the opposite. I was very fortunate to have a warm, loving and stable family home; both my parents were hard-working and law-abiding with high moral standards and honest grounded values, wholly committed to family life. The only time they socialised and used alcohol was the weekly Saturday night visits to either the Irish Club or the Catholic Club; they would normally be home before midnight, often a bit tipsy.

On special occasions, other Irish relatives would return to our house, and as is the tradition, would sing songs into the early hours, with the customary "Sshh!" to anyone who would dare talk while the singer was in full song (no matter how bad or out of tune they were!). My brothers, sister and I used to sit on the stairs listening to the performances; I remember all the words of the more memorable songs even today (they were mainly Republican songs reminiscing about 'the struggle'). However, once I left the safe and protective environment of my home, I would often hook up with friends in the locality and we frequently 'stretched' the laws of acceptable behaviour, getting involved in regular gang fights, being chased by the police, and even designing home-made 'napalm style' Molotov Cocktails by mixing petrol and jelly cubes, which often acted as a great equaliser when outnumbered by rivals! Regardless of how much of a positive home life a young person has, once they are out in the local community things can get a little messy; growing up on a council estate can often be a daily navigation between bad and worse, my local area would definitely be described by contemporary criminologists as an 'at risk' environment. I would return home at the allocated time, after cleaning up at a tap behind some garages, with the standard response of 'playing football' when asked by my parents where I had been – if only they knew! My antics came to an abrupt halt following a particularly fierce street brawl with another gang which left me hospitalised with two nasty slash wounds in my back that required dozens of stitches, and an evening in intensive care due to heavy blood loss. After I recovered, I chose the righteous path at the 'Y junction' that my peers and I inevitably faced; as well as playing rugby, I took up climbing and mountaineering; my energy and exuberance now channelled thankfully in a more productive, rewarding and law-abiding direction.

My eyes were extremely painful all day; fortunately I didn't need a poo as that would definitely not have been an enjoyable experience, going out into a storm fully fit was always interesting, but doing it while unable to see would have been hilarious; even using the pee bottle inside the tent created much amusement, "Left a bit... a bit more, fire!" The excruciating pain in both my eyes, and being storm-bound in a tent on the Dyer Plateau, struggling to stay warm in probably the coldest temperatures I have ever experienced, all left me feeling a little sorry for myself. Once that sullen mood had its cloak around me, my mind inevitably wandered to thoughts of Sandra, I had to be strong and steer my head away from any negative feelings and maintain as positive an attitude as possible, which I just about managed to do.

Friday 14th December

12:00 pm Another lie-up day, eyes seem to be recovering well, ready to get working again but the Dyer is not being friendly today.

4:00 pm Weather now the worst since we arrived, had to give in to nature and poo – what a blooming kafuffle going out and digging the poo-pit, Asti and I both in hysterics (the only way to cope I guess!) as I get all my outdoor gear on and head into the 'hell' that is waiting outside, it amazes me how much snow can get inside a tent when both of us think we are really slick with our tent exits/entries. Wind has picked up to about 60 mph and air temp on thermometer showing minus 35C, knocking up minus 60C wind-chill outside while squatting, my poor bits and pieces didn't know what hit them as I did the quickest crap in the history of human existence; had to take a glove off for about a minute, hand white and numb, only frostnip in the fingers though – you would not want to be out in that weather for too long. After leaping back into the tent in a maelstrom of snow and wind, my head and face completely covered in frost, Asti calmly says in his dry humorous Highland way "Aye, it's nearly as cold as Scotland, I may have to think about putting on a jumper on if a go oot..." indeed. Trying to read with hands and face inside the bag to try and escape the cold, hard to turn the pages with woollen mittens on, once that stove is off, this tent is twice as cold as a deep-freezer within minutes. Asti's last words in the tent as we were both shivering uncontrollably were "I think ma snot's frozen again."

"Me too, both nostrils."

Another 'lie-up' day with a wind raging outside followed. The walls of the tent were taking a battering, we both sat smiling about how resilient these old tents were proving. BAS has been using this 'pyramid' shape and style of tent since it started doing field research projects decades ago, and they have certainly stood up to the conditions; the only thing that has changed has been the improved quality of the cotton, and the devices which we use to secure the guy ropes. What certainly hasn't changed is how uncomfortable it is going out for a number two in such appalling conditions. I have detailed the methods used previously, so won't go into that again; what was improving quickly was my skill and speed in completing the task. Maybe the appropriate governing bodies should incorporate it as a new sport in the next winter Olympics – 'Speed Shitting in Blizzard Conditions', using a large wind tunnel fan in a giant freezer. I feel confident I would be on the podium, possibly sporting a gold medal.

The snow blindness was slowly easing; the uncomfortable pain was subsiding and fortunately the person throwing sand into the back of my eyeballs had shown mercy on my stupidity and that element of the pain had eased off. As was the norm when we found ourselves tent-bound in storms, Asti and I spent the day chatting about a variety of things, but mostly joking about the horrendous weather blasting the walls of our tent, and the antics involved in going out to use the toilet. He didn't carry out his threat of going out in just his tee shirt; not even this hardy Highlander would last too long in the harsh conditions raging outside. It was now as cold inside the tent as I have ever experienced; when the Primus stove was lit for cooking the food, the temperature remained just above freezing and we could strip down to our thermals and be reasonably comfortable. But within five minutes of turning the stove off, the temperature quickly plummeted to match the still outside air temperature; I was wrapped up in the best cold weather equipment available, but trying to sleep in minus 35C was often all but impossible as I shivered in my sleeping bag. Regardless of these conditions, both Asti and I appeared to be adopting a reasonably positive and sangfroid attitude to the testing conditions we currently found ourselves in. I guess there was not anything we could do about the situation other than to accept it and soldier on with a smile, albeit breathing through frozen nostrils.

Saturday 15th December

7:00 am Very difficult sleeping last night, intensely cold, even lighting the stove first thing is a mission at minus 30C indoors, "Whose turn is it?" has been a common birdsong the last few mornings! Tent-bound all day, holding the number two in, good job the rations are designed to keep you regular at 3-day intervals.

5:00 pm Braved the storm and went outside to check nothing has been blown away (and to have a break from the tent), all skin covered up, the most extreme conditions I can remember, visibility down to ten feet, wind gusting at 70 mph, walked only to the 'doos and back (definitely would not fancy a night in the open in this!), the tent is beginning to get buried in drifting snow, we'll have to move it if this continues for a few more days. Back in the tent, with an abundance of blowing snow to wake Asti up! More reading, chatting, and eating, polished off A Catcher in the Rye – a great classic, and a second read in a week. Being holed up in the tent can become a bit tedious and psychologically testing once you've rested enough, luckily Asti is a cool guy and we both know how to cope with it, had some decent chats, I caused him much more amusement with more tales of my teenage antics! Back in the sanctuary of the tent wrapped up in my sleeping bag, I could be anywhere in the world (as long as it was very cold and windy), it's when venturing outside; one realises what a hostile, alien and unforgiving place Antarctica is, I guess when nature bares its teeth here, there can't be anywhere on the planet more inhospitable. The technology and materialism of man seems so irrelevant and meaningless in such a powerful place; I truly feel as though I am on another planet, and could not be further away from Sandra if I tried. Hope she isn't being smooth talked by potential suitors, need to get out working, tent fever around the corner! Chatted with Asti about girlfriends back home, he dryly said, "Och, mine will be probably shagging." – Thanks mate, that doesn't really help matters!

Being 'tent-bound' in a remote location is an interesting experience, any mountaineers or outdoor enthusiasts who have been cooped up within the confines of a small tent for a few days or weeks, with storms raging outside, will have an appreciation of what a unique experience it is, and a great test of preserving harmonious relationships, especially with the additional element of coping with the sub-zero conditions. Initially, the daily itinerary is very rudimentary i.e. sleep as late as possible, eat breakfast, sleep some more, eat lunch, read, perform ablutions, eat more food, read some more, cook dinner, play cards, listen to music (if you have any) and chat as much as you can about every topic known to man (this, of course, dependent on the conversational level of your tent companion), then try and sleep through the night. On a trip such as ours, we had limited fuel and food, so could not cook continuously for hours on end. Related to this was the ever-present risk of carbon monoxide poisoning from the paraffin stove; although there was a ventilation 'dongle' at the apex of the tent, there was often a build-up of noxious gas if one left the stove on for too long. Additionally, we had 24-hour daylight, and our trip through the 'night' from Auriga had upset our body clock a little; to combat this we had both fashioned eye patches from a piece of black cotton cloth to replicate darkness and assist us in sleeping through the night-time daylight.

I had brought along three books; as well as *A Catcher in the Rye*, I also had Hunter S Thompson's brilliant but acerbic *Fear and Loathing in Las Vegas* and in sharp contrast to this, Tolstoy's wonderful *Anna Karenina*; however, already I had read each one twice due to our extended time at Fossil Bluff and the five lie-up days since arriving at Auriga Nunatak, so filling in time in the tent positively was always a mission. Once we had eaten, slept and exhausted conversation, I would set myself such spectacular tasks as taking all the matches out of the matchboxes, counting them a few times, and individually putting them back in the box the opposite way around; dismantling the stove and putting it back together; counting the stitches in the fabric on each corner of the tent, a couple of times in case you omitted one on the first count. I once also started taking the radio apart, but on quick reflection, aborted that task after ten minutes, as it was our only means of communication, and so the consequences of messing it up were fairly harsh. Ultimately, there was only so much of this fantastically amusing stuff that you could do for days on end, so donning all the gear and venturing outside into the storm to 'check the kit' was sometimes an unpleasant but necessary option, undertaken really just to break the monotony and stave off tent-fever and lunacy.

Following on from our conversation during the tent-bound days, it became clearly obvious that we had similar philosophies when it came to lifestyle choices. Neither of us really bought into a materialistic way of life or needed traditional status symbols to gain credence in society; we both shared the view that any money we earned was probably better spent on travelling and experiencing new cultures and landscapes, rather than on a shiny new car, an expensive watch, or costly 'designer' clothing. Huge sprawling shopping centres, which might equally be termed 'homogenous hell holes' depending on one's outlook, have become a ubiquitous sight almost everywhere in the world. Normally built outside cities, tarnishing the countryside with their ugly structures, on land often previously graced by green fields, they now present flat black expanses adorned with abundant parking spaces for the hordes of hapless spenders. While mulling over this, I remembered the words of the great Pakistani humanitarian and philanthropist Abdul Sattar Edhi, "When you stop living for luxuries, you understand the true meaning of life." It is said that he only ever owned two outfits of clothing... I suppose you need to have at least one spare when the other is in the wash. Venturing outside the tent into a ferocious Antarctic storm reinforced both our personal views of the unimportance of consumerism and of 'keeping up with the

Joneses'; such things seemed insignificant, trivial and futile when in such an awe-inspiring, powerful and foreboding place.

Another detrimental aspect of being tent-bound in the mountains is that it allows too much time for one to brood over relationships back home. Having a beautiful girlfriend back in England did cause me some pause for thought during tent days; as much as people try to avoid it, once you have had all the fun you can with a box of matches or a cooking stove, it is inevitable that one's mind will wander to things back home, and I did find myself mulling over Sandra. While talking about this with Asti, his dry and somewhat pragmatic response about the potential infidelity of his own girlfriend was obviously his honest sentiment about the issue. That did very little to assuage my own anxieties; I really needed to keep my mind focused; 'What will be, will be'.

Sunday 16th December

7:30 am Early weather schedule with Rothera, wind still blowing, but maybe easing up I hope, it needs to, we are both not wired or designed for being indoors too long.

12:30 pm Weather improved dramatically, as if by magic, the wind dropped completely, so up and on the skidoos to do more glacier poles; we have not seen a single crevasse up here, now travelling un-roped as a result – calculated risk (if we do come across one it is likely to be hundreds of feet deep so we probably won't live to tell the tale if we drop into one!) Eyes feel much better today.

7:30 pm Had a personal airletter from Sandra read out to me at the end of the radio sched with Rothera (hope the other field parties were all not listening). I thought it was a bit mushy, hopefully only I, the radio op, and Asti were going to hear it, Asti was having his read out as well. It was a lovely letter from Sandra but sadly carried bad news. My next door neighbour had died suddenly, he was an Irish building contractor who I had previously worked for, he was an honourable, tough and hardy man from County Mayo, I thought he would live forever. I had grown up beside him and am close friends with the sons; their mum has been the ill one, wonder how they will cope, having lost my own mother when I was 24 I understand the grief of losing a parent. It's a tough thing, especially when you have a close family... life goes on, I guess. I will try and send a telegram.

10:00 pm Out to do a few more glacier poles, I think we both feel morally and ethically obliged to work hard after being tent-bound for a couple of days, back in the tent for midnight and a welcome cup of hot chocolate. Once the stove is off, and we have settled down into our sleeping bags, the silence is very apparent and like nothing I have experienced before, not a single audible sound, to the point when you think you can hear your heart beating. Gazing up at the apex of the tent and my mind drifting to home and Sandra – wish she could see the beauty of Antarctica; she would understand why I am here.

Over breakfast the storm continued to rage outside, then shortly after midday, and pretty much without any indication that things were about to change, the wind suddenly stopped battering the sides of the tent and a calmness descended. Being inside the tent cooped up in such a confined environment with a deafening wind relentlessly pounding the walls of the tent is always going to be a struggle, stepping out into a wide open spacious, calm and beautiful outdoor environment, as cold as it was, cleansed one's mind and spirit immediately; from dystopia to utopia in the space of minutes just by stepping through the tent doorway. We quickly got our outer clothing on and headed outside, me ensuring I had my Bolle ski goggles on. The sun was now shining brightly high above us, and my eyes were still quite fragile from the snow blindness; the last thing I needed was to expose them to direct sunlight right now. Asti and I were in good spirits and so far had not tried to kill each other. I say this in jest, but having spent the last three-and-a-half days (around 85 hours straight) in just each other's company in the tight confines of a small tent in such a desolate and isolated location, struggling to sleep in extreme cold temperatures and a howling wind, it was surprising we remained in such good spirits. The psychology of how one copes in such situations to me is reasonably straightforward; always fall back on humour when things start to get a bit frayed. Fortunately, Asti had the same approach and I think this, and our generally positive approach to life, were the fundamental reasons we kept our morale up.

The remainder of the day was very productive and we had two lengthy spells measuring and extending the glacier poles, with a short break in-between for dinner back in the tent and the radio schedule with Rothera. During the radio transmission with base, I had an 'airletter' from Sandra read out to me, part of which carried some sad news that a neighbour I knew really well had recently passed away. The airletter is read out at the end of the schedule, all the other field parties could easily listen in, but there was an unwritten agreement that everyone goes off air when a personal airletter is read; this wasn't an ideal way of communication, but it was better than not hearing anything at all. The news about my neighbour left me feeling saddened; he was one of the Irish contractors I had worked for some years previously. With the help of the base radio operator, I managed to get a telegram to his son prior to the funeral to pass on my condolences. Part of the airletter read out by the radio operator was a bit romantic and 'mushy'; this could be a tad embarrassing depending on who was with you in the tent, but Asti did the honourable thing and just carried on reading his book while we both heard the letter being read out. If any of the guys in the other field parties did leave their radio sets on and break the 'rule', they would never say anything as that would certainly be taboo, Asti and I always switched the set off without any discussion if another field party was having one read out; it was undoubtedly the righteous thing to do.

Monday 17th December

7:30 am My turn to light the stove, not too bad as the temp has risen up to about minus 18C, tropical! Radio schedule with Rothera, we can expect a plane (Neil – oh dear) sometime this morning. Neil arrives about 10:00 am, he came in to make another really low pass over the tent, I was ready for him this time and fired one of our emergency signal flares towards the plane, which incredibly hit the nose and caused a scary wobble – oops! As usual after circling around and landing on the ski-way he jumped out, apparently unfazed, calmly responding; "That was fun, Con, where did you learn to shoot like that?" However, there did seem to be a slightly anxious glint in his eyes! Plane loaded with more ice cores and away at 10:30 am.

11:00 am Out to work on more glacier poles, working our way well through the grid in this decent weather, travelled 70 km and measured/extended 38 stakes by 7:15 pm – finished them all at last, we were riding on bone-shattering 'sastrugi' but managed to get them all done.

__7:30 pm__ Radio schedule. Let Pete know all the grid glacier poles was complete but some ice cores remaining – Murray chipped in to say he was flying back from FB and could come and get the ice cores for Rothera, but also air-lift Asti and I across to Fossil Bluff first. I hope this is the case; it will be bone breaking going the 80 km to Auriga in the solid sastrugi we had late on today. Been arsing about on the skidoo earlier today behind Asti, driving full blast across the back of him between poles – nearly knocked him off twice, felt like I had it 'planing' on the flatter sections, still probably only about 80 kmh.

Due to the weather remaining pleasant and warming up to a balmy minus 18C, a long productive and rewarding day found us completing all the glacier poles and getting most of the ice core boxes off with Neil when he came in at mid-morning, leaving just half a dozen to be collected. During the radio schedule with Rothera, the New Zealand pilot, Murray, interrupted the transmission to let us know that he would be leaving Fossil Bluff later with an empty aircraft and could divert to collect the remaining ice cores, all our kit, and fly Asti and I back to base.

This was great news; during the day when we were finishing extending some poles on the western side of the grid pattern we had encountered some heavy 'sastrugi' over a significant area. Sastrugi is a surface condition on snow and glaciers caused by wind, they are wave-like structures that develop and increase in size in constant wind, similar to what happens to sand dunes in the desert; these wave-like patterns can freeze solid and can sometimes be more than a metre high. Travelling over such frozen structures is an interesting but slow process as you bounce off the tops and then into the troughs of these frozen white waves; the driver is often thrown around the skidoo like a rodeo rider on a bucking horse. We were not sure if the weather would hold out up on the Dyer until tonight and wondered if we would have to descend back to Auriga Nunatak, taking the few remaining ice cores with us on the sledges, and be collected there where the weather might be more favourable, just as it was when we were originally dropped off. This would be something of a problem because the worst of the sastrugi (or best, if you were a glaciologist) lay in the direction we would need to travel to get to Auriga; let's wait and see. The surface conditions on the eastern side were in sharp contrast to the sastrugi-ridden chaos to the west; the snow was completely flat, and this resulted in me driving the skidoo as fast as it could go. Free of the burdening sledge, I got it up to about 80 kmh, weaving across the back of Asti's tracks like a naughty child with a new toy, and on two occasions clipping the back of his sledge carrying the glacier equipment, much to his annoyance. We were now at the tail end of the project, so I guess I was in a celebratory mood and a tad giddy.

This mischievous mood nearly caused a critical problem earlier on when Neil came in to collect a batch of ice cores. We could see and hear him approaching from a long way off; as was the norm with him, he would give us a low pass either before he landed or after he took off. Some of his low passes could be very scary for the uninitiated. For those field parties he knew enjoyed his antics, he would really push the envelope and pass very low above one's head. I saw the plane descend low on the glacier about two kilometres out; by the sound of the engines and the angle, height and speed of the big red Twin Otter, I knew he was making a full speed low pass directly at us. This is where my sense of mischief could have ended in disaster; I had taken one of the emergency rocket flares out of the survival box and I fired a signal flare towards the plane as he approached. This was intended to go somewhere near to the plane to give Neil a bit of a shock, and obviously not to actually hit the aircraft, Unfortunately, it hit the nose cone directly and surprised him as it bounced past the cockpit windscreen in a red flash with a smoking tail. This unexpected fiery object zooming past his window dislodged his focus and concentration for a moment, causing the aircraft to tilt slightly sideways, its left wing tip only about five metres from the snow as the plane hurled towards us at high speed. "Oh shit!" came out simultaneously from our mouths as we froze for a fraction of a second, terrified that the worst was about to happen; an enormous Twin Otter hitting the snow in a catastrophic crash due to my idiotic action would not look good on my CV. Fortunately, the somewhat expert shot did not deter Neil too much; he regained control a moment after the impact, the aircraft blasted over our heads and on landing he adopted his usual attitude, congratulating me on my excellent flare marksmanship.

Tuesday 18th and Wednesday 19th December: Dyer Plateau to Thompson Rock

7:30 am Plan has gone a bit wonky, Pete went against Murray's suggestion to clear the Dyer, but then at midday we heard that Murray was coming to collect the last of the ice cores later on today, and Asti and I were to drive the

280 km overland to Fossil Bluff – that means find a route off the Dyer, get through the crevasse filled Batterbee Mountains, then find a way down one of those chaotic glaciers, and across the frozen sea channel, oh – oh!

8:00 pm *Murray in to collect the last ice cores, three guys from Fossil Bluff squeezing in with the boxes on their way back to Rothera. All wished us good luck with the trip, no one's done it before, they tell us. Asti and I were puzzled why the decision was made; however, we were both excited about it, and understandably anxious about a trip into the unknown.*

10:00 pm *Due to the settled weather, we decided to pack up camp and get going on the trip, make a fast dash before it turned crap again, we didn't want to get caught in those blizzards while down in the mountains. Mind blowing scenery all the way to Thompson Rock, we gave it 'big licks' all the way as we knew it should be safe on the flat plateau, saw the odd crevasse but only one big open one, the surface contrast was great so we could see the ground well and keep up our speed, only problem was navigating without any features until Friedman Nunataks came into view after about 40 km – due to there being zero wind, had to use clouds on the horizon with a bearing on the 'doo and kept an eye on the rear tracks to ensure they kept in a straight line; using clouds to navigate - that's a first!*

Only mishap was the back sledge overtaking the rear 'doo and tipping Asti off as it flipped over when we slowed down after spotting a crevasse – don't really want a broken leg up here, we decided earlier against putting chains on the back sledge as it caused far too much drag – oops. Hit Friedman Nunataks in no time; a few crevasses appearing, had to cross a wide one, rested and ate/drank at Mount Cadbury, a truly spectacular location, then on to the south side of Mount Bagshawe, near Thompson Rock at the lower end of the Batterbee Range. Camped after a very tiring 12 hours and 130 km of skidoo travel, collapsed into my sleeping bag at 2:00 pm after an exhausting 30-hour day; had some food and slept like a drunk baby, my thumb is numb from holding the throttle down. Temp has really warmed up as we have slowly descended off the Dyer, stripped down to thermals as we pitched camp. What a fantastic day.

Asti and I had been successful on the Plateau; we had extended all the glacier poles and extracted all the ice cores from the buried chamber, and now all but a few were back at Rothera courtesy of the planes that had landed to collect them. We were a little puzzled as to why we couldn't also be flown back as well as the ice cores. We discussed why a decision had been made for us to travel overland to Fossil Bluff. We thought we could have sat it out on the Dyer for a few days until an aircraft could get us. After a short conversation, we mutually concluded that the base commander, Pete, was a kindred spirit and he would have relished the opportunity to undertake a trip that had never been done before. We guessed he may have deliberately planned this so we could undertake the journey of a lifetime, and get collected from Fossil Bluff instead of flying back to Rothera from the Dyer. Once we accepted the idea and got our heads around the task ahead, we each embraced the notion with a big grin on our faces, albeit with a certain amount of trepidation. The maps we had were limited in respect to the terrain they showed, in particular in their coverage of the major crevassing once we reached the Batterbee range; an interesting journey lay ahead for us.

Murray arrived to collect the remaining ice cores at 8:00 pm. He had three lads hitching a lift back to Rothera; they all wished us well, and they also dropped some spare jerry cans with petrol for the skidoos. Two of the guys who were also field assistants appeared envious of our journey ahead, but gave us a wry wink and a smile as they said goodbye; they were more than aware that any route down from the Dyer would be tricky, to say the least.

Once the plane had taxied and departed, Asti and I made the decision to pack up and get underway immediately; as usual, we had to take full advantage of the good weather. During the day, we had spent some time inside the tent using the USGS 1:500,000 map to plan the best route from the Dyer to Fossil Bluff. We had been fortunate to see a lot of the terrain in the area from an aerial vantage point during our flight up to Auriga Nunatak, so we knew that we had to avoid certain routes, such as the chaotic Ryder Glacier; although that would be a more direct route, we knew it would be impassable for a full unit. We opted instead to head south-west, staying on the Dyer for a while until we reached Friedman Nunatak, skirt around the ranges of Carina Heights and Puppis Pikes, then past Mount Cadbury on to Thompson Rock at the southeast side of the Batterbee Mountains, and from there find a route through between Mount Bagshawe and Butler Peaks to the Rowley Corridor. We planned to then try and get down one of the steep glaciers onto the Sound. Once there it should be plain sailing across the flat glacier to Fossil Bluff. It was a trip no one had ever undertaken before, so we were very excited about it!

An interesting aspect of this journey was going to be navigating accurately during the initial stage; the direction we were heading had no definite features to aim for whatsoever, being just a white desert as far as we could see. The mountains would not come into view for quite a while, and so we would have no specific landmark to line up on with the compass bearing. We took a compass heading from the map that would bring us about two kilometres to the east side of the first significant landmark, Friedman Nunataks, but we knew these mountains would not be in view for about an hour. The method to maintain a straight line on a bearing in such terrain is to constantly look back at your skidoo/sledge tracks and ensure they are in a straight line. We did not have any GPS hand-held units with us as there were none available when we left Rothera, so this was the only way to maintain a bearing during daylight. Modern adventurers have access to GPS; our navigational techniques did seem somewhat archaic in comparison to the technological devices available today. However... as we were experiencing near-perfect weather without any wind whatsoever, we saw some clouds low on the horizon that were in the direction of the compass bearing we intended travelling. Asti and I sat on the skidoos for about fifteen minutes looking at them against a fixed point we had each picked on the windshield of our skidoos to work out if the clouds were indeed motionless. Staying as still as possible and staring ahead, we both agreed that the clouds were not moving. We picked one that was exactly on our compass bearing and set off. This was possibly a navigational first, and it certainly was for me!

The weather remained superb as we embarked on our journey. The temperature, though, was still very low and the cold bit at my face as I took the lead skidoo towards the cloud on the horizon. I had a balaclava on underneath the helmet, but as the visor was scratched I had it raised and had my goggles on underneath. The wind was really biting at the small part of exposed flesh just at the top of my cheek bones, so after ten minutes, I had to pull the visor down to avoid frostnip in my exposed cheeks. Although this reduced the effects of the cold, it did restrict my view ahead due to the scratches on the visor. We knew from our experience of travelling around on the Dyer while extending the glacier poles that the chance of encountering crevasses at this elevation was remote, so until we could see Friedman Nunataks I decided to go fast and we ate the ground up quickly. While travelling towards the cloud on the horizon, I would also occasionally look back at our tracks to ensure we were going in a straight line. We were, and so it seemed navigating using a cloud could work after all (but only on windless days, and definitely not to be encouraged for use by novice hill walkers!).

Travelling along the featureless white desert towards the small cloud that sat low on the horizon against the intense blue backdrop of the sky felt very much like a surreal experience. A two-tone of white and blue ahead, separated sharply and horizontally by the skyline, and only the drone of the skidoo engine noise through my helmet and the vibration in my hands distracting my senses. After about an hour and almost 50 kilometres of distance travelled, the dreamlike state was fractured as the top of Friedman Nunatak slowly rose into view on the distant horizon; we had made good speed to this point and should be able to maintain it. We rested briefly, soaked up the fantastic view ahead, and swapped over positions, both joking about cloud navigation being the way forward, as we had hit Friedman bang on the mark.

From where we stopped, we would now be heading down off the plateau towards Carina Heights, which we could just make out in the distant southwest; it was only a small gradient so we opted against putting chain brakes on the back sledge, as this created considerable drag. The decision had to be balanced against the danger of the sledge gaining speed and passing the back skidoo should the convoy have to slow down – this always had interesting outcomes when it happened, the chief one being whipping the back skidoo over and dismounting the driver; always fun to witness, but not if you're the victim. As I was now on the rear skidoo, I intended monitoring the gradient of the slope carefully!

Asti led for the next leg towards Carina Heights, the weather was holding out and the vista of the coastal mountains could now occasionally be made out in the far distance to our right. We travelled fairly quickly, but we were both aware that as we were now on slightly undulating ground, presenting occasional downhill gradients, there was an increased chance of encountering crevasses. As the weather and surface contrast were just about perfect, we should be able to crack on at a good speed and easily spot them in plenty of time. However… following another changeover, I had now returned to the lead skidoo and after ten minutes of driving, I spotted quite a large and unexpected crevasse about 50 metres ahead and had to give the 'stop' sign with my left hand in the air, admittedly without a great deal of notice to Asti!

Consequently, and as predicted due to the absence of a 'slow down' hand signal, I looked around and saw the rear sledge pass Asti's stationary skidoo two metres to the right of him, still travelling at about 50 kmh. Asti's grimacing face, clearly mouthing the words, "Oh fuck" momentarily indicated that he knew exactly what fate had in store for him. The connecting rope from the sledge to the back of his skidoo whipped tight as it passed him, and instantly pulled his skidoo at ninety degrees, tipping it over just as he leapt from it onto the snow to avoid injury, before it was dragged forward for a few metres, acting as a brake for the runaway sledge – maybe we should consider the chain brakes if it gets steeper!

I scanned the ground around to check it was safe, dismounted and walked over to see if Asti was okay, "What the fuck happened there? Did you no' think about slowing down first!" he screamed; he clearly was okay. Once he got up, dusted himself down and saw the large open crevasse ahead, he warmed a little more to my decision-making.

This was a minor setback, but still time-consuming as the sledge had also tipped over and all the kit had become dislodged, causing it to be unstable. As a result, we had to unlash everything, take it all off onto the snow, leaving a bare sledge, and then reload all the gear back on and lash it tightly down. As usual, we saw the positive side, and looked upon it as a bit of exercise and a welcome break from kneeling on the skidoo freezing our nuts off. It was always a little difficult trying to keep the sledge from being top-heavy; there was an abundance of gear to load – jerry cans containing the skidoo fuel, food boxes, radio boxes, cooking box, first aid, tents, survival gear etc., all of which had to be loaded with the heavier equipment on the bottom layer to try and maintain a low centre of gravity.

Because of the sledge mishap and the glaciers ahead having downhill gradients, we reluctantly put the chain brakes on the front runners of the rear sledge. Although this would cause resistance, we didn't want to risk a repeat performance and potential injury. Asti took the lead skidoo as we set off, skirting around the open crevasse and crossing it on a reasonably firm snow bridge where it narrowed to about a metre-and-a-half (the open crevasse either side of the bridge had no visible bottom to it) before continuing towards the northeast tip of Carina Heights; we also took a compass bearing just in case the weather changed. Crossing crevasse bridges is always slightly unnerving, the glaciers we were travelling on are hundreds of metres deep, as the ice moves over undulating ground, fractures can develop on the surface (these fractures on a glacier are referred to as crevasses). Some crevasses can be just a metre or less wide and not very deep, however, on steeper gradients they can often be huge gaping chasms many metres wide and scarily deep; blowing surface snow will often build up to form bridges across the gaps of smaller crevasses, this snow can be deep and firm enough to walk on or drive a skidoo across, but sometimes they can be shallow and fragile, hence going across them was often unsettling.

The next legs of the journey were relatively uneventful, once we arrived at the northern part of Carina Heights, the next 20 km leg took us past the eastern flanks of these amazing-looking peaks whose upper reaches and summits protruded from the glacier that blanketed the ground around them. From the southern section of Carina, we headed south west for the 30 km section to Mount Cadbury, with the beautiful summits of Puppis Pikes breaking through the glacier to our right; looking southeast we could also see the small isolated Elliot Hills in the far distance. Puppis Pikes are a series of rocky pinnacles reaching up for about two hundred metres from the surrounding glacier, some of them connected by snow covered ridges; as we approached them, initially we could only see four of them that ran diagonally across our right flank (from the south west to the north east). As we drove past the south end of this ridge, at least eight more of these huge rocky pillars came into view. The scenery was utterly spectacular all around and we were rewarded with the snow flanked and majestic Mount Cadbury as we stopped beside it to take a well-earned and welcome break.

Despite the relatively easy terrain we travelled through, the concentration levels needed on both the lead skidoo (scanning the ground for crevasses) and the rear skidoo (keeping the connecting ropes at the right tension and looking out for the rear sledge) had been very intense. There had been a few other small crevasses that we had crossed; in the fantastic weather, they could be seen from a reasonable distance and the majority had solid enough ice bridges, which we negotiated across relatively safely.

Nonetheless, between Puppis Pikes and Mount Cadbury we encountered one crevasse that looked to be extending far too wide in either direction to skirt around, and it was about fifteen feet across. The skidoos are only about six feet long, which meant the whole weight of one would be on the snow bridge if we crossed. We decided to dismount a good twenty metres ahead of it, rope up and go and 'probe' the bridge to test its thickness. This practice entailed something I have never seen outside Antarctica. Using a long thick wooden broom handle which has a heavy duty blunt carpenter's chisel attached to the end of it (referred to as a 'bog chisel'), one walks towards the crevasse holding said bog chisel in front, and 'probes' at the snow bridge at the edge of the crevasse to assess its depth (when climbing in the Alps, this is nearly always done with the shaft of an ice-axe, it is a very different ball-game down here!). With a crevasse the width of the one we intended crossing, I had to lean forward with Asti keeping our connecting climbing rope taut, and probe along the width of it, getting as close as possible to the far edge where the bridge met the top of the solid crevasse wall on the other side; it looked to be a 'goer', but I reckoned it might be only about 30 centimetres thick in the centre.

On wider crevasses, this procedure often meant walking on the snow bridge itself as you gingerly paced across (or crawled to spread one's weight) roped up to your partner who remained on safe ground behind you, with an ice-axe at the ready to drop on and be the 'anchor' in case the lead person went through the bridge. You would then be testing the depth and making rough mental calculations as to whether or not the bridge would take the 300-kilogramme combined weight of a skidoo and rider – scientific calculations no, 'guestimating' yes! The crevasse bridges are generally arched-shaped underneath, and when one reaches the middle point of the bridge, the probe can often go straight through a couple of inches of snow and Davegle unnervingly in the void below as you probe into fresh air. As has happened on more than one occasion, you yourself can drop through at the central weak point, which always tends to wake you up and get the adrenalin pumping as one's legs dangle into the abyss below.

Consequently, this crevasse bridge we crossed did entail an episode of me using the emergency 'fast as fuck' hand signal to Asti as I went full throttle across in the lead skidoo. I certainly had no intention of the skidoo and I lingering on the mid-section of that crevasse, and I could feel some jerking on the connecting ropes as I hammered the skidoo across. I suspected there was some drama behind, but stopping at this stage was most definitely not an option and would only have made things worse should Asti be struggling to cross. Once I went far enough on the opposite side of the crevasse to a point where I knew the full unit was clear, I slowed a little and looked back over to see Asti smiling and shaking his head. He told me a little later that his skidoo had slumped into the snow bridge after my skidoo and the first sledge had destabilised it. Luckily it held just long enough for him to get across (with the help of my pulling power). The sledges were not really a problem as they were long enough to cross without any difficulty, but they did often cause the bridge to weaken a little. When a crevasse bridge 'slumps' as you drive the skidoo across it, this is caused by the snow being compressed down due to the weight coming on top of it. When that happens, one can only hope that this compression of snow does not create so much pressure on the bridge that the whole thing collapses; it is certainly a strange and disconcerting sensation when a slump occurs.

We were now at an elevation considerably lower than the Dyer and the temperature had increased to a 'sweltering' minus 15C. The stop at Mount Cadbury gave us some time to rest, take on board food, and more importantly water, as we were both feeling dehydrated. I had filled up a water bottle before we broke camp and stashed it under the skidoo seat, optimistically thinking the heat from the engine might filter back and keep it from freezing; no blooming chance, as it was now a solid block of ice. We had the stove going quickly in a wind-break by the skidoo and after melting and consuming plenty of water, I hydrated some freeze dried meat granules to go with a portion of boil-in-a-bag rice. This was made reasonably edible due to the addition of the 'all-spice' flavouring I mixed into it. The meat granules came in three flavours, lamb, beef and chicken and my theory was that it was all really from the same place – the sweepings of an abattoir floor – and had meat flavours added to it when it had been freeze dried for shipping. All of this was of no importance, as ultimately it was pretty awful tasting, though with the addition of the all-conquering bag of 'all-spice' that had journeyed with me all the way from a wonderful Pakistani supermarket in Bradford, it was just about edible.

While we were sitting down having a rest and eating, we had some time to really soak up the scenery around us. We were just a few hundred metres from the base of Mount Cadbury, its pyramid-like snow covered flanks rising from the surrounding glacier. We could then see down to the south west towards the Batterbee Mountains and Butler Peaks, which we needed to get between to access the Rowley Corridor. The sky was a rich blue, which made the glacier clad peaks and the dark jutting summits look even more stunning. During the trip from the Dyer our focus had been on travelling safely and so we had been unable to immerse ourselves in the surrounding landscape; we just snatched momentary glimpses. It was so rewarding now to have the opportunity to linger on the views around us. Gazing upon such overwhelming and spectacular scenery made me realise that some things are just not quantifiable. Our conversation was somewhat stilted as we sat on the skidoos which we had drawn up level beside each other, but this didn't seem to be a problem as we both had a smile on our face gazing at the majesty around us; no words were needed.

We could have sat for an age in this incredible environment; once the skidoo engines had cooled there was not a single audible sound, without a breath of wind it was complete silence. Back home in urban environments there is never absolute silence, even in the early hours of the morning; maybe a vehicle passing, trees rustling in the wind. But sat here it was so totally silent. I felt sure I could hear the pulse of my heart pumping the blood around my body; this lack of sound just added to the impact and power of the stunning setting we felt privileged to be sat in.

Alas, we had to get going and set off for Thompson Rock, with Asti taking the lead. Due to the undulating terrain with long downhill sections, we reluctantly left the chain brakes on the back sledge and had to live with the drag it caused; we had got this far without injury and were both aware that Asti had been fortunate to remain unscathed when the heavily laden out of control sledge pulled his skidoo over earlier.

Thankfully, we did not encounter any major crevassing during the remaining part of the journey to the proposed camp below Mount Bagshawe. We were forced to slow down as we crossed quite a few that were only a foot or two wide, which didn't entail any 'stop and probe' action. As we approached the single jagged nunatak of Thompson Rock projecting skyward from its glacial blanket, we decided to skirt around the left of it rather than through the gap between it and the steep rising sides of the much larger Mount Bagshawe. The hanging glaciers on the upper reaches of Mount Bagshawe and the fresh avalanche debris on the corridor between its base and Thompson Rock made us think that trying that route was not worth the risk, and we were proved right. As we flanked around the eastern side of Thompson Rock, a huge house-size slab of ice and snow cracked off a section of hanging glacier high up on Bagshawe and came hurtling down and crashed into the corridor that we had avoided, shattered icy debris flying in all directions; wisdom had prevailed. Serious injury, or potentially loss of life, would most likely have been the outcome had we been underneath the tons of ice that came thundering down.

We drove for another twenty minutes until we found a location between Butler Peaks on our left and a safe spot with Mount Bagshawe rising above us to the north-east, but out of the way of any potential avalanche runs. We knew the southern edge of the Rowley Corridor was just a few kilometres further west, but felt it wise to stop and camp here as the ground toward Rowley looked tricky and we may have to take one sledge at a time. Looking at the map, there was another direct route south of Butler Peaks which went down the Conchin Glacier onto the Sound. However, like the Ryder Glacier north of the Batterbee Range, this was very likely to be impassable for a full unit due to huge crevasse fields, some so wide they would easily swallow an office block – a non-starter really. Alongside this, we were both feeling completely exhausted. We had been on the go for about thirty hours, and on the skidoos for the last twelve, which had entailed maintaining extremely high concentration levels. No other people had visited this area before, which made it a truly unique trip for us and felt really satisfying. Although there had been a few mini-dramas, we were both in one piece, and more importantly, we were in great spirits, able to maintain our sense of humour and having a laugh, particularly about blowing up the bloody air beds in our shattered states after being on the go for so long.

I have been involved in many activities in the past that have been mentally and physically challenging. These have included two-day mountain marathons, fell racing, triathlons, cycle races, road marathons and even the gruelling Parachute Regiment 'P Company' selection; however, as I collapsed into my sleeping bag that afternoon, I believed I was the epitome of tiredness and exhaustion. Even so, "Try another ten-hour shift laying water mains in the winter months, my friend," I could almost hear my old Irish contractor pals say.

Wed 10:00 pm *Up for a very late breakfast, muesli, hot chocolate and the ubiquitous chocolate bar, checked all the kit, oiled and fuelled the 'doos, and then checked the map to find a route down once we got on to the Rowley Corridor. There is a choice of three glaciers to get down onto the Sound, all look hectic with heavy crevassing, the scale of the map is not great and we have a few satellite photos dropped off for us, however, it's definitely going to be a 'let's have a look' trip. Maybe try a recce down the Norman Glacier with a half unit, then back up to do the business, far too hairy with a full unit. This looks like it could be the most 'interesting' journey I have ever undertaken in the mountains, back to bed and see what tomorrow brings.*

Following one of the most wonderful sleeps I can ever remember, I awoke late in the evening for some 'breakfast'. Although it would remain light enough all through the night to travel further, we decided to try and work out the best route down onto the Sound and get more rest for what was potentially a challenging day tomorrow. One aspect of travelling in Antarctica that is very different to the more popular mountain areas around the world is the availability of detailed maps. The only map we had with us was the United States Geological Survey (USGS) that covered the western part of the Dyer Plateau and also the area on both sides of Sound; one of the pilots had been kind enough to drop this off for us back up on the Dyer. The map's scale of 1:500,000 gave no real detail of the glaciers other than showing all three possible routes with their crevasse fields, some more extensive than others. In addition to this, we had a few aerial photographs of the area, but these were lacking in the detail we needed to plan a safe route (although I'm not so sure the word 'safe' can really be used to describe what lay ahead). After some discussion we opted for giving the Norman Glacier a whirl, this decision was based more on a 'pin the tail on the donkey' method rather than anything more scientific, although it did look slightly less crevassed than the other two potential options of the Armstrong Glacier, or the horrendously crevassed McArthur Glacier north of the Norman. We agreed that the smartest thing to do was go out on a half unit to try and recce the best route down. If that didn't present too many problems, we could get everything down in two trips taking one sledge at a time; although this meant that we would have to negotiate a return trip twice. The choice of having a second sledge at the rear was not really worth considering; an out of control tail sledge on a heavily crevassed steep glacier was not a very appealing option.

After eating our not too exciting breakfast/dinner/supper combo and agreeing on the route the next day, I had gone out to check that all the kit was secure for the night, and re-fuelled the skidoos as well as oiling all the track bearings for the trip tomorrow; going out of the tent also gave me a chance to soak up the incredible scenery on a beautiful but very fresh night, with the midnight sun hovering on the horizon. Even though I had been out in the mountains for a few weeks, it still remained quite a surreal experience having daylight around the clock. We had been working off our wrist watches to try and maintain some kind of day and night routine, but often when standing outside the tent, looking around, it was difficult to guess what time of day/night it was without referring to a watch. I had been thorough in checking and oiling the working parts of the skidoo, as we certainly didn't want anything to go wrong mechanically while working out a route down the glacier, I could only imagine the drama that might ensue should one of the skidoos breakdown while crossing a fragile snow bridge on a wide crevasse – prevention was undoubtedly better than cure on this proposed journey, hence my giving the skidoos an extra careful check. With both of us excited and eagerly anticipating what tomorrow might bring, we crashed out for some more rest.

Thursday 20th December: Mount Bagshawe, Rowley Corridor and the Norman Glacier

9:00 am Up at what feels really early (still feeling tired from yesterday) packed all the gear below the stunning Mount Bagshawe and set off for the Norman Glacier. The weather feels incredibly warm compared to the Dyer – it feels tropical at minus 15C, my shoulders and back feel a little burnt due to me being topless for an hour yesterday while we were setting up camp, the wind was cooling when it came, but the sun seems to penetrate the thinner clean air easily down here (also need to be aware of the depleted ozone – again – don't forget the snow-blind saga!). Left the campsite in a full unit at 11:00 am and headed for the Rowley Corridor, big avalanches coming off Bagshawe and the surrounding peaks due to the rising temperatures, fortunately we are not in their path. We think we may be the first people ever to come through here (will check when we return to base), and definitely the first ever to attempt a descent of the Norman Glacier (I wonder who 'Norman was?). Travelled about 20 km to stop at a nunatak at the head of the Norman Glacier and made camp, had to go steadily due to a lot of major crevassing to the north. Truly spectacular scenery and viewed by very few, if any, other humans, possibly the most mind-blowing scenery I have ever seen (I seem to be saying that a lot recently, but this has to be THE view of views!). I hope the photos come out and do the place justice and portray what this landscape is really about, it will be good to share them with Sandra on my return home and maybe it will help her understand why I come down here.

3:00 pm Prepared a half unit for a recce down the Norman Glacier, had a brief radio sched with Pete at Rothera who described some aerial photos of this area that he had managed to find in the base archives, didn't really shed much light on the route, the USGS map we have used to get here is 1:500,000 scale, so not much help other than where the mountain ranges and glaciers are, no details of crevassing at all – unknown ground ahead! We nipped up a small peak at the head of the Norman to give us an overview, there were crevasses all over but we could only see the top section due to the glacier dropping away – we plotted a rough line and hoped for the best – fuck it! We flipped a coin on who would take the lead, winning did seem a lose-lose situation, at the front you may go straight down a big hole, at the back you may drop down a slot that has been weakened by the front 'doo and the sledge! The Norman Glacier is about six miles long, we got about halfway down with only two incidents of crossing dodgy crevasses, only just got across what initially looked like a small slot, then it partially collapsed and looked much larger, I veered quickly right to avoid it, it opened up more on Asti, causing some Celtic cursing! The other was across a huge snow bridge on a monster which I checked out on foot first, it slumped when I crossed, Asti said it dropped away at one side as he went across. Frustratingly, we met thick cloud coming in from the Sound so had to head back up with Asti leading this time.

Return trip a bit 'interesting! The lower crevasse we had opened up coming down had partially collapsed, Asti went hard right and increased speed doing the agreed 'fast as fuck' signal with his right hand, and he only just got across, the sledge then bounced in and out. No time to think about it roped together and I went in-between two enormous holes that were either side of the remaining fragile bridge with full power on the throttle, just as I bounced out the other side; the whole bridge collapsed behind me and I briefly glanced backwards to see an enormous crevasse with no bottom in sight, looks like we may have to re-route that section! As it collapsed I heard a manic laugh and realised it was me, this shit really tests one's sense of humour, and definitely puts the central nervous system on 'high alert!' It was a very sketchy and unnerving part of the journey and I breathed a sigh of relief after getting across – no time for photos in these bloody situations! A couple more dodgy slots caused a bit more emotional trauma, but back to the camp safely at 9:00 pm, probably recce the lower route later tonight if the cloud below us on the Sound clears up.

Cloud didn't clear so we will have a look tomorrow. Probably the best day so far with BAS.

This leg of the trip was incredible and a day that I am sure will live with me for the rest of my life. It stimulated an array of human emotions; exhilaration, intense anxiety (and fear), euphoria, relief, maybe some momentary heart failure, and in the early part of the day, blissful happiness.

The weather was settled and felt warm in comparison to our experiences back up on the Dyer. Once decamped we headed down onto the Rowley in a full unit, being acutely aware of some big avalanches that were occasionally coming down from a hanging glacier on Mount Bagshawe, and some heavy crevassing on the north side of the Corridor. Asti and I were in great spirits – as exhausting as the previous days had been, we remained positive and enthused about embarking on this adventure into the relative unknown, and we had also been getting along well, which is not a given when one is being tested physically, mentally and psychologically to the level that we had.

We camped just below an isolated nunatak at the top of the Norman Glacier and were rewarded with spectacular views in every direction, we had descended about 4,000 feet from the Dyer and the temperature was now up to about minus 15C, which felt quite toasty compared to just a few days ago. Asti and I were still unsure if any other humans had ever set foot in this remarkable valley. We found out later that this area had been surveyed from the air in 1969–74 and was named after David N. Rowley, a senior pilot with the British Antarctic Survey. The Norman Glacier was named for Shaun M. Norman, a base commander with BAS at Stonington Island 1966–68. No records exist of anyone travelling through here by land before our own journey.

I spent a little time taking photographs with my 35 mm Olympus OM10 that had a reasonably reliable manual winding mechanism in cold weather, and managed to capture some great and unique images. While we had been laid up in the storms, I had been dwelling on Sandra; if she could see the photographic evidence of such spectacular scenery that currently surrounded me, it might help her understand my drive to be in such an amazing place. She and I would often go hill walking in the Lake District and she had a real appreciation of natural beauty; my current location would hopefully make her jaw drop on seeing the photographs, and possibly let me off the hook to a certain degree for leaving her back in England. Once I had a good selection of shots, I got wrapped up and laid on the skidoo looking down the Rowley Corridor; it had to be one of the most beautiful natural sights I had ever seen, with jaw-dropping splendour in all directions.

What made the whole experience feel so special was that we were the first people ever to travel through here. The pure white glacier of the Rowley Corridor is about 30 kilometres long and 8 kilometres wide, hemmed in on the east by awesome deep-brown rock towers and on the west side by the coastal mountains, to the north by the chaotic and impassable-looking McArthur Glacier, to the south east the lower section of the Batterbee Mountains through which we had entered the Corridor earlier; and then further south behind us lay the dramatic Butler peaks. All these mountains stretched skyward from the deep glaciers that kept their lower reaches entombed. I was so taken with the view and feeling quite euphoric that I hadn't noticed Asti was also sat on his skidoo, similarly having his brain drenched with the beauty around us; we seemed to be having quite a few of these kindred spirit, speechless moments, smiling in awe together at our majestic surroundings.

For me the only thing that had been missing throughout the trip so far from a natural beauty perspective, was the absence of sunsets. I have always been a huge lover of this wonderful free gift that nature gives us. Due to the sun only dipping onto the horizon during the long Antarctic summer, and not setting over the landscapes for another few months,

I could only imagine what extra depth such colours might give to this view. As a keen amateur photographer, I have often gone the extra yard to capture sunsets, which has entailed camping out on the top of Lakeland peaks back home in England to get both sunsets and sunrises. Winter months can often present the most vivid colours, so I have had more than a few lonely chilly nights on various mountains, solitary vigils which frequently provided me with superb pictures, and a complimentary cold backside.

What also occurred to me as I sat soaking up the view was how surreal it all seemed. Just a few years beforehand I had been working in civil engineering as a team leader repairing burst water mains for a local authority in Leeds. If only my former colleagues could see the environment I was currently in; it really was an incredible change of life that I had undertaken. I had handed in my notice from what appeared (to most) a secure and well paid job to embark on a world trip, which culminated in spending a full winter mountaineering on the South Island of New Zealand. Prior to me leaving my employment, many people there had voiced their concerns, "What if… What about...?" etc. I just smiled and shared a bit of my positive philosophy with them about life being a journey, hopefully without being too patronising. Although there are plenty of people who will not leave their comfortable surroundings, or venture beyond mainstream holidays and outings, this is no reflection on their qualities as a person; each to their own, I say.

My own view is that the greatest rewards can often necessitate taking great risks, and that to experience real authenticity, the world is better viewed and experienced through one's own eyes, rather than via a television or computer screen. A great inspiration for me to travel came from my elder brother, Ed, whom I have mentioned earlier. He would frequently send postcards to us all from his global travels with the Navy; they were always very respectful to our mam and dad, and often protective to my elder sister Gail (such as "If there are any dodgy lads bothering you, sis, let me know") and those to my younger brother Damian and I were filled with amusing anecdotes. When he came home on leave, he always used to wrestle me to the ground in our garden with a big smile on his face; this he said was to make me tough and ready for whatever life might throw at us. When I was about 15, I was ill in hospital in an oxygen tent suffering badly with bronchitis. On learning this, Ed's postcard from Costa Rica read, *"Sorry to hear I missed your confirmation Damian, and Cornelius, hope you're out of hospital when I get back, I'm gonna punch your chest in, that should sort things out!"* Such a wonderful sense of humour! I took up martial arts for a few years in my mid-teens to assist in getting the upper hand when it came to garden wrestling. When Ed heard about this, his postcard read, *"Heard about the 'yee ha, ha cha' stuff, don't think so, I'll still get you, buster,"* which he inevitably did.

Had it not been for his influence, I am sure I would not have got to see the remote mountain landscapes and experienced the differing cultures that I have, and possibly never have ended up here in Antarctica. I could talk for an eternity about my elder brother, but will leave it with one last tale of a great 'Ed' moment which happened while he was home on leave from the Field Gun Crew. He came to watch Damian and I play rugby against a team of steelworkers in Leeds. We easily won the game, and in the bar afterwards, the opposition captain made an attempt to salvage some pride. He approached where all my teammates, Ed, Damian and I were sitting. He had with him a huge lump of a man who I would describe as the lookalike of the character Mungo from the movie *Blazing Saddles*, "I'm the Yorkshire arm wrestling champion, any takers?" he gruffly boasted, the semi-coherent words coming from a face that looked like it had been used to hammer steel into shape.

Ed gave me a nudge and a wink, "I'll give it a whirl, big fella" he calmly said to the huge unsuspecting victim.

"C'mon then, shorty," grunted Mungo as they sat down at the table, many of the opposition team now gathered around, eager to witness their pending victory. In less than a minute, Mungo's left arm, and then his 'stronger' right arm, were unceremoniously whacked down hard onto the table. Ed modestly walked back to our group with a big smile on his face and to a huge cheer from us. We tragically lost Ed to a sudden and unexpected illness in 2012; the world is a sadder place without him.

The dreamlike 'other world' environment of the Antarctic also reinforced my belief that to really find out about oneself, and to truly be in touch with who we are, we have to test our limits, and step way beyond comfort zones. I recalled being in the English 'garrison town' of Aldershot a few years previously getting tested at a number of levels; up to my knees in half-frozen mud along with three other guys and my old friend Paul Briggs, all of us on our last legs laden down with webbing, weapons and a metal 'stretcher' on our shoulders, onto which someone in their wisdom had welded some tank track to give it an extra 'dimension and challenge'. Beside us was a tough Para Corporal screaming obscenities at us to get moving (off beat encouragement, I guess) and to carry on trudging through the mud and freezing water for another few miles.

There appeared to be no purpose to the task other than to test our determination, physical fitness and mental tenacity – which it most certainly did!

After about half an hour or so, we knew we had to begin the inevitable 'Journey of Prospective Doom' – as it had humorously become known – down the Norman Glacier to recce a possible 'safe' route as a half unit, put some tracks in and then get the camp down. We were acutely aware of the potential problems ahead. The maps we had did not have any real indication of crevassing; if we were going down on foot or skis this would not be such a problem as it would be much easier to negotiate through any crevassing. However, we were both experienced in skidoo and sledge travel and knew this could be much trickier, especially if it meant retreating, or weaving our way through the glacier. We had a quick radio schedule with the base commander, Pete, back at Rothera to see if there were any better scale maps of the area to assist us. None were available, so we headed out on the half unit in mid-afternoon, both now fully caught up in the spirit of adventure giving each other a wry smile just prior to setting off. Pete had wished us good luck, he was a mountaineer himself who loved adventure and I guessed he was very envious of where we were right now; he and other staff back on the base would be eagerly monitoring our progress. Asti and I had earlier climbed up a small peak at the head of the glacier to try and gain a vantage point to see what lay ahead and plot the best route we could. However, the top section of the glacier looked riddled with crevasses and we couldn't see too far down due to the gradient of the slope. The phrase 'carpe diem' sprang to mind.

As described in the diary entry above, we had flipped a coin to see who would take lead and rear skidoo. I was victorious in the coin toss and opted for lead skidoo on the way down (get it out of the way!). We agreed that we would switch for the return trip, and Asti would then take the lead skidoo when we came down the next time. Either position presented its own differing problems. The lead driver had the responsibility of negotiating a route down a ten-kilometre-long glacier, ridden with crevasses that were hundreds of metres deep, some covered with bridges of an unknown thickness that might/might not hold the weight of a skidoo and rider, while others were wide open, with gaping chasms that went down into icy deep blue and black depths. The driver of the second skidoo had his own problems to negotiate, which had the equal potential of inducing 'pant filling' anxiety. The sledge that was roped between the two skidoos had to be kept at the right tension so as to not jerk the lead skidoo and affect the lead driver's concentration; it also had to not be allowed to gain too much slack and veer off course. The main problem for the second skidoo, which Asti had experienced earlier near Mount Cadbury, was the danger of the lead skidoo and sledge weakening fragile crevasses as they crossed, leaving the crevasses on the verge of collapse as the rear skidoo went apprehensively across (or as in most cases, shot over at full throttle!).

If we found ourselves on a steep section, with an abundance of crevasses around, making a circle with a half unit to retrace the way in was going to be difficult. The prospect of going through a bridge, or down a crevasse sideway with skidoo and driver (while making a turn and momentarily running parallel with a crevasse) did not bear thinking about; the skidoos weigh about 230 kilogrammes and the sides of crevasse walls are brick hard, going down one bouncing against the walls with the skidoo was invariably going to leave one smarting, hence the need to keep the connecting rope taut to make sure if either of us went down a slot, we shouldn't (shouldn't!) go too far down. Added to this was our isolated location; should either, or both, of us get injured, then there could be a serious problem regarding treatment and evacuation. We also only had one functioning radio, which, in our infinite wisdom, we had left back at the camp to avoid risking losing it and the sledge down a crevasse. Asti and I had discussed this earlier; we reckoned that although there was the chance that one of us might get hurt, the other could administer first aid and drive back the few miles to camp on the inbound tracks (dangerously on a solo skidoo) and then radio the base or Fossil Bluff, who might or might not be able to assist, depending on the weather and flying conditions. Although we both were skilled in first aid and treating minor trauma injuries, we weren't blooming doctors; one really was out on a limb down here.

Regardless of all these concerns, our options appeared limited to just the one, as we knew no aircraft were available to get us, and it also would be very tricky for a plane to land on the Rowley because of the extent of the crevassing. Even so, it was also very apparent to me that, although the journey ahead was causing a significant amount of anxiety, we were both keen to make the first descent (and ascent) of the glacier.

We headed down with me leading; the ground had a moderate decline near the top section, but after two hundred metres became steeper in places, which I knew meant I would be soon coming across the crevasses we had seen from the ridge outlook earlier. The first one I approached seemed fairly innocuous initially, but then, just as I was on top of it, the bugger partially collapsed to reveal a wide crevasse. I veered away from the cavernous hole and held my breath, knowing Asti would be cursing as the sledge would also probably widen it. I gained enough distance to know that he was across and looked around; there had definitely been some drama as I had felt the link rope jolting hard. Even above the noise of the engines I could hear him shouting, "We kin nay come back up over that fucker!" I didn't say at the time, but I wasn't sure we had any other choice but to return over it somehow; negotiating a different route uphill through these crevasses would be asking for serious trouble! There were plenty more slots of a foot or two wide which were child's play. This was all seeming pleasant enough until I slowed down at a monster that appeared to cut all the way across the glacier as far as we could see to either side, mostly revealing open horrendous drops, but with a few snow bridges intact here and there.

Asti came forward and agreed we needed to rope up and have me head across on foot over one of the better looking snow bridges with the bog chisel and 'test' it out for thickness; it appeared to be about six metres wide, so once again would need to be able to take the full weight of skidoo and driver. I walked tentatively across and back, probing the snow depth every couple of feet; at the bridge's central weakest point it felt about half a metre thick, but held my weight standing up. It was a goer I thought, and then I returned to the lead skidoo and drove across the bridge, not too slowly I might add. It slumped slightly with a very unnerving 'vwum' sound, so I increased speed for the sledge and Asti to follow; the less time on this bugger the better, I felt.

Being on this slumping crevasse for that very brief moment was a very strange experience. All my senses seemed so intense and fine-tuned for that half a second or so; the underlying acute knowledge that if it collapsed it was highly likely I could lose my life, or be badly injured; every aspect of my entire self, physical and psychological, was acutely focussed on that exact moment. I don't ever remember my senses being so amplified before; it would be very interesting to see what one's heart rate and blood pressure is in such a concentrated moment. There is no doubt that the brain had activated my adrenal gland to send that powerful drug coursing around my system. Once we had crossed the bridge, Asti shouted that it had all dropped away on the right hand side, leaving only a narrow corridor to get back across – blooming great news! We had about fifty metres of ground ahead that looked reasonably safe, so Asti brought his skidoo up alongside mine, making sure not to drive over the connecting ropes. We had a brief discussion about having to go back up that way. Asti wryly informed me that the last crevasse that opened up had left a bridge only three metres or so wide to cross, and in either direction left and right from where we looked, it was completely open, leaving us only that fragile bridge to get back up – lovely jubbly!

We had come only a few kilometres, and as we returned to the task ahead of descending further down the glacier and contemplated our next move, thick mist and low dark cloud had crept in from the Sound and was now licking its way up the glacier towards us. It would be impossible to try and negotiate a route in such poor visibility; luckily we were on safe enough ground to do a tight 180 degree turn. We swapped positions, with Asti now on the lead skidoo for the hellish return trip over what we already knew were very sketchy crevasses. For a moment, just prior to setting off back up, I paused and once again had a sharp awareness of the surreal and quite bizarre situation I found myself in compared to what I had been doing only a few years ago. Here I was in incredibly spectacular surroundings in the Antarctic wilderness, on a dangerous crevasse-laden glacier, where no other humans had ever travelled down before, about to drive across chasms hundreds of feet deep with bridges that had already given us a warning about what may happen if we mess with them again, and if things were to go 'pear shaped', we were pretty much on our own; "So… you're not so bloody clever after all," I sarcastically said to myself.

It appeared Asti was also having a 'moment' as he looked over his shoulder and gave me the nod. Then, with a little shake of his head he went off. Although we were both full of adventurous spirit, I guessed he was having an intake of breath, and probably saying something along the lines of, "Aye, this is gonna be fucking interesting!" The calm weather and glorious blue skies above seemed a tad irrelevant, as our brains, which would normally be busily appreciating such a beautiful day, were otherwise engaged as Asti was heading directly at the remaining section of snow bridge. Without any hesitation, he blasted straight across it, while vigorously doing the only hand signal I was expecting at this juncture, 'fast as fuck!' I was desperately trying to keep the connecting rope at the right tension; I didn't want to be jerking his skidoo backwards while he was midway across the crevasse – that would definitely induce some colourful Highland language.

I was also intensely monitoring what happened ahead to the bridge while Asti crossed it; unfortunately, the very unreasonable and selfish section of bridge collapsed even further as his skidoo seemed to slump in and out of its ever-reducing span. *For fuck's sake*! My thoughts shouted at me as the sledge then hammered across the partially collapsed section, causing even more of the bridge to fall away – blooming smashing! There was now no other option but to continue full throttle; all this was happening in just a few seconds, but it did feel a bit like slow-motion. I was well past the point of no return and pressed the thumb throttle as hard as I could (nearly dislocating my thumb, such was my urgency), heading for the narrow remaining section of the snow bridge. The front ski of the skidoo went in a downward direction into the slumping snow bridge that was now only about two metres wide with the huge crevasse completely open on either side without any bottom in sight. *Shit, that's not good!* flashed into my acutely focused mind. I leaned slightly back and pulled upwards on the handle bars, the engine still at full throttle. As I felt the bridge below me slump even more, I bounced out onto the other side at the precise moment the whole of the bridge fell away into the bottomless-looking crevasse. The back of the skidoo tracks was left hanging just over the edge – fantastic! Strangely, I recall just letting out a kind of manic laugh at the outrageousness of the situation; a basic coping mechanism I imagine (I also think I should have maybe worn a nappy, there was definitely some 'touching cloth' action at the critical point!).

We then faced having to get across the other snow bridge that Asti had earlier shouted we were certainly not returning across, this induced more heart stopping moments as that also partially collapsed when I crossed it. Although this weakened bridge did not collapse completely as the last one had, a section to the side of me dropped away while I was right in the middle of it; even though I was going full throttle, my brain certainly registered the chaos that was happening, as once again, I could hear myself swearing through gritted teeth, and I imagine, a tightly grimaced face.

The descent of this glacier was proving to be quite challenging, and getting all the kit down was going to be fun; it was no surprise to learn that no sledge team had ever been down it. We arrived back at camp about 9:00 pm with a certain degree of relief, but we both remained confident that when the weather cleared we would find a way down to the bottom of the glacier, staying well clear of the horror inducing crevasse we had only just scraped across. Although we planned to give it a try tonight, the lower half of the Norman remained draped in a thick mist, so we deferred further adventures until the next day.

While having some late dinner in the tent, we ended up in hysterics at our earlier shenanigans, and how lucky we both felt at getting back up the glacier unscathed. We also agreed that it really had been an incredible day.

Friday 21st December, Mid-Summer's Day: Rowley Corridor and Norman Glacier

6:00 am Up nice and early, still thick cloud below us on the lower section of the glacier so unable to recce the bottom section. Slept well last night, dreaming about Sandra, consciously my mind is acutely focused on the task in hand and getting safely to FB, I guess subconsciously I am missing her. Good weather up here so we took a half unit for a trip around some spectacular nunataks we had seen from camp about 6 km north on the upper reaches of the Rowley Corridor. We came across some heavy crevassing so parked the 'doos, roped up and climbed one of the smaller peaks, nice to get the heart rate going again, saw three snow petrels. Superb views from the top, to the west is MacArthur Glacier, it looks beautiful but horrendously crevassed – huge holes and slots everywhere, impossible to travel through; I hope the lower half of the Norman Glacier is nothing like it. Soaked up the view for a while, felt philosophical and named it 'Mid-Summer Nunatak'. Descended and circumnavigated the spectacular nunataks (which look similar to the Dolomites in Italy), sneaking past some huge crevasses on the return trip and got back to camp at 2:00 pm, a really enjoyable 6 hr trip.

Following a great night's sleep, we arose nice and early, I had been experiencing some very intense dreams about Sandra; bearing in mind our current situation one would have thought my mind would be entirely pre-occupied with completing this trip safely. Maybe Freud was right about us having no control of the unconscious and I was not being honest with myself about how much I was missing her.

Because the Norman Glacier and the Sound were still blanketed in cloud, we decided to spend the time productively and go out on a recce trip up the Rowley. However, as we would not be able to see down the Norman, in truth we were going on a fun trip for ourselves (classed as a 'jolly' by BAS staff). Travelling out as a half unit for our 'jolly' recce trip was fantastic; the Rowley Corridor is about 30 kilometres long and 8 kilometres wide, hemmed in on the east and west by awesome rock towers and mountains, the heavily crevassed Macarthur Glacier further north, and the Batterbee Mountains to the southeast. After only a short while travelling up this pristine white glacier, our way was barred by huge crevasses that looked to be cutting a significant way diagonally across the Rowley.

They were snow-bridged in places, but as they looked to be about 20 metres wide and potentially hundreds of feet deep, we didn't want to risk crossing; we both felt we had enough of a challenge ahead of us! Fortunately, we were close enough to park below some isolated and amazing-looking nunataks that we had seen protruding from the middle of the glacier as we travelled up the Corridor. We roped up and ascended about 300 metres to the top of the closest peak. We got up it fairly quick; we were both thankful for the exercise, and the climb wasn't technical, just involving some steep scrambling in places. We took it in turns to lead each rope length, but as there were only a few short sections that required the placement of any gear to protect us in case of a fall, we moved swiftly, and the route did not take us as long as we initially anticipated it would, reaching the top within an hour. It was also exhilarating and refreshing getting our hearts, lungs and leg muscles toiling hard again, each of us working up a sweat on our way to the top of this spectacular nunatak.

As we sat on the summit soaking up the view breathing heavily from the exercise, and sucking in the purest air I can ever remember, I decided to give this beautiful unnamed peak the grand and fitting title of 'Mid-summer Nunatak'. It was great to be sat on solid ground; after being permanently on snow for so long it did feel a little strange being on rock again. While we gazed silently, three snow petrels came flying up the face of the peak and darted just over our heads. They must have been nesting somewhere on the face and were spooked by the extremely unfamiliar sight of two humans; such beautiful birds, and hardy, as they were a long way from their food supply at the coast, more than a hundred kilometres away. They are a bird that breeds exclusively in Antarctica, easily identifiable by their pure white plumage, and a small black beak flanked by two coal-black eyes. Below us stretched the Rowley Corridor, the crevasses that had halted our journey northward were much clearer now, some looking large enough to accommodate an office block. We could see back up the glacier to the 2,200 metre Mount Bagshawe that we had camped below on our way in and directly across the glacial valley were 600 metre rock towers that reminded me of the Italian Dolomites, where there are similar looking peaks, the only difference being that no other people had set foot here before, and there was not a man-made thing in sight. Not a speck of vegetation clung onto them, just rock, snow and ice; other than some movement in the glaciers this landscape had not changed for thousands of years.

Soaking up such amazing mountain scenery inevitably provokes in me feelings of fulfilment, contentment and a real love of such incredible natural beauty. I'm sure this is not the case for all, and it is likely there are many people who are not so 'in tune' with the mountains, or those who don't appreciate the splendour of an untouched landscape. Maybe those with a more mainstream lifestyle, weighed down by all the trappings of the developed world, might react to such scenery with a "But there's nothing there".

My approach, on the contrary, would always be "But there's everything there"; each to their own I guess.

Asti was sitting on a rock close by with a satisfied smile all over his face gazing across the valley, his single quiet comment of, "Aye, that really is so fuckin' beautiful," was certainly a strong indicator he was on my wavelength on this issue; I suppose there was really never any doubt or debate about that!

After taking in the scenery for a while, we headed back down to the skidoos on the glacier below. From our vantage point on the top it looked like we could travel slightly further north and squeeze between the nearest crevasse and the foot of the nunataks, then travel full circle and pick up our trail in. We did manage to squeeze down a 50-metre corridor between the nunataks bergschrund and the nearest crevasse out on the glacier (a bergschrund is crevasse that forms at the base of mountains, when the glacier pulls away from the stagnant ice that clings to the rock, some bergschrunds can be more than a hundred metres deep). Against normal glacier travelling rules, we had to take a line parallel with a huge crevasse for about a quarter of a mile; fortunately, we could clearly see where the edge of the crevasse met solid snow. Unnervingly we could also see down into the gaping chasms where the snow bridges had occasionally collapsed; it looked very deep – not somewhere we wanted to unwittingly drive our 230 kilogrammes skidoos down, with us attached to them. We were rewarded with outstanding scenery all the way back to camp. Just as we arrived, the cloud appeared to be slowly breaking up on the Sound; it looked like our very enjoyable trip up the Rowley was to be replaced by whatever the Norman Glacier had awaiting us.

Friday 5:00 pm The cloud and mist eventually cleared from most of the Sound in late afternoon so we went to recce the bottom half, I thought yesterday was unnerving but this afternoon nearly made me break out the morphine to calm me down. Asti led down this time, snow bridges collapsed on two occasions just as I got over them, as the second one collapsed I'm sure I actually felt my heart skip a few beats! We eventually got a reasonable route recced to a few hundred metres from the bottom that weaved through some large crevassing, we'll have to bring the sledges down one at a time, which means two return trips – lovely jubbly! Back at the camp for midnight, a fantastic but long and tiring 18-hour day; weather permitting we will get all the kit down the glacier tomorrow and then negotiate a route across the Sound. Sat outside the tent soaking the view up at midnight, I have become accustomed to having no darkness whatsoever, it will feel strange seeing dark skies and stars after months of permanent daylight, midsummer night at midnight and it's just started snowing heavily in broad daylight – quite bizarre! As I dozed off in the tent my mind drifted to my working days a few years ago, what a change!

The improvement in the weather down on the Norman after the great trip down the Corridor met with mixed feelings, we now had to give it a whirl down the newly titled 'Glacier of Impending Death'. Although it didn't live up to its title exactly, it was a journey that made yesterday's adventure something of a walk in the park! The same thing that happened on the monster crevasse yesterday occurred twice more while we were going downhill with Asti in the lead. We had taken a completely new route, avoiding yesterday's tracks, but the same monster crevasse stretched the width of the valley and was impossible to avoid; we only just got across as a similar bridge collapsed underneath us – I should have volunteered to take the lead again as my nervous system was getting a tad frayed, bouncing in and out of fragile crevasse bridges that were collapsing behind me was not conducive to maintaining a healthy mental state.

There were numerous more one to two metre crevasses, all seemed to have weak bridges due to the relatively warmer temperatures than we had experienced on higher ground, one was three metres across that we struggled to find a bridge solid enough to cross. After much deliberation we blasted across a somewhat dubious bridge with the now familiar 'FAF' hand signal. There then followed a route weaving through a chaotic crevasse field until we eventually reached a point close to the bottom of the glacier at about 10:00 pm; this had been slow and methodical work, the crevasses were not huge, but often seemed to be fracturing off at unusual angles, which meant us taking a meandering route through them, entailing many stops, and an abundance of Highland cursing. However, more cloud had floated in again and glued itself to the final lower section of the Norman, barring further progress for now. The view across the Sound to Alexander Island over the low laying cloud was magnificent; crossing this 30-kilometre-wide frozen sea channel that currently lay mostly hidden underneath the patchy cloud blanket was a problem that would have to wait until we sorted our current situation out.

There was little time for celebration. The weather was still clear, so we took on board some chocolate and water and headed back up. It was ten kilometres to camp and I had already had a mental plan for which bridges to attempt to cross, I had been really focused on looking at alternatives right and left of those that were fragile and had partially collapsed as we crossed them on the way down. Asti and I both agreed that there could be no room for hesitation going back uphill over snow bridges, and I warned him that it was going to be 'FAF' all the way. Although this seemed somewhat reckless, it did feel to us both the only thing we could do; going slowly over those weak bridges would be asking for trouble

Two hours later we had reached the top of the glacier and I slowed and stopped on some safe-looking ground; Asti drew up beside me and we both must have had similar expressions; ecstasy mixed with shock and horror. I had not let up on the throttle at any point crossing the crevasses, but had stopped or slowed for few breaks on the safer ground between crevasses to calm down and prepare for more extreme trauma. Perhaps more by chance and good luck than skill and sound judgement, the crevasse bridges I had opted for in split-second decisions had all nearly held; those that collapsed were only a few feet across and Asti had shot over them. Although we were ecstatic that we had got up safely, we were both acutely and very worryingly aware that we now had the delightful prospect of two return trips up and down the bugger; we could never take a full unit down so it had to be one sledge at a time, having another sledge at the rear of the second skidoo, with nothing to control it during the descent, was unthinkable on such dangerous ground (although we could use the chains on the front runners of the second sledge, they did not provide enough friction on steep slopes to adequately slow a heavy laden sledge). Back at camp we had a hot drink, some boil in a bag rice, and relaxed under the midnight sun on a midsummer night; it had been beautiful weather all day (which unsurprisingly we hadn't been too focused on). The temperature had remained around minus15C, so it was pleasant enough to sit outside the tent wrapped up in down jackets. However, this was about to change. Having been sat down soaking up the view for only thirty minutes, light snow heading in from the north-west slowly began falling. Within ten minutes it was blizzard like; Asti's pragmatic observation of, "Och, well that's fucked it," summed it up.

That was today's bloody tracks snowed over; all that work done in vain. But this is the Antarctic, I guess… 'life is a journey, indeed'. It was pointless worrying about it, like any problem that is beyond one's control, fretting about it achieves nothing except causing unnecessary stress; if problems are able to be solved, sort them out, if not, forget about them. Tomorrow would be another day at the office, hopefully to be survived unscathed!

Saturday 22nd December: Rowley Corridor

Unfortunately a lie-up day, unusually heavy snow, windy and bad contrast all day, even more unfortunately, the tracks we put down yesterday will have disappeared. These in-tent days are not great at the moment, I get too much time to think about home and Sandra, and am often feeling a little sad and melancholy, the confined space of the inside of a tent is not a great place to feel emotionally low. Three days before Christmas and I am camped in a mountain pass in the middle of the Antarctic Peninsula when I should be out buying presents for my girlfriend – nobody forced me here and I will have to make up for it next year, I guess – out of the tent to get blown around while having a speedy toilet break.

After the previous two days of intense excitement, being back inside the tent due to the blizzard raging outside was something of an emotional comedown. Our adrenal glands had been working overtime over the course of the last two days and now we were back in 'lie-up' mode until the storm abated. Although our bodies needed some rest, we also wanted to crack the full descent of the Norman

Glacier and get across to Fossil Bluff. We were also aware that the storm outside would have highly likely blown away all evidence of our tracks from yesterday's route-finding trip; we accepted this and adopted a positive approach that hopefully the falling snow would also build up the depth of the snow and strengthen some of the crevasse bridges. After half the day had passed and with no sign of a let up in the blizzard's ferocity, I could sense my focus was slipping and my mood becoming a tad gloomy thinking about Sandra back at home. It was not healthy to ponder on this in the environment we were in, and the melancholy feeling was probably accentuated due to our being on a bit of a comedown from the previous day's excitement. I decided to go outside for a blast from a good old-fashioned Antarctic storm to clear my mind, and also very quickly clear my bowels, which as usual, was an extremely swift process. I earnestly hoped tomorrow would bring more clement weather.

Sunday 23rd December

Another blooming lie-up day, the storm continues to blow outside, went out to check the gear, about 10" of new snow; although it will have definitely have covered our route, it may have filled in and strengthened the crevasse bridges. Checked the skidoos, we have done 530 km since we were dropped at Auriga. Occupied the day reading, chatting with Asti, eating, rehydrating – coping with being tent-bound is certainly an interesting psychological test! Spoke on the radio sched with to my old friend Bruce who was with a field party about 400 miles away, the signal was quite feint, gave him my best regards and wished him "Happy Christmas".

Our prediction of the falling snow covering our previous tracks was looking to be true as I went outside to check the weather. The snow was falling, but only lightly now, and there looked to have been about ten inches laid overnight, which was pretty much a guarantee that the previous tracks we had made would now be covered. On the positive side, this might have made the crevasse bridges less terrifying. Although the falling snow was easing a little, the wind was still fierce, blowing snow and spindrift around high into the air. Any travel in such poor visibility was out of the question. Asti and I were by now well-versed in our storm-bound routine and just got on with things as best we could, both of us hiding our frustration as we sat at the top of the beckoning Norman Glacier. I alleviated the boredom of being tent-bound by checking all the kit was secure around our camp to make sure nothing was at risk of being blown away. Some of the 'katabatic' winds have reportedly gusted in excess of 300 kmh (although so far we had been really fortunate and not had anything more than about 140 kmh); although this can be a tad unsettling when one is in the tent riding it out, we had been confident that our secure pitching of the tent would withstand the weather, and so far we had been right. While I was by the two skidoos I had a quick look at the speedometer dial to see how far we had travelled since we were dropped at Auriga Nunatak by the aircraft; we had journeyed more than 500 kilometres since disembarking the Twin Otter, which included the relatively safe day trips completing the glacier-pole project back up on the Dyer, but also incorporated a few 'tricky' miles along the way; my instincts told me we had a few more interesting sections ahead of us.

At the end of our 7:00 pm scheduled radio contact with Rothera to give them a progress update, I managed to get patched through to Bruce Crawford, an old friend who was working with a field party about 650 kilometres to the north of our location. I had first met Bruce two years previously through our mutual friend Andy Tugby, when Andy and I were undertaking an outdoor education course at Telford College in Edinburgh. Bruce was a wonderful, friendly guy, always smiling and full of positive energy. He owned and lived in his apartment in the city and Andy was renting a room there. We quickly became friendly, mainly due to our mutual passion for the mountains. At the end of the course I headed off with Andy to work at the summer camp in New Hampshire in the States, and I bid my fond farewells to Bruce in Edinburgh, unsure if our paths would ever cross again. Six months later, after I had just boarded the RRS *Biscoe* which was docked in Grimsby about to head south with BAS, who should come walking up the gangplank but Bruce. Neither of us had ever spoken about any interest in coming down to work with BAS or were aware that the other had applied for the vacant posts that were advertised in a climbing magazine, and now here we were on the Antarctic Peninsula, both of us sat storm-bound in our tents having a brief chat on the field radio; that could be ranked as an excellent definition of a strange coincidence, there being currently only a very small number of people on the planet doing what we were.

Monday 24th December, Christmas Eve: Rowley Corridor and Norman Glacier

7:00 am Clear weather so we recced a new route down the Glacier, about two feet of snow has fallen and most of the bridges seemed a lot more stable as we crossed many crevasses, only one major collapse but plenty more of the 'FAF' hand movement. Great feeling getting to the bottom, had to drop the half unit sledge at the base and head back up to the top of the glacier and pack the camp for the second sledge and bring that down, all packed away and left the Rowley Corridor at 3:45 pm, what a memorable place, so pristine and beautiful, I wonder if anyone else will ever set foot here in the next 100 years? While halfway down, saw a Twin Otter that came close by and gave us a wing wiggle, not sure who was flying. The second sledge was heavier so opened up a few holes that Asti's lead skidoo had weakened, throttle down and bounced in and out of a few that were about 6–8 feet wide, one 12 ft crevasse had a narrow bridge that I just squeezed across, most of it collapsed as the sledge bounced in and out – hold the breath and full throttle again!

11:30 pm All the gear and ourselves safely down the Norman Glacier at last, a first descent, that feels good! We decided to un-rope the 'doos, and went with a sledge each – although the frozen sea channel has 200 metres of ice above it, it is highly unlikely to have any crevassing – we hoped! The journey across was great with no major incidents, but once in the middle felt like we were on a different planet, there were lots of different shades of blue and white, then occasional melt pools that you couldn't tell the depth of until you were going through them, I had one that half buried the 'doo, so full belt to get it out in a huge spray of water before the engine had chance to cut out, I don't really want to be knee deep in freezing slushy water at this stage of the game! We came across some big cracks just at the base of the Eros Glacier where it met the Sound, managed to weave a circuitous route around them and eventually got to the sanctuary of Fossil Bluff at 11:00 pm, only seven hours to get from the head of the Norman Glacier, across the Sound to the hut – can't blooming argue with that! The guys at FB were pleased (and relieved) to see us. The entire trip from the Dyer to Thompson Rock, around Mount Bagshawe, through the Rowley Corridor, circling Uniform Nunatak, down the Norman Glacier (many times) and across the Sound, has to be the trip of a lifetime – 6 days (2 lie-ups) and 280 kilometres.

***1:00 am** To bed on Christmas Day in the sanctuary and relative civilisation of Fossil Bluff, if only Sandra, family and friends could see this location – a very white Christmas indeed!*

It is Christmas Eve morning and here I am, once again privileged (and on occasion terrified) to experience an incredible day in the mountains and glaciers of this beautiful and unspoilt continent. We awoke to clear blue skies with no wind blowing whatsoever. Although it was still relatively cool at about minus 15C, this was perfect travelling weather for us and we both felt that if it held out, we should get a decent route down the Norman Glacier. We could then return to decamp, get everything to the bottom of the glacier and plan a route across the Sound; with a bit of luck, we could make it to Fossil Bluff before Christmas Day. With giddy excitement, albeit mixed with a certain level of nervous anticipation, we quickly wolfed down some basic breakfast, melted as much drinking water as we could and prepared the half unit for the next chapter of the Norman Glacier odyssey. Wisdom told us not to take the tent down just yet; we were both fully aware that things can change very quickly in this part of the world. As predicted, the significant snowfall had now covered all the tracks we had previously laid, but this in no way held up our progress, as I already had a mental image of how we would negotiate the best route down due to the previous forays we had made. At about 8:00 am, we drove to the head of the glacier with me taking the lead skidoo, the adjoining ropes once again coalescing the two skidoos and sledge as one unit. I took the initial few hundred metres quite steadily, as the small crevasses we had encountered on Friday were now invisible; this kept the speed of the skidoo low as I had to scan left and right for the tell-tale signs of any slots in the snow. In good light, crevasses that have bridges across them can often easily be seen, the snow may be slightly slumped where the bridge is, or when you look to the left or right, there may be areas where the bridge has collapsed. This morning, though, the two and three feet wide crevasses we had crossed on Friday were now completely invisible due to the heavy snowfall.

This gave a slight false sense of security, only because we knew that some of the crevasses that lay ahead were very wide, in particular the one that spanned the width of the glacier and previously caused our hearts to be in our mouths. We wanted to be able to identify the wider ones to choose the best spot to cross, but going blind across wide snow bridges that we knew hid deep crevasses just feet below was not ideal. After we had travelled a distance to the point where I thought we had encountered the first large crevasse where the bridge had given way on Friday, I slowed to a snail's pace; when we passed this way before, I had made a mental note of roughly where the crevasse was in its relation to a point on the jagged ridge to our north. This foresight, combined with slowing right down, appeared to be a smart decision, since as I edged forward, the open crevasse slowly came into view ahead. It was exposed across most of the ground left and right, but fortunately a decent looking bridge had developed across the 6-metre-wide gap due to the heavy blowing snow.

The majority of time in the mountains, decisions are made by assessing all the risk factors, weighing up the positive and protective factors, then making a balanced decision on the available information; however, this morning's decision-making felt more like 'cross one's fingers and hope for the best'. I turned the nose of the skidoo in line with the snow bridge and, with just ten metres between the front of the skidoo and the edge of the bridge, I gave Asti the 'FAF' hand signal, hit the throttle and blasted across. Although this felt a tad reckless, from the previous days' experiences my confidence that the bridge would support us was reasonably strong (reasonably). The bridge slumped as I hammered across it, and as usual I kept going fast until I knew I had gained enough ground for the sledge and Asti to be across, which was in itself a tad unnerving, as I was now speeding across snow that could have bridges on unseen crevasses. As I slowed down on what appeared to be safe ground, Asti shouted down to me that it had held, but that his skidoo had slumped into the crevasse a little; good fortune prevailed. Although this was another hairy encounter, most of the smaller open crevasses we had met on Friday higher up on the glacier were now covered; this gave us hope that the chaotic bottom section ahead may be now much safer due to the heavy snow storm. The last couple of miles of the glacier had indeed improved for us; before travelling down this we had a few minutes rest at the halfway point where the glacier levelled out a little before steepening down towards the Sound. We took this opportunity to look out across the George VI Sound and plan a potential route across the 30-kilometre expanse from the base of the Norman Glacier to the sanctuary of Fossil Bluff hut.

The weather remained excellent, which gave us a fantastic view across the ice covered valley. The George VI Ice Shelf is completely flat, with the dramatic mountains and glaciers of Alexander Island as a backdrop. Dotted all over it were different size melt pools of varying shades of blue, some the size of football fields, others just a few metres across. These iridescent pools shimmering as the light reflected off them; it really did present as a scene from another planet, and we had to get across the bugger. While we were gazing across the Sound, the tell-tale engine noise of a Twin Otter gradually started entering my ears; the distinctive sound was coming from the south as it slowly increased in volume. I scanned the sky and quickly made out the blood-red aircraft flying low and easily visible against the mountain backdrop. The plane had most likely been dropping equipment off for a different field party in another area, or was moving staff around; whoever was flying must have heard about our little adventure, because the aircraft deviated from its northern path and came in close to the head of the Norman Glacier and gave the wings a wiggle as it roared past us just a hundred metres away.

The pilots were a great bunch and some of them were not averse to occasionally bending a few rules; they had varied backgrounds, ranging from ex-fighter pilots, to commercial airline pilots and stunt pilots. All had a common desire: to fly in this great white wilderness. Before coming into the field, I remember chatting and joking with Neil about the hierarchy in aviation while I was co-piloting a short flight with him from Rothera. He said he wasn't too keen on the stuffiness and snobbery when he was a pilot flying with a major airline on long haul Boeing 747 flights. He added that he had always felt he would get involved in some kind of wilderness flying; he most certainly had achieved that goal. He was also an accomplished stunt pilot who flew the 'Pitts Special' bi and triplanes; this explained a lot when watching him throw the Twin Otters around the sky. Listening to him talk about his flying career made me wonder how things were in the social calendar of pilots back in the land of 'civilisation'; what events they may be obliged to attend, whether there was hierarchical snobbery among them and how things might be organised at occasions such as a pilots' convention; would the pilot's rank and airline be reflected in the treatment from the hosts? I could imagine the waiting staff at some swanky event walking around with two tier canapé trays, and just before offering the bite-size delights to the pilots, a brave sarcastic waiter asking who they flew with:

"Second Officer, short haul with Ryanair."
"Bottom layer only, sir, the sausage rolls are excellent, sourced from Iceland, I believe."
Conversely, *"London to Singapore with Cathay Pacific."*
"Top layer, sir, I understand the salmon and caviar rolls are delightful, fresh in from Loch Linnhe."

The aircraft veered away to regain its flight path and we re-focused on the task ahead. As expected, the last couple of miles on the bottom section of the Norman Glacier had indeed improved for us as a result of the heavy snowfall. However, this bottom section of the Norman still obliged us with a few surprises; we managed to get safely to the lowest part without any serious dramas, the snow covering down here seemed to be even deeper than what we had encountered on the upper section of the glacier, where the snow had filled the tops of many of the open crevasses. Unfortunately, or fortunately if you were a crazed adrenaline junkie, even though there had been heavy snowfall on the lower part of the glacier, there were still some wider crevasses that presented dubious bridges, resulting in a few shaky moments. About 500 metres from the point where the sloping glacier met the Sound, we came across another monster crevasse, similar to the large crevasse many kilometres behind us at the top end of the glacier. It also looked to span the width of the glacier and brought me to an abrupt halt – so close yet so far. Looking across to the far left and then to the right, it became quickly obvious that we wouldn't be able to find a route around by the base of the mountains as there was chaotic surface moraine there, with huge boulders blocking any possible route and treacherous looking bergschrunds waiting menacingly at the base of the steeply sloping ridges. However, just 30 metres to my right I could see there was a decent-looking snow bridge across the crevasse. I was still about 20 metres from the edge of the chasm, and so, turning towards Asti, I signalled my intention of going towards the bridge to have a closer look. He gave me the thumbs up as he could also see the potential way across.

The skidoo engine slowly ticked over as I cautiously turned the ski on the front of the skidoo and edged towards the snow bridge; as I got closer, I stood up, holding the handle bars with slight pressure on the throttle to gain as high a vantage point as possible. Inching forward, I began to peer into the crevasse and saw that the bridge across the 3-metre-wide gap looked to be of a decent depth; I estimated it to be about half a metre deep at the narrowest point of the arch, with safer looking snow on the other side – easy peasy. One deep breath and the 'FAF' hand signal to Asti, full throttle action ensued, and the bridge held, with only a slight slump as the sledge and Asti's skidoo crossed it. Another thirty minutes of downhill travelling found us having to cross a few more crevasse bridges that spanned across slots just a metre or two; however, these had decent bridges that held up well to the weight of the skidoos and sledges. This made me feel a little more relaxed about coming back up, compared to Friday's intensity; having just two doubtful crevasses to cross seemed something of a luxury. Nevertheless, we had to cross them twice and we both knew the second sledge we had to bring down was much heavier than the half unit sledge that we were about to leave at the base of the Norman. We paused at the base of the glacier and I gave Asti a pat on the shoulder, both of us sporting broad smiles; we were overjoyed that we had managed to find a route down. Although we didn't say anything about it at the time, it felt extra special knowing we were the first people ever to have travelled down the beautiful, but very dangerous Norman Glacier.

As we rested briefly at the bottom, I quickly pulled the stove out from under the storage area below the skidoo seat and melted some snow for a quick hot drink and an energy boost of chocolate and biscuits. We were wise enough not to rest on the laurels of our achievement, as this mission was far from over; the trip back up to our camp might well present further dramas, so taking food and fuel on board was essential. Plus, as we sat with our backs to the Norman Glacier, looking out across the wide expanse of the King George VI Ice Shelf to Alexander Island in the distance, where the sanctuary of Fossil Bluff teased and beckoned, we were conscious we still had to get across that barrier. We looked at each other and it dawned on us that there was indeed plenty more to do and no time for complacency. This little adventure was far from over. That thought reminded me of the wise adage about mountaineering, *The top of the mountain is only the halfway point, you still have to get safely down.*

We un-roped the sledge, made it secure with snow stakes at the base of the glacier and connected the front and rear of our skidoos together for the trip back up. While we sat for ten minutes enjoying the much needed hot tea and chocolate, and soaking up the amazing view ahead of us, I did a quick mental check to try and analyse how I was really feeling; the most prominent emotions seemed to be elation and euphoria. Although the trip down had some heart stopping moments, I did not really feel too stressed by it all, which surprised me bearing in mind the location I was in; but I was sure that could possibly change in the hours to come.

In the nerve-wracking moments crossing the unstable bridges there are probably some people who might have looked to the heavens and said a quick prayer. However, I'm not really a religious person even though I was brought up in an Irish Catholic household, where attending church and 'confession' was part of my childhood routine. Unlike most of my peers with Irish parents, my own parents were quite liberal in their approach and during my early teens when we came out of church on a Sunday morning, I would mischievously ask questions such as, "Mam, can I ask you something? If that priest is 'drinking the blood of Christ', does that make him part vampire?" and "So this God character who created the universe, was he having a bad day when he created cancer and malaria?" My parents soon realised I was never going to conform to any mainstream religion and eventually said that they didn't think I was getting much out of it, so by the age of fifteen I was given the option of not attending. From a personal perspective, and with all due respect to those who do adhere to their chosen religion, one particular aspect of Catholicism that I didn't enjoy, was attending 'confession' on a Saturday morning. I used to hook up with my next door neighbour, Pat, who was also from an Irish family and dressed in our smart pants, clean shirt and freshly polished shoes, we would stroll down to the Cathedral which was, and still is, in Leeds city centre.

On the journey there we would discuss what we were planning to say to the stranger on the other side of the semi-transparent grill when he asked us what we had to confess to, this before he dished out his obligatory punishments. These generally entailed having to go to one of the pews, kneel down, and quietly recite the Lord's Prayer a couple of times to cleanse ourselves of our sins, quite often a few Hail Marys were thrown in for good measure. Our response to the priest's question was always the same, "Bless me father for I have sinned, etc. I have been cheeky to my parents a few times since my last confession father and also arguing with my brothers and sister." I knew from previous experience this would not involve too much kneeling time in the pew mumbling my punishments; if I had shared with him what I really had been up to over the previous two weeks out on the estate with the 'wrecking crew', I may have developed some serious knee discomfort, maybe even calluses, and certainly not made it home for tea (that's 'dinner' to those not brought up on a northern council estate). I wonder how many Hail Marys or the Lord's Prayer are recommended in the priest's 'sentencing guidelines' for throwing home-made napalm petrol bombs (simply mix jelly cubes with the petrol) at the feet of rival gang members to dissuade their forward progress? As I grew older and left behind the misdemeanours of my teenage years, I found I didn't need any religious texts or icons to refer to when helping others. My inspiration to do good things came from tangible positive role models around me and also from looking inside myself to realise that benevolent actions bring their own rewards and life is far too short to be unkind to people.

Travelling back up the glacier (albeit without any prayers to protect me, or the prospect of divine intervention should things go pear shaped) and with just the skidoos roped together and no hindering sledge between us, we found the uphill ground quickly covered and the snow bridges holding well, Asti took the lead up and did not hesitate in following our tracks across them. The bridges across the two larger crevasses held okay, and as we reached the head of the glacier on what we knew was safe ground, Asti slowed and beckoned me forward. I pulled up alongside his skidoo for a quick 'on-site' meeting to catch our breath and gather our senses back. The brief discussion was about the two weakened bridges on the wide crevasses; if we thought they could hold another trip across them with the heavy sledge, and whether or not there were other options available, or if we should walk and probe them

242

before the final trip down. The discussion was very brief indeed.

The weather remained excellent – abundant blue skies with hardly any wind – and looked promising for at least the next few hours. This reinforced our decision to break camp and get everything down to the base of the Norman Glacier; if the bridges remained intact, we should find ourselves at the base of the glacier soon enough. Our camping and decamping was now finely-tuned and little conversation was needed as we both quickly and enthusiastically engaged in the task of taking the tent down, and loading everything onto the sledge, ensuring all the boxes and equipment were lashed down tightly (the last thing we needed was a problem with the sledge on the way down). We attached the heavily laden sledge between our two skidoos with the thick rope, bid our farewells to the spectacular Rowley Corridor, started up the skidoos and set off for the penultimate chapter of the Dyer to Fossil Bluff odyssey. As we sat on the skidoos, we both gave the camp area one last look to ensure nothing at all was left other than our tracks ('take only photos, leave only footprints'), and off we set.

It was Asti's turn to take the lead, my concentration levels were highly focused as we headed downhill. Keeping the thick connecting rope at the right tension was a little trickier due to the heavy weight of the sledge, maintaining tension on the rope was easy, but I didn't want too much tautness as that may have meant I was causing Asti's lead skidoo to brake. What was at the forefront of my mind as we slowly covered the few hundred metres of the top section was guiding such a heavy sledge across the already weakened bridges on the two big crevasses; letting it go slowly across would mean leaving it for too long on the bridge and risking a collapse, going too fast without adequately controlling the connecting rope carried the risk of the sledge slipping sideways and dropping into the chasm. Neither option was very desirable; however, I felt sure Asti would opt for 'FAF' action, as I probably would in his position.

The next two hours will remain etched in my mind for a long time. Although Asti kept a reasonably sensible pace over the safe (ish) sections of the glacier, when we approached the wide crevasses he casually gave the now very familiar 'FAF' signal without even looking back over his shoulder. The bridge on the monster crevasse on the upper section held well enough, even though as I sped over it my peripheral vision on both sides registered, for that brief moment I was on it, that just feet either side of my skidoo, there was a bottomless-looking dark chasm. The smaller crevasses we didn't give a second thought to as we drove over the bridges. In any other circumstances in other popular mountain regions around the world, crossing these crevasses would have involved placing anchors, roping up and gingerly probing with an ice axe on foot; however, today there seemed to be an acquiescent attitude to crossing them. As we eventually approached the huge crevasse near the bottom, my mind honed in on both Asti's movements, and the adjoining sledge between us; his arm raised and beckoned vigorously forward as he accelerated at the narrow bridge that was our last barrier to getting safely down the Norman and onto the Sound. His skidoo appeared to slump as he drove across. A fraction of a second behind, the sledge caused the bridge to drop a little further into the crevasse as it bounced out onto solid surface over the crevasse lip; I held my thumb hard on the accelerator as I aimed for the centre of the ever-reducing snow bridge, hoping Asti would keep accelerating so that the adjoining rope didn't develop slack and tangle in my front ski at the critical moment. I hammered across it with gritted teeth and a grimacing face; I'm sure I felt my heart forcing its way up my throat. What surprised me once again, just as had also happened last week on the big weak crevasse bridge that collapsed, was that I distinctly heard myself laugh out as my skidoo bounced in and out of the now horrendously slumped snow bridge, most of it tumbling into the gaping chasm as I reached the safe ground. It is certainly strange how the mind works in times of acute stress; manic laughter appeared to be my personal coping mechanism, but what I was certainly sure about was that I most definitely didn't think this situation was in any way funny.

After speaking to others who have found themselves in tight situations, I understand this is a common reaction when people find themselves under intense pressure or in life threatening situations. I was recently on a flight back from Qatar and struck up a conversation with a friendly laid back guy in the next seat to me. He was an ex-Royal Marine on a trip back home from working as a private security contractor in Baghdad. We were having a cheerful chat about scary experiences and he relayed a tale about being in Afghanistan while still in the Marines; he was pinned down in a shallow ditch with two pals while mortars were exploding all around them (and as often happens, the mortars were coming from his own side). What was interesting and felt so familiar to me was what he told me about their reaction and how they coped with their dire situation – all three of them were laughing manically as shrapnel, rock and dirt whizzed past them. I do wonder if it might be a coping strategy exclusive to British people; our sense of humour is said to be unique, so perhaps this particular way of coping is also. Following my pained laughing session I drew my skidoo up alongside Asti's and spoke to him. He also joined in the laughter, but it was similar to mine, not at all the same laugh you make when you hear a funny joke. "Well at least we never have to come down that fucker again!" he stated through a wild smiling face.

"That's a shame, I wish we had another sledge to go back up for," was the only sarcastic and mildly amusing thing I could think of to say to try and lighten the terror we had both just been submitted to.

We took on board some more food and water while studying closely the best map we had, deliberating about the smartest route across the 30-kilometre-wide Sound to the hut at Fossil Bluff. Now that we were down on the glacier, we did not have the privilege of an elevated position to plan the best way across. Although we had looked at the expanse of the Sound when we had a brief stop halfway down the Norman, all our concentration at the time was turned to surviving the bottom section of the descent, we had not paid close enough attention to what came next.

What we should have done was taken some compass bearings to avoid the huge melt water pools that were dotted all over the Sound, rather than looking in awe at it like a pair of stoned Californian surfers admiring a huge breaking wave, "Wow, that's really beautiful, man!"

We now decided to connect each sled individually to our skidoos and not travel as a 'full unit', choosing instead to travel across separately but staying close to each other should there be a problem; the glacier was completely flat and because we were many kilometres further south from where we had flown over the horrendously crevassed snout of the glacier where it met open water, we did not expect to come across any crevasses; another 'fingers crossed' risk assessment. What we were also unsure about was how deep the water might be in the melt water pools, although we would undoubtedly try and avoid going through them, when we were high up on the Norman Glacier we saw that there were so many it might be tricky not having to go through at least the odd smaller one. Not being roped up as a convoy would allow one skidoo to tow the other out if one of us ended up in deep water with the engine possibly cutting out. Well, that was the plan.

As I sat savouring the sweet tea and my six-year-old chocolate bar, I gazed back up the Norman Glacier, smiling with mixed emotions while pondering once again on the journey so far. The most prominent feeling was one of relief at having survived some quite hairy moments on the chaotic glacier, but there was also a strong sense of achievement at having accomplished a first descent (and numerous blooming unplanned ascents). Although during both the descents and ascents it often felt like there had been a significant element of over boldness in our approach, I was of the firm view that we had to adopt this attitude, otherwise we would still be camped up on the Rowley Corridor, wondering what to do next. Looking back up the imposing Norman Glacier, I smiled again to myself as I reflected once more on how my life had changed compared to a few years before. My working life back in Yorkshire repairing burst water mains in a big city was certainly the sharpest of contrasts to my current circumstances, and I felt I had to pinch myself to ensure I was not dreaming; this really felt like I was on another planet. Looking back to the time I made the decision to leave a well-paid 'secure' job and go travelling, I recall pondering over the future, but right now I wondered why there was any hesitation. I guess Mark Twain was right when he said, "The two most important days in your life are the day you were born, and the day you find out why."

My right thumb eased the throttle forward as we fired up the skidoos and set off across the eerily beautiful flat expanse of the Sound, initially driving parallel with each other until we encountered the maze of melt pools. The trip across was great fun compared to the 'interesting' hours we had endured earlier in the day. As predicted, we ended up driving the skidoos through the smaller melt pools when the gaps on the solid surface between them became narrow. This didn't present any problems as the pools were generally just a foot or so deep, allowing our skidoos to drive through them easily, spraying water and slush out to the sides. The temperature was hovering around freezing, so the water that had melted to form the pools was suitably cold and often had a thin veneer of ice. The pools had formed in shallow indentations on the glacier surface, all very beautiful, presenting differing shades of light blue, glistening light bouncing off the surface water. Some that I avoided looked to be more than a hundred metres across; the water towards the centre of these mini lakes was likely to be quite deep, and as relatively relaxed as we both now felt, I didn't particularly fancy swimming out of chest-deep freezing water and walking back to Fossil Bluff. I optimistically blasted quickly through one that was about twenty metres across and caught my breath as the deep water started slowing the skidoo down and began coming up over my boots up on the metal foot well. Fortunately, the engine carburettor was just a little higher than the water level and the engine stayed running as I shot out the other side; getting the skidoo stuck, part submerged in freezing water at this stage of the journey was not an appealing prospect. Asti was experiencing similar fun dramas (does that equate to a comedy?) as he, too, had to surge through some pools that had deep water, but fortunately his skidoo also did not pack in and we covered the strange and other worldly like thirty kilometres of the King George VI Sound relatively swiftly, arriving at around 10:00 pm at the head of the Eros Glacier, where the deep floating ice of the Sound met Alexander Island. Reaching the other side again gave us a huge sense of satisfaction, but, we didn't want to be too reckless at this point, just a few kilometres from the warmth and sanctuary of Fossil Bluff transit station. The merging glaciers of the Sound and the Eros Glacier would undoubtedly have some crevassing where they met, and we might still have to cross those. Asti and I pulled our skidoos up alongside each other, and after having a quick chuckle about the strange and quite unique crossing of the Sound and its melt pools, we decided not to rope up a full unit for the last mile or so. We could now see the hut in the distance, it was currently to our south west due to our having had to deviate north when we met some unexpected small crevassing as the Eros Glacier met the Sound; the crevasses were only a few feet across, but as we were now un-roped from each other, we chose the smart option of going around them.

From our current position and looking at the surface terrain between us and the hut, we both felt confident that we could get there safely travelling as two half units if we went at a steady pace. We also knew we would now have the prospect of help from the guys at the hut should either of us go through a hidden crevasse. In retrospect, our physically and mentally exhausted state after such an immensely taxing and lengthy day was responsible for this somewhat unwise decision. The journey down had seen us experiencing some truly life threatening situations, now we were on flat and relatively safe ground, I think we both just wanted to be in the safety of the hut. Fortunately, today we were jammy enough to have an outcome where fortune favoured the brave (and extremely tired) and we successfully weaved our way through some minor visible crevassing until safely pulling up outside the hut an hour before midnight. With the sun still shining brightly, we found a small smiling welcome committee who looked pleased and relieved to see us in one piece. In true Antarctic tradition, Asti and I didn't give each other a big hug or make a song and dance about it, we just gave each other another 'manly' pat on the shoulder, and casually remarked to the lads it had been an interesting trip, as they helped us secure the skidoos and sledges before going inside to the relative luxury of the wooden hut for much needed food, hot drink and sleep, and maybe even a beer if there were any at the hut.

While we were tucking into some beautiful food – at least compared to the repetitive rations we had been eating for the last month – we joked with the guys about the trip down and the 'fun' moments on the huge crevasses. As usual, there was much jesting about us taking our time and making a meal of things; it certainly was the custom down here to minimise things. Dave was still at the hut looking after arrangements there. With him for a few days was one of the doctors from the base, an Australian guy called Miles, who presented a somewhat serious attitude and persona much of the time, but balanced this with a dry sense of humour. It was great sitting around a table, tucking in enthusiastically to some delicious spaghetti Bolognese and chatting with them, catching up on the progress of the other field parties and what had been happening both here at Fossil Bluff and back at Rothera Base. Although there were a few cold beers to be had, after drinking just one I was more than ready to hit the sleeping bag that was beckoning seductively from the relative comfort of one of the bunks in the hut. It had been one heck of a day and my body and mind were more than ready to collapse into a deep sleep. As I headed towards the bunk, I chuckled at the expected comments from Dave, "You blooming lightweight, have another beer, all you've done is sat on a skidoo for a few hours getting a suntan"; I did enjoy his sense of humour.

Tuesday 25th December, Christmas Day: Fossil Bluff

9:30 am Bit of a lie-in, still feeling quite drained, both physically and psychologically – the concentration levels have been very intense, especially the trips up and down Norman Glacier. My first Christmas away from home for a long time, it's certainly quite novel waking up on the edge of a permanently frozen sea channel, about 300 miles from the base, and 12000 miles from England. A far cry from last Christmas morning waking up beside Sandra, probably not wise to dwell on that right now, it will make me sad. Just four of us at the hut, Asti and I, Dave, and Miles, the base doctor who had managed to bag a few days at FB. Dinner was a combined effort; bearing in mind the limited ingredients we managed three courses – not confident of a Michelin star award. A tipsy toast to nature late on, spoilt by people being cold, or wanting the loo!

The surroundings I awoke to on Christmas Day morning were in sharp contrast to those the previous year. Here I was in a sleeping bag on a wooden bunk in a small hut that was the only structure for hundreds of kilometres in every direction, surrounded by mountains and glaciers; last year I had been in a warm bed beside a beautiful woman in a house in a large city in Europe. I looked around the small room at my three other unwashed stubble-chinned comrades slowly awakening after all having a celebratory lie in and smiled to myself; life certainly is a journey. It took quite a while for me to gather myself and get up; the last few days had been so intense I was feeling unusually tired and lethargic. Not just physically, but also mentally I was feeling fairly wiped out.

No flights from Rothera were due in on Christmas Day, so all of us were looking forward to the unusual luxury of having a day off, especially with the conditions remaining good outside; there had been plenty of non-working days while Asti and I were up on the Dyer, but only as a result of horrendous weather raging outside the tent. The concept of people back home often being rigid around working times and patterns seemed distant right now, which really made me appreciate the unique aspects of life down here and the positive work ethos that prevailed. Obviously, I recognise that things back home are different and that workers need to have terms and conditions of employment; otherwise there would be the danger of being left open to exploitation. However, the working environment down here was far from 'normal' and the weather was always the deciding factor as to when we worked. No one ever seemed to comment on the long hours and lack of time off; the philosophy amongst the staff was definitely one of kindred spirits, and I certainly felt privileged to be working in such an amazing environment. It was just a case of 'get on with it'. Most of us were aware of the cost implications of getting field parties into the mountains and the vast array of support that was needed; consequently, I felt a moral and ethical obligation to work as hard as possible to get things completed. The summer season was relatively short, so a nine to five mentality would be hardly conducive to getting things done. Asti and I had experienced some days on the plateau that entailed working the same number of hours in one continuous stint that many people back in England would work in a full week. Yet in contrast to this we had also sat (unwillingly) stormbound in the tent doing nothing for days on end. It is not everyone's cup of tea, I imagine; but as I once heard, 'Life begins beyond the comfort zone'.

Making the most of the day, I had a much needed wash and shave, grabbed a cup of coffee, some cheese and biscuits, put on some warm clothes and headed outside to savour this very unusual Christmas morning environment. Compared to some of the conditions we had experienced up on the Dyer, the weather today was beautiful; the sun was shining brightly, and with just a light wind blowing and a 'balmy' air temperature of minus 10C, I should have brought my sunbathing shorts. I positioned myself on a wooden box with my back resting against the external wall of the hut looking out across the Sound to the spectacular Peninsula, and soaked up the sun and remarkable surroundings; the flat polka dotted expanse between me and the coastal mountains and glaciers reminded me what an incredible day yesterday had been. Looking directly out east across the Sound I could make out the heavily crevassed McArthur Glacier edging steeply downhill. Even from where I was sat some thirty or so kilometres away, I mentally confirmed what a smart decision it had been not to try and make a descent of that monster. It hadn't altered much when I had looked across to it prior to setting off for the Dyer and it looked like it would present a near impossible task on foot, never mind travelling as a full unit. In my mind's eye, I roughly retraced our previous day's route across the flat glacier. The hundreds of different size and varying shades of blue melt pools really made it seem like a scene from some uninhabited planet. It was impossible to make out our skidoo or sledge tracks; we had been travelling on snow some of the time, but mostly either going through slushy melt pools or on the hard glacial ice, and so had barely left any marks on the surface. To the south-east I could just about identify the base of the Norman Glacier as its snout met the Sound, the Batterbee Mountains rising majestically at the rear, with the high point of Mount Bagshawe easily visible in the centre of the range. Sitting basking in the glorious sunshine, and feeling so warm I had even discarded my fleece (hardy Glaswegians would have been down to their underwear by now), I began to feel a contented smile spread over my face; here I was sat in the relative comfort and safety of Fossil Bluff hut, but only twenty four hours earlier Asti and I had been having our nerve endings cheese grated while doing battle with the Norman Glacier, which right now, as I gazed across at it, looked incredibly innocuous. As I was sat feeling contented, and (unusually) a little bit smug if I am completely honest with myself, Dave came out with a coffee in his hand to join me. As we both enjoyed the spectacular vista in front of us across the sun-drenched glacier, Dave remarked, "Bit of an epic that one mate, nice one," and took a sip of his hot drink. I glanced towards him, smiling expectantly, waiting for a punchline, but he just smiled back and winked; now I really did feel a sense of achievement, the joker had been temporarily silenced.

The rest of the morning was spent sorting all the kit out, giving the skidoos a quick once over and grabbing some more very welcome rest on the five-star luxury of a bunk with a thin mattress. Dave and I prepared a Christmas dinner of sorts, and Asti and Miles located some tinned chocolate sponge pudding that had been brought inside overnight so it could thaw out in time for the festivities. This and condensed milk would be our delicious desert. While they were undertaking this complicated culinary challenge, Dave and I concocted a cottage pie from freeze dried beef granules, dried onions and tinned potatoes; tomato soup was the posh entrée, with some fruit biscuits to dip in. Most of the tinned goods were well beyond their sell-by dates, but due to their being stored in boxes outside the base, they remained frozen until brought inside; some of the tinned butter that Asti and I used on the Dyer was seven years out of date, but tasted fine (or as fine as tinned butter can) and our stomachs held up okay. I'm not so sure the high street supermarkets back home in England would engage in such a practice; in sharp contrast they work at the opposite end of the scale, each day collectively discarding tons of perfectly edible food.

As expected, Dave had managed to acquire some surprisingly reasonable red wine to accompany our sumptuous dinner; he was one of these guys who would fall in a sewer and come out smiling, with an aroma of a fine aftershave emanating from him. Various toasts were made throughout our culinary spectacular, with more wine appearing as each bottle emptied and my wine glass somehow remaining consistently healthy; Dave would have done well in biblical times with tricks like that. There was an old cassette player that had a radio built in and we managed to get a weak signal for the BBC World Service, and we listened in as a recording of the Queen's Speech earlier in the day came squeaking through the small in built speaker. This coincided with a very relaxed 7:00 pm radio schedule with Rothera, so we gathered around the small set, chuckling while trying to listen to Queen Elizabeth impart her worldly wisdom, while keeping one ear on Dave relaying my and Asti's safe return to Fossil Bluff. Being all a little tipsy from the surprisingly pleasant wine, there was much joking while we listened to the speech, which Miles of course loved, being a citizen of a former colonial outpost, (but still in the Commonwealth, as we reminded him, pointing out whose head was on the country's postal stamp. I think there was even humorous mention of his convict forefathers; I blame it on Dave, and the wine). After much laughter and the obligatory game of Monopoly, which I recall Miles won and gave all the streets Australian names, with Bond Street obviously becoming 'Bondi Street', the less than delicious chocolate pudding and red wine combination resulted in us all feeling full and tired. There being no flights scheduled to come in, the remainder of the evening was spent relaxing and reading, with occasional bursts of witticisms from Dave. Before I knew it, Christmas Day was merging into Boxing Day.

However, before Christmas Day finally came to an end, late in the evening we all extricated ourselves from our slumber and went out at supper time to give a toast to the mountains and Mother Nature, each with a glass of port (from a bottle which Dave produced from his magic hat). The sun still shone brightly, but was now dropping lower towards the horizon resulting in a sharp drop in temperature. Standing on the outside deck of the hut with the three other guys and toasting the stunning landscape in front of us was a beautiful moment; once we sipped our Port, we all just gazed ahead in silence, seemingly entranced by the scenery around us. The lowering sun was now creating shadows from the mountains, leaving shafts of light streaming across their adjoining glaciers and making the view even more breath-taking. I felt a profound sense of mental wellbeing and I recalled a section from a famous quote that seemed to sum up the current situation, "Not everything that counts can be counted."

"Let's get back inside, it's bloody freezing."

"Yeah, and I need a crap." These exclamations, however, fractured the majestic silence; oh well, so much for the 'spiritual' moment.

Photographs

Dyer Plateau - Camp 2

En route to the Dyer Plateau

Approaching Friedmann Nunataks

Full Unit near Carina Heights

Near Camp 3

Puppis Pikes

Rowley Corridor - Camp 4

Mount Cadbury

Head of Norman Glacier

Atop Mid-summer Nunatak, Rowley Corridor

7. Back to Base

Asti and I loaded all the gear onto a Twin Otter flown in by Murray, who seemed happy to see our faces as we waited with all the gear on the glacier. With a wry smile and his gravelly Kiwi accent, his only comment was, "Heard you two had an epic... Don't break my plane"; he had obviously not forgotten about my near miss when loading the skidoo onto the plane weeks earlier. The flight back to Rothera was in brilliant sunshine, which provided more remarkable views; as we were climbing up off the glacier runway at Fossil Bluff, Asti and I sat atop some kit and both peered out of the right hand side of the Twin Otter looking east across at the Norman Glacier. The Rowley Corridor and the Batterbee Range slowly came into view, then the Dyer far beyond in the distance as we climbed higher. We glanced across at each other, both wearing a huge big grin; what a trip.

The Twin Otter touched down perfectly on the ski-way above Rothera, the journey back was as spectacular as when we had headed down to Fossil Bluff a month earlier. The coastal mountains looked dramatic as they met the crystal-clear water of Marguerite Bay, white icebergs dotting the surface, some flat and the size of football fields, others huge with sharp edged towers. These taller ones were always at risk of toppling over if they drifted near to the coast and the bottom of them struck rock; only about 10–20 percent of an iceberg sits above the water line, the bulk of their mass is hidden below.

At the glacier above Rothera, Ray the plumber arrived having driven the Sno-Cat up to collect us and all our equipment. The tractor-like vehicle had a large wide sledge attached to the back of it, so we managed to get all the kit and our two Nansen sledges loaded in one go. We thanked Murray for the lift back and he just grunted his response as he climbed up into the passenger seat of the cabin, his P-bag (containing a sleeping bag and survival equipment) chucked on top of our equipment on the sledge. Ray had helped us load all the kit on and he just smiled as he lashed down his and Murray's P-bags. Murray was a likeable guy, but sometimes he could blow a bit hot and cold, without anyone being able to predict his emotional temperature at any given time (although I found his capriciousness actually quite amusing). Asti and I attached the two skidoos together and we set off in convoy behind the Sno-Cat back along the elevated glacier, with the saw tooth Reptile Ridge looking as dramatic as ever up to our right as we slowly made our way back down the short distance to Rothera. We had been tempted to not link the skidoos together, but on second thoughts we agreed it was the bright thing to do; as well travelled this route up to the glacier airstrip was, crevasses had appeared there and it would be a tad embarrassing to go into one so close to the base, especially after having survived reasonably unscathed during the Dyer to Fossil Bluff trip.

Pete, the base commander, was waiting for us at the bottom of the ski-way, and it was good to see him, a friendly character who always seemed to take things in his stride. A calm demeanour was certainly a pre-requisite for holding the position he had; having responsibility for the safe day-to-day running of the base and all the field operations was no walk in the park. We spent ten minutes chatting and updating him on events from the Dyer down to the hut, as usual joking about the epic moments on the Norman Glacier. He agreed that it sounded like a 'fun' time, but also looked genuinely relieved to see that we had made it without any major incident or injury. Asti and I left the skidoos outside the mechanics shed, collected our kit and headed into the base. A lot of the scientists and field assistants were still out in the mountains and glaciers, and as it was the middle of the day, the majority of the base support staff were going about their duties. So there was hardly anyone about as we dropped our kit off in our rooms, went upstairs into the canteen and grabbed some soup and bread; eating fresh bread was an absolute delight after living off rations and we savoured every morsel.

The next thing I was eagerly looking forward to was to get a hot shower; it was now a month since I had anything that resembled a proper wash, so it was something I could hardly wait to do. Just as Asti and I were discussing exactly that, Oz, the assistant base manager, came into the canteen to greet us, congratulate us on the successful completion of the project and also to chat about the trip from the Dyer. As the discussion was drawing to a close and we were getting up to go downstairs to get the much-needed shower, he dropped what felt at the time, like a massive bombshell, "By the way, you do know there is a fault with the water system and showering is banned temporarily."

"Oh bollocks!" was the only thing I could bring myself to say in response; that was the long lingering hot shower that I have been looking forward to for the past month right out the fecking window. Oz just smiled and walked away.

"Really sorry boys. It should be sorted in a few days' time", oh well, another one of life's little surprises that we had to take in our stride. Hot showers, fresh running water and good sanitation systems are things that most of us take for granted back home in England. Yet once these things are taken away for a significant period of time, one quickly realises that such activities are in fact a luxury. Although something as trivial sounding as the lack of a shower for a few more days might sound, it left me feeling somewhat deflated; my body was in dire need of a hot soapy scrub. Undeterred, I went downstairs to the bath room, stripped off, filled the sink basin up with hot water and had a full body wash. Although it wasn't steaming water cascading down over my head and cleansing my somewhat smelly body, it had to suffice for now.

The rest of the day was spent sorting all our field kit out and returning items to their various homes. Before I knew it, dinnertime had arrived, and so after a quick change of clothes, including the fantastic feeling of fresh cotton underpants and socks, I made my way back to the base canteen for some magnificent fresh food and some great conversation with an array of people, all very interested to hear about the trip from the Dyer. It had been decorated with a few Christmas trimmings to add a little festive cheer. Although we all accepted that we were here to work and the holiday period didn't apply down here, there was an air of celebration. After dinner, quite a few staff retired to the bar that adjoins the canteen for a few Boxing Day drinks; while I was sat there, Steve the electrician came into the bar with a large plastic container full of chunky lumps of ice. He sat beside me, produced a small bottle of gin and got a couple of glasses from behind the bar, along with a bottle of tonic water, "Looks nice, but I'm not a big a G and T fan Steve".

He smiled at me, "You really have to try one after I tell you where this ice came from." The ice in the bucket, it turned out, was from one of the ice cores from the Dyer; last week, while Steve had been helping unload the boxes from a Twin Otter up on the ski-way, one of the boxes fell off the aircraft ramp causing the box to split open and the ice core to land on the surface snow. As a result, the ice core was contaminated and unfit for scientific research. Resourceful chap that Steve is, he commandeered the large cylindrical ice core and stored it outside the base to bring in and use to put in drinks. How could I refuse?

As I loaded the drink with the beautiful ice, we chinked glasses and toasted, "To the last thousand years..." To be honest, as novel and unique an experience as it was, I couldn't really tell any difference; it didn't suddenly make me fond of gin either.

The remainder of the season was spent engaging in a variety of tasks around the base and undertaking short trips into the field supporting other teams with resupply and an additional pair of hands if required. One task that brought me down to earth with a bang was working on the water desalination unit; this ingenious machine turned sea water into drinking water and had a filtering system within it that, over time, became clogged up with algae. When Ray, the plumber, came into the canteen one morning looking for a volunteer to assist him with a 'quick job on the base, my enthusiastic approach saw my hand being raised. As I left the canteen with Ray, Steve the electrician's smiling comment of "Have fun", made me instantly doubtful about what I had volunteered for. An hour later, as I lay squeezed in a large plastic conduit in two inches of water, scraping loads of stinking green algae off a large filter, I gave myself a firm mental reminder to ask first before sticking my hand up.

I was also keen to get as much co-piloting done as possible and I would be in the canteen each morning quickly demolishing my breakfast and then hanging around, lingering on my coffee, until any pilots came in requesting volunteers; there were a handful of staff who also enjoyed getting up in the air with the pilots, so competition was often strong. This reminded me of my young schooldays when we would eat our puddings quickly at dinnertime, waiting expectantly for the head dinner lady to make the eagerly anticipated call of "Seconds!"; we would have our pudding plates ready in our hands, feet poised at our tables like sprinters in the starting blocks. The second syllable had scarcely left her lips when there would be a stampede of boys to the far end of the serving table where the scraps of apple pie and custard remained. Strangely, no one opted for 'seconds' from the swede, cabbage or cauliflower stations. However, back on the base this enthusiasm for flying was not always replicated amongst the ardent and aspiring co-pilots; when Neil entered the canteen with a request, quite often silence enveloped most of the normally keen volunteers, and until the wild man found a victim to join him on his exploits, heads and eyes were firmly focused on the empty breakfast plates, or suddenly began perusing an old newspaper. Although co-piloting was exciting and provided those in the aircraft some of the best views and scenery on the planet, trips with this ninja pilot often entailed heart stopping moments. I quite enjoyed his antics, so subsequently spent a significant amount of time in the air with him, enjoying almost every moment; I think, though, that I developed some premature grey hairs in the process.

Rothera Base sits on a large rocky outcrop on the eastern side of Adelaide Island, there is a variety of buildings dotted around, with the main building that houses the accommodation, science labs, canteen and aircraft control room at the central point facing up the ski-way towards Reptile Ridge and the highest peak of the island, Mount Gaudry, which lies further back towards the centre of the island. If I wanted to get away from the busy hub of the base for some quiet time, I would sometimes go to the rear of the main building, walk for a few minutes and then find a comfy rock to sit on near the water's edge, facing out across the bay towards the coastal mountains in the distance.

Every view from the base provided great scenery, but I was particularly fond of looking out across the expanse of crystal clear water to the dramatic glaciated peaks on the mainland, with their variety of different shaped and sized icebergs scattered across the surface. One Saturday evening after dinner I had gone out of the building and wandered around the back to take in a short dose of Antarctic scenery before retiring to my room. After walking approximately 200 metres to the water's edge, I was sitting in my favourite spot, wrapped up in my down jacket, the sun on my back and the lack of wind producing a pond-like sea surface ahead of me. It was then that I was fortunate and extremely privileged to witness an amazing marine animal encounter.

A small tabular iceberg had caught my eye soon after sitting down and getting cosy. It was only about eight metres in diameter and just thirty metres out into the sea directly in front of me, with the coastal mountains affording a spectacular backdrop in the distance behind. These small flat icebergs were a common sight in the bay, but what attracted my eye to this one was that two crabeater seals were perched in the middle of it and for some reason looked a bit jittery. The reason for their anxiety soon became apparent; two huge orcas slowly breached the surface alongside the small iceberg, gracefully – but probably extremely menacingly from the seals' point of view – beginning to circle slowly around the ice floe. I was transfixed, as I watched and waited, wondering what might unfold before me. The only noise was that of the seals moving as close to the centre of the ice as possible, and the breathing hole on the top of the orca's heads making a soft sound each time they exhaled. My focus was interrupted when I realised that I was possibly about to see something amazing occur, but didn't have my camera with me to record any images of it. There then followed a swift internal discussion; I normally carried my camera with me when wandering around the coast of the base, but hadn't done so this time, as I had been heading to dinner earlier and wouldn't need a camera. It had been a last minute idea to come out for some fresh air at my favourite spot. Now I had a dilemma: to race back to my room and get the camera and risk missing something potentially spectacular; or just to sit and watch events unfold and record the images and memory solely in my head? Even though I am a keen photographer, I quickly realised that I had no option but to wait and watch things pan out; it might be that nothing happened, but if something did and I was being an eejit running up to my room, then I would regret possibly missing out on something that might be really special.

I had seen orcas a few times on the way down on the *Biscoe*: the time in the Lemaire Channel had probably been the best occasion so far; and also once from the same spot where I was now sat, I had seen a pod of orcas pass about a hundred metres from shore. But I had never witnessed any of the predatory behaviour which I was seeing right made now. I had made the right choice.

The two orcas both submerged simultaneously about ten metres from the iceberg, just twenty metres from where I sat, their colossal shapes now between the iceberg and my position. Shortly after disappearing, their noses slowly reappeared beside each other under the edge of the iceberg on the side that was facing me, their bulky bodies in a near vertical position, the deep water so clear it was easy to see their black mass with the white flashes beneath the surface. In unison, these two powerful animals began making upward thrusts with their tails and powerful bodies, their noses nudging the edge of the large heavy ice floe up at an angle in an attempt to cause the two terrified seals to slide off into the water and become the orcas' dinner. Their potential meal was slightly different to the lovely chicken and rice with a delightful tarragon sauce I had consumed just thirty minutes earlier; I suppose orcas are not really built for a kitchen and their fins would not have enough dexterity even to turn on the gas rings to start cooking the seal meat, never mind preparing an accompanying garlic shrimp sauce.

The petrified seals were now digging their small claws frantically into the centre of the ice to avoid sliding off and the inevitable swift demise that would follow. Meanwhile, because of the weight of the ice, the orcas were only managing to get the floe up to an angle where the seals could just about maintain their grip on the ice. The battle continued in this way for about ten minutes, the orcas seemingly undeterred by their lack of success in dislodging their prey, the two seals desperately clinging on as their lives hung in the balance by just a few degrees. After another ten minutes the orcas appeared to accept defeat and broke off to swim away; they headed off to the east but after thirty metres submerged again and I did not see them resurface. I chose to stay in my spot for a while, reflecting on the incredible sights I had just witnessed, and to enjoy the scenery a little longer, wondering if the seals on the ice flow would eventually settle back down. They looked extremely relieved a few minutes after the orcas departed, but appeared to remain a tad anxious, with their claws only slowly loosening their grip on the ice; understandable I suppose after such a close encounter. Their claws digging into the ice reminded me of the time I had been co-piloting with Neil, and how long it had taken me to prise my fingers away from the arm of the passenger seat armrests after he had landed on the ice floe in Marguerite Bay and skied off the end down towards the sea, pulling the Twin Otter up with only seconds to spare; I had developed seal empathy.

It was starting to feel quite cold, as the sun dropped low and the air temperature began to dip. Just as I slowly rose to turn and make my way back into the accommodation block, thinking that the encounter was over, the two seals, having now waited about twenty minutes since the orcas disappeared, slowly began moving towards the edge of the ice floe to re-enter the water. They both still looked apprehensive as they edged towards the lip of the ice, each of them pressing their bodies up on their front flippers and scanning nervously in all directions. I was reasonably confident that the orcas had gone in search of dinner at another restaurant. However, I am no animal behaviourist; within two seconds of one of the seals deciding to literally take the plunge and enter the water, the now tranquil and calm scene in front of me was suddenly and violently shattered as the seal was abruptly tossed into the air in an explosion and wild spray of water. The head of one of the orcas appeared in the frothy spray and chaotic surface water, its large sharp-toothed mouth agape. The seal landed back in the water right beside the Orca, who quickly bit into it and dragged it under the surface, the clear blue water now stained with the bright red blood of the seal. The strength and power of the Orca was vividly demonstrated; the seal must have weighed in excess of 200 kilogrammes and yet it was tossed into the air like a small rag doll. The orcas were indeed a bright and extremely patient animal, regarded as one of the most skilled hunters in the ocean and at the apex of the predatory food chain. Although it was sad to see the seal killed, witnessing such a dramatic natural event felt particularly special.

Keen to share this wonderful experience, I made my way back into the canteen. This was now empty, so I carried on into the bar and pulled up a stool beside Steve and another guy and calmly relayed what I had just seen. As expected, I received a response of, "Really, and was Elvis on the back of one of the orcas?"

After a few more derisory comments, their envy at what I had seen eventually dissipated and they asked to hear more about it, to which I obviously smilingly responded, "No way, you had your chance to hear it, but blew it because you couldn't stop yourselves from taking the piss, because you were so jealous you missed it!" Leaving them to sweat for a few minutes, I finally recounted the events to them; it would have been cruel not to share what I had witnessed.

The final week on the base was a hive of activity, as scientific parties returned from the field, some with interesting tales to tell; I had co-piloted on a few pickups and it was great helping colleagues load all their kit into the Twin Otters and to see the relief on their faces after safely completing their projects. The sense of relief always appeared to be a little more pronounced when picking up the geology parties who had, like Asti and I, spent time travelling through mountain ranges with dangerously crevassed glaciers; I could certainly empathise with them. I had also been in the aircraft picking up field parties who had been completing static glaciology projects; although these assignments presented their own difficulties, the teams generally remained in one camp on flat glaciers, and so were not exposed to the risks involved when travelling up or down badly crevassed glaciers.

Thankfully all the field parties returned to base safely and, as was the custom, there was an end of season dinner and a bit of a knees up afterwards in the bar; this inevitably involved a good old sing song. I had brought my acoustic guitar with me from England on the *Biscoe*. I regarded myself as something of a novice musician at the time, but fortunately there were one or two more accomplished guitarists who could play much better than I and drown out the din I was making; everyone appeared to enjoy it, joining in raucously with the choruses of an eclectic mix of tunes. I thought it was a really fun way to end the season; having been brought up in an Irish household, all parties invariably involved singing, it was a great way for gatherings to have fun.

Just a few days before leaving the base, I managed to get out on a fantastic day's climbing with my old friend Bruce from Edinburgh. It is often quite frustrating for climbers working in Antarctica not to be able to get to climb on the beautiful rock faces that were in a huge abundance; science was our purpose in being here, so it was reluctantly accepted that one could not really go out climbing, putting oneself at risk. However, as it was nearing the end of the season, all the field parties were safely back and most of the major jobs had been completed, when the weekend arrived and we had an afternoon of free time, the rules were relaxed a little. If you made the base commander aware of your plans to go and climb on a reasonably local crag, then there generally wasn't much resistance to your plans, as long as you made sure you continued to employ all the usual basic skidoo travelling rules, i.e. never travelling without the skidoos roped together, even if you were only going a few miles. It is easy to get complacent and relaxed after being for a certain time in really remote and dangerous mountain ranges, thinking that being so close to the busy base of Rothera would reduce the chances of going through a crevasse bridge.

During the last week, two guys had been going up to the landing strip on the glacier just a few miles away when an accident happened; they had not roped the skidoos together and had been travelling side by side on the well-used route on the glacier below Reptile Ridge. On the way back, one of the lads needed a pee so he stopped the skidoo and stepped off onto the innocent and safe-looking snow surface beside him. Ordinarily, you would tie yourself into the skidoo but he had not done this, and as he stepped off he went straight through a weak metre-wide crevasse bridge that he did not know was there. He fell about ten metres until he got wedged where the crevasse walls became narrow. Fortunately, he was not injured; the amusing part of the incident is that after fifty metres or so, his mate looked to the side of the skidoo he was travelling on and realised that the other skidoo and rider were no longer there. He slowed to look around and could only see the stationary skidoo back along their tracks, with the rider nowhere to be seen. After looking in all directions and not finding his mate was anywhere in sight, he knew something was obviously wrong; when he drove back to the stationary skidoo, he pulled up on the opposite side of where the rider had stepped off, now even more confused that he could not see him. He was an experienced guy, who soon realised that something was definitely amiss, and was smart enough not to step off of his skidoo onto the ground around him. He was close enough to the rider-less skidoo to lean across and get onto that without stepping onto the snow, and as he looked over the other side of it, he saw just a small hole about three feet in diameter. Quickly leaning back over to his own machine and turning off his noisy skidoo engine, he immediately heard the comedy-like calls of a voice shouting up from the darkness below, "I'm down here, and stuck!" It all ended well, but was a firm reminder to us all that we had to be on our guard; no matter how close we were to the base, crevasses can develop anywhere on a sloping glacier. I had bent the rules and ridden a lone skidoo up to the ski-way a couple of times since returning from base, and so had been quite fortunate (I never stopped for a pee though).

Bearing this in mind, Bruce and I loaded up a couple of day sacks with all the climbing kit, some food and water, and headed up the ski-way on two skidoos (roped together, of course). The weather was great; the sun was shining brightly and the temperature was just a few degrees above freezing. We were planning on putting a new route on a big near vertical granite slab just a mile or so past the aircraft ski-way; it was a pure rock route, so we would be climbing with gloveless hands. The relatively warm weather was a definite requirement for this type of climb; I didn't want freezing pinkies on my afternoon off work.

The afternoon was really enjoyable and it felt great to be climbing again, the route wasn't too difficult and we graded it 'VS' (very severe). We took it in turns leading the pitches and after a couple of hours and about a hundred metres of superb climbing, we got to the top of the wall, then rested for some food and water on a fantastic ledge looking out over the glacier. The funny part of the climb was me making the decision to change from my plastic mountaineering boots into my rubber-soled rock climbing boots that I had in my rucksack, this while halfway up a pitch I was leading. I'm not the greatest of rock climbers and was struggling to get purchase on some of the smaller holds with the bulky mountaineering boots; changing footwear dangling in my harness hundreds of feet up on a vertical rock wall caused amusement to Bruce and I, especially when I nearly dropped one of the heavy boots down onto Bruce twenty metres directly below me, just catching it at the last moment.

Although I had climbed up a new route on the snow and ice glacier wall at the back of Fossil Bluff, I had never put up a 'first ascent' on a rock climb before, so this was something quite special for me. We also abseiled down from the top of the route as the scramble down the gulley off to the right was full of big loose boulders and neither of us wanted to get crushed at this stage of the proceedings; it was a really enjoyable day to bring the season to a close. At the bottom of the route, Bruce and I joked about how it was only a year before that I had left Edinburgh, both of us wondering if we might ever bump into each other again, and here we were putting a new route up together on a rock face in Antarctica.

Just two days later, I had all my kit packed and was ready to jump on board the *Biscoe* and head north. This was about as concrete as my travel plans were at the moment; there had been a mix up about who was flying back to the Falklands on the Twin Otters and I had missed a slot. At this time, the most I knew was that I would be boarding the *Biscoe* at Rothera and getting taken as far as King George Island at the north end of the Peninsula. Many other countries had research stations on the Island and while we were making our way up there, Pete back on Rothera would negotiate with these bases to find one that would allow a few of us to stay as guests until a more definite plan was arranged for further travel north.

8. King George Island and the President of Brazil

Walking back up the gangway onto my old home of the RRS *Biscoe* gave me mixed emotions. I was so sad leaving the base and the wonderful people I had met there, but I was also looking forward to getting back home. Interestingly, there seemed to be, lightly entangled with these emotions, some tangible thoughts of returning. When I was initially given the job, I had told Sandra, family and friends back home that it would be a fantastic 'one time' experience. However, the impact that the stunning beauty of Antarctica had made on me was now raising some questions whether the trip should actually be a one-off. Some of the people who were spending the winter at Rothera waved us off. These were the ones who had the coming dark winter months to look forward to; they had the task of keeping the base running and preparing all the gear for the next season. There had been handshakes and a few hugs as we said our farewells at the jetty. Not many words were spoken but it was clear that there were a lot of emotions being suppressed; I think the old tradition of men not showing their feelings was still very present down here in this bastion of exploration.

After a couple of days sailing back the 600 kilometres plus up the west side of the spectacular Peninsula coastline,

I was dropped with a few other staff at King George Island which lies in the archipelago of the South Shetland Islands at the north-west tip of the Peninsula; the *Biscoe* was continuing to other parts of the Peninsula to undertake some marine biology research. I had been experiencing a mixture of emotions on the journey up the Peninsula; exhilaration when gazing out at the dramatic mountains and pristine glaciers, but this felt to be twinned with a slight feeling of gloom and sadness. I soon realised what was causing these contrasting feelings; it was simply that I was unsure if this was the last time I would be seeing this unique continent and amazing landscape. There was no British research station here so the Chileans, who have a large base there, were kind enough to offer us some basic accommodation at Teniente Rodolfo Marsh (now named Base Presidente Eduardo Frei Montalva) until we had our plan finalised for how we were getting further north. King George Island is home to many research bases from a variety of countries including Argentina, Brazil, Chile, China, Ecuador, South Korea, Peru, Poland, Russia, Uruguay and the United States. No country has any sovereignty rights in Antarctica due to agreements made within the 1959 Antarctic Treaty and different countries have allocated areas to work, whose boundaries often overlap; on King George Island many countries worked alongside each other, and seemed to operate together reasonably harmoniously.

The few days on the base gave us time to relax; the Chileans were incredibly hospitable and interested in hearing about the work I had been involved with while located deep field on the Dyer Plateau. The resident chef on the base was a wonderful character called Joao, who managed to cook fantastic meals with a very limited larder.

The base was located above the Antarctic Circle, so some people who had travelled and worked further south within the Circle would often joke that those working above it were not fully fledged 'Antarcticans', but I didn't buy into this philosophy; those who worked here were also in a magnificent Antarctic setting, regardless of its being above the Circle. However, they were certainly blown away by my story of the trip from the Dyer to Fossil Bluff much further south. While on the Island I also met two 'lively' Russian marine biologists while I was wandering around on their nearby Bellingshausen base. They were sitting outside one of their small accommodation buildings chatting as I was strolling past. Their English was just comprehensible and, as is the tradition with most things Russian, they invited me in for a drink. It was a Saturday evening so it would have felt quite rude to decline. These two friendly young bearded PhD scientists had built a small vodka distillery and took great pleasure in inviting me in to try a glass; after one tumbler accompanied by a hearty *'nostrovia'*, we began chatting about life in Antarctica. For the first few minutes I was trying to bravely mask the shock my body was experiencing from the firewater I had unwisely imbibed; their chuckles at my discomfort were poorly stifled and soon I could hide my pain no longer; laughing through a contorted face that probably looked like I had been sucking a lemon while having the juice squirted in my eyes, I blurted out, "Guys, that stuff is not really suitable for human consumption!" Boy oh boy, how they giggled. After one further tumbler of pain and more grimaced laughs with these two unique characters I departed, my legs and ears tingly from the 80% proof concoction they had shared with me. As I walked away, I wondered if the eyesight of these two amiable guys was going to outlast the season.

The morning after my attempted vodka suicide, I was woken from my comfortable bunk in the Chilean accommodation by the sound of helicopters approaching. They were easily identifiable as Bell Hueys due to the distinctive noise their chunky main rotors make as they cut through the surrounding air. I had completed a military parachute course in northern Florida some years previously and we had been ferried around the Everglades in these old workhorse helicopters; their characteristic noise is hard to forget. I was also a fan of the classic anti-war movie *Apocalypse Now*, in which Hueys played a memorable part, the brilliant Robert Duvall as the indestructible colonel heading up his 'Aircav' unit of Hueys (he loved 'the smell of napalm in the morning'), their distinctive sound thunders out of the screen as he stood unscathed and immaculately clad on a war-torn beach and uttered the prophetic line, "One day this war will be over, son." The 'flash bang wallop' films of today with the compulsory apocalyptic orgy of huge fireball explosions, collapsing buildings and predictable muscular heroes saving the day (and always getting the girl), seem like a dreary franchise requirement in comparison, but surprisingly very popular; even so, I'm sure an articulate eight-year-old with an average imagination could easily write the script for a contemporary 'blockbuster'. Curiosity got the better of this cat and I was soon up from my bunk, quickly dressed in some shabby clothing and nosing around outside the accommodation building to check out what was going on with the Hueys. The three helicopters landed in a clearing by the main building; as I was watching them, their rotors slowly coming to a halt, Jose, one of the Chilean scientists who I had met earlier on our visit, walked across to me and explained he had heard the occupants of the aircraft were from Brazil.

It was indeed a delegation of Brazilian VIPs, who had flown down to King George Island on a public relation visit to Antarctica; they had come to the Island to visit their base here, the 'Comandante Ferraz Antarctic Station'. It emerged that one of the occupants was the President of Brazil himself, who at short notice had apparently requested to come and see the Chilean base. Additionally, and to my horror, he had heard that there were some BAS staff staying as guests here on the Chilean base and he wanted to meet some of us. The Chilean base commander had volunteered me for this task, as it appeared I was the only BAS person they could currently find on the base... lucky me. It turned out to be quite a pleasant experience, but also highly amusing; the President and his entourage (more on the 'entourage' very soon) disembarked from the helicopters and made their way to the main building where the canteen was situated. Jose insisted that I go straight across to meet the party, as it was quite literally a flying visit, and so unwashed, sporting two days stubble and with a mouth full of slightly furry teeth, I headed across to meet the presidential party.

President Fernando Collor de Mello was a distinctive, approachable chap who spoke perfect English, with a face that could have graced a glossy men's magazine, striking features below a well-groomed jet-black head of hair. With his contingent of tough-looking security men hovering close by, we sat and had some tea and Rich Tea biscuits as I explained what I had been up to further south with BAS. Maybe he requested this brand of biscuits from the Chileans for my benefit so as to add something English to the meeting, but I don't really like them. With all due respect to the manufacturers, Fernando and other fans of this traditional tea accompaniment, I believe there are far superior biscuits to be had, especially for dunking action… chocolate Hobnobs in particular. I rest my case. As I was dunking the bland biscuits into my tea and encouraging him to do the same, with the obvious warning of the dunk being very time limited to avoid 'soggy drop-off' and sludgy tea, he was telling me about his interest in the important scientific research that Brazil and all the other nations were undertaking down here in Antarctica; although his voice was reaching my ears perfectly okay, none of what he was saying was really registering. And there was a good reason for this.

Within his 'entourage' were two gorgeous-looking females; ten minutes earlier, when the Chilean base commander was introducing me to the President and his party, the smell of a lovely fragrant perfume wafted into my nostrils. I then caught sight of the two beautiful women for the first time, as they stood just behind the President and other members of the visiting group. One of them had long dark hair, the other a blonde 'bob' haircut, and both of them had stunning facial features emphasised with perfectly applied make-up and subtle red lipstick. When the party had disembarked from the helicopters earlier, I had not spotted the women as most of the group were wearing bulky overcoats and there was still snow blowing around as the rotors slowly stopped turning, which slightly obscured my view as the groups hurriedly made their way into the canteen block. I was introduced to both of them and tried to maintain my composure and remain professional as I shook their hands and kissed them on their cheeks which they offered in customary South American fashion (I somehow couldn't imagine that happening back in England in a similar situation). However, I felt like an adolescent schoolboy who has just watched the new beautiful French student teacher walk into class. As I spoke with the President, I did my best not to stare at the two striking-looking women now bereft of their bulky overcoats, dressed completely inappropriately for Antarctica in leather boots, tight leggings and fur jackets. I am not sure how successful I was; I think the Labrador-like tongue drooling on my chin might have given me away; it had been a few months since I had seen a female, and certainly none as stunning as these two beautiful ladies (I'm also unsure as to what relationship or role the two women had within the group; one could only speculate). Within half an hour the visit was concluded and the helicopters were lifting off the small flat gravelled area they had been temporarily parked on. As the three Hueys flew off, Jose, who had also been speaking to the President and his party, was stood beside me outside the canteen. Dryly, he asked, "So Con, did you notice those two lovely-looking ladies accompanying the President?"

"How very observant and funny Jose, I'm sure they didn't catch your eye either, and you might want to roll up your tongue." We both smiled, the wonderful scent of perfume lingering in both our nostrils.

9. HMS Endurance and a Return to the Falkland Islands

That evening the Chilean base commander informed me that I had transport arrangements to get back to the Falkland Islands; HMS *Endurance* would be passing the following day and the Navy had agreed to let the Captain bring the ship in to collect Paul and myself and drop us off at Stanley. From there I would get a military aircraft back to England. As I sat reading in my bunk that night I reflected back on my journey so far. It had certainly presented some epic moments but now I was nearing the end of this trip; although I felt sad to be leaving such a stunningly beautiful place, I was also looking forward to getting back home and seeing Sandra. However, I didn't have any confirmed employment to go back to at the moment and the money I had saved while working down here would not last for too long. Once I got to the Falklands I would ring Sandra. I had only spoke to her once using a satellite phone while I was co-piloting one of the Twin Otters on a morning fuel run to the Fossil Bluff; it was only a relatively brief chat but it was great to hear her voice (it was also my most expensive phone call ever, about £185, I think). The trip back up on the *Endurance* was enjoyable and interesting in its own right, a Navy Lieutenant greeted us on board as we arrived on the ship the next day after a landing craft came in to collect us from a small jetty. We had said our farewells to the wonderful people from the Chilean base and Paul and I were berthed down below decks with a small detachment of Royal Marines from 45 Commando. They were a great bunch of guys and made us feel welcome while we were on the ship. A few of the Marines were familiar faces to Paul and I, as we had met them a few weeks previously when the *Endurance* had berthed at Rothera to unload some stores for the base. While the ship was moored there for a couple of days, a mini 'winter Olympics' was organised for the Marines to compete against BAS staff. At the time, most of the field staff were back on the base, therefore allowing a team of eight to be selected from the many willing and able volunteers.

As one can imagine, plenty of the base staff were highly skilled in winter sports, and also, surprisingly for the unsuspecting Marines, we generally had excellent fitness levels. Consequently, we won just about all the events except a short cross country ski event, in which one of the Marines just pipped our guy. I recall them returning to the ship looking a little shell-shocked at what had just happened; a bunch of civilians beating them at their own game. Paul and I were polite and respectful enough (and sensible enough) not to remind the guys about it while living below decks with them. I don't think we would have been victorious in an unplanned below decks dust up; they looked like that would be something they were highly skilled at!

A curious part of the trip back to Stanley was the way in which the officers on board dealt with us. It is not often that the Navy has civilians on board while they are out at sea, so they couldn't decide how we should address them in front of the rest of the crew. I would have rather taken meals with the Marines and the ship's crew in their mess. However, it had been arranged prior to our arrival for us to use the officers' mess. My desire to eat in the crews' mess was for the simple reason that the officers' mess seemed a tad formal for me at this stage of the proceedings, but Paul and I went along with it, me deliberately addressing the officers by their first names over dinner without preceding it with their rank. They seemed to accept this; however, one morning when I was up on the decks walking past one of the officers, I greeted him by his first name within earshot of two of the ship's crew. He diplomatically pulled me to one side and asked very politely, "Look, old chap, it's all rather strange having a pair of civilians on board, we don't mind you using our first names in the mess, but I would be awfully appreciative if you would use the officers' titles when addressing them in front of the crew."

I politely responded that I understood fully and I would comply with his request during the rest of the trip, which indeed I did, but amused myself by over emphasising the title when addressing the officers around the decks e.g., "Good morning, Loootenant Jones," which I think they found slightly annoying but also a little amusing; the Royal Marine and sailors certainly chuckled. I think the Captain was glad to see the back of my anti-authority humour when I disembarked at Stanley. One particularly pleasant aspect of the trip back up to the Falklands was that mother nature decided to be kind to us and Drake Passage was like a village pond compared to our trip down across it months earlier; Paul and I had been warning the Marines to expect a rough ride, and much to their amusement, quite the opposite occurred.

Spending the last couple of days in the southern hemisphere before my journey north was relaxing and pleasant. Things had been very hectic on the base following our memorable trip on the Dyer, so it was great to relax for a short time and unwind with no pressure on me whatsoever. I was accommodated in a B&B in Stanley that was operated by a lovely couple from Scotland who had been on the Islands since just after the war ended. The chap was a civilian engineer who had extended his contract a few times and both he and his charming wife loved the ruggedness and natural beauty of the Falklands. She wanted to work while they were down here so jumped at the opportunity and challenge of running the small guest house, which she did very well. She was a fantastic cook; the meals on the base and on the ship had been more than adequate, but this food in the guesthouse could have graced a decent restaurant table. I complimented her after every meal, which was not a thing I think she heard at every meal time. I also made a point of praising her on how lovely she looked, which she genuinely did, which was another thing I don't think she heard too much of. As pleasant as her husband was, I'm not so sure his somewhat traditional outlook on life included paying her compliments; but then again, one never knows what occurs behind closed doors.

The weather was again favourable, so I made the best use of the time by taking a walk up some of the local hills west of Stanley that I had seen, but not visited, when I had walked up Mount Tumbledown on my previous visit to the Falklands on the way down to Antarctica. Just as I had found on Tumbledown, some of the hill tops still bore the remnants of the conflict; once again as I sat on the top of Wireless Ridge soaking up the vista around me, my heart felt deeply saddened as I imagined the bloody carnage and loss of life that had occurred here not many years previously. I tried to put that from my mind as I made my way through the rugged hillside back into Stanley.

Paul was staying in another bed and breakfast close by, so next morning I arranged to go out for a run with him. We looked at a map and decided to head out of town on a small road for about three miles and then return the same way, picking up the pace on the last section. Again the weather remained pleasant, cool but sunny, so the run was really enjoyable and also quite taxing. I felt in good physical shape; I had been exercising a lot at Rothera after returning from the field, and also been doing circuit training with the Marines while on the ship, and so was looking forward to a good run. We really did 'pick up the pace' the last mile in; my lungs were bursting and my heart nearly beating out of my chest as we came to a halt near the war memorial, after pretty much sprinting the last 400 metres. With my hands on my head taking in deep breaths, I struggled to gasp out the words, "Cheers mate, that was a cracking run," not looking anywhere near as physically taxed as I was feeling.

Paul responded with, "No worries, I loved it too, you don't mind if head out and do it again," and off he trotted. I regarded myself as having good fitness levels, but Paul was in another league, one of the fittest, and nicest guys you could ever meet; I knew he had competed in Iron Man triathlons in the past; he told me he once did two Iron Man races back to back – which means more than 4 miles of swimming, 224 miles on a bike and 52 miles of running in total. Our six-mile run must have seemed like a warm-up stretch in comparison.

After another couple of days wandering on the Island, having a beer or two in the nearby bar, chatting with locals and enjoying great food at the guesthouse, I said my goodbyes to Paul, who I think was heading to South America, and to the hosts, making sure to give the wonderful hostess a big hug and kiss. I hitched a lift in an Army Land Rover (I must have been forgiven for my misdemeanours on the way down), and travelled west to the busy military airbase at Mount Pleasant to board my long flight back home.

10. Arriving Home

The plane touched down at RAF Brize Norton after a long and tiring 21-hour flight back from the airbase on the Falklands. I had boarded the quite dated Vickers VC10 at Mount Pleasant airport, flown up to Ascension Island in the mid-Atlantic to experience quite a scary landing on their runway, hung around for a couple of hours to refuel, then carried onwards north for the second leg back to Brize Norton. Ascension is a small British Overseas Territory located in the Atlantic Ocean about 1600 kilometres from the coast of West Africa and 2400 kilometres from Brazil and has a tropical desert climate. As I climbed down the stairs onto the tarmac to stretch my legs, it felt like I had stepped into an oven; the still air temperature was about 35C and the sweltering heat was reflecting up from the light coloured concrete runway. My body was becoming a little confused by these huge temperature variations; only recently my body had been experiencing minus 30C in bitingly cold Antarctic storms. Landing here had been a bit of a nail biter due to the RAF pilot aborting his first landing attempt at the very last minute. The single runway at 'Wideawake Airfield' is roughly at a north-west to southeast angle, running from the coast inland, therefore, the pilots only have two options to choose from in their approach.

Those with a basic understand of aircraft flight will understand that the preferred landing for a pilot is into a headwind; however, with a single runway, the options are limited. The day we landed, there was a very strong southerly wind blowing across the runway, and so the pilot chose to come in from the north west to land at the head of the runway near the coast, keeping the plane facing slightly south into the wind, and 'crabbing' sideways, until the wheels were just about to touch down, then straighten up for the landing. The first attempt was a complete shambles; as I looked out of the side window and saw the coast quickly meet the start of the runway, I knew we were too high, and had also been pushed too far to the left of the runway by the gale force winds coming up from the south. Just as the wheels were about to touch, the engines hit full throttle and we climbed away. There was an audible sigh of relief from inside the plane as other passengers who had also been nervously looking out the window and realised we would have overshot the runway, knew the pilot had not risked the landing and taken the appropriate action right at the last moment; Ascension was our only landing option. The second attempt was spot on; however, although I have experienced a significant number of dubious plane landings on my travels, I can't recall my whole body being thrown forward so hard and a seatbelt biting into my stomach so much, due to the pilot's very enthusiastic application of the aircraft's brakes, and the front wheel apparently stopping just as concrete met dirt. We eventually came to a halt after taxiing to the refuelling station; we showed our support to the RAF pilot and navigator for their efforts with a healthy cheer as they emerged from the cockpit door, both looking relieved and slightly bemused.

Nine hours after leaving Ascension our landing at RAF Brize Norton was a very straightforward affair by comparison with no dramas whatsoever, the pilot completing a smooth textbook landing. We all disembarked onto the tarmac and headed towards the customs/arrivals building. I was still in a military environment and didn't know any of the other passengers; other than an elderly couple I had spoken to while we were in the Falklands, they were all military personnel returning home after their stint in the southern Atlantic military outpost. The continued presence of a military base in such an isolated location such as the Falklands does create some debate these days. Without getting too involved in any political issues, I might lean towards the suggestion that it may be to do with the vast amounts of untapped minerals that lie within the Antarctic, and the geographical location of the Islands make them a perfect stepping stone should any mineral exploitation tragically occur in the future. Hopefully, the Antarctic Treaty will always deter commercial drilling and mining from ever occurring on the beautiful continent; but with the rise of global capitalism, diminishing mineral sources elsewhere on the planet and the lack of pursuit of alternative renewable power sources, who knows what the future holds for the great white continent?

Following an interesting debate with a military customs officer about the two ice axes attached to my rucksack (at one stage of our discussion it was very tempting to un-attach one of the axes to literally emphasise my point), I found myself at a bus stop awaiting transport to Oxford train station. It felt quite nostalgic being back at the RAF base; the last time I had been here was about eight years earlier while undertaking a military parachuting course. I have fond recollections of the course, that surprisingly to many, is run completely by RAF instructors, and is arguably the best military parachute training school in the world; all British military personnel doing basic parachute training come through this establishment, including special forces. While I was doing my parachute course there was a small detachment of US soldiers from the 82nd and 101st Airborne Divisions qualifying for their British 'wings', an arrangement which was often reciprocated; a year later I was fortunate enough to gain my own American 'wings' jumping from the back of Chinook helicopters over the Everglades in Florida.

Much to our amusement, and the annoyance of the RAF instructors at Brize Norton, these guys from the States insisted on shouting "AIRBORNE!" every time they jumped out of the aircraft door, including the door of the mock fuselage of a Hercules aircraft that was inside a hangar and used for practising 'aircraft exits'; with only a metre or so drop to the floor, it really was quite funny to witness; those American soldiers just can't seem to stop themselves, it must be all the gung-ho movies they watch. I also recall parachuting into a four-day exercise while in Florida working alongside guys from the US 82nd Airborne Unit. As myself and a small platoon of British paratroopers were climbing up the ramp of the Chinook helicopter that was going to drop us from 1200 metres over a large forest clearing, all of us laden down with a heavy container, I noticed the American troops did not have any with them and were therefore jumping 'clean fatigues' i.e. just two parachutes and no equipment whatsoever. Prior to exiting the helicopter, our containers would be attached to the front of the parachuting harness on some 'D rings' just below the emergency parachute. Within these bulky containers is webbing, ammunition, food, water, and a weapon strapped onto the side. Although they are an essential part of military parachuting as their contents will keep you alive, they are very uncomfortable to parachute with, adding an extra element of danger. Once you have exited the aircraft and done all round observations to ensure you are not about to collide with anyone else, the container is dropped from the D ring and dangles on a fifteen-foot-long cord which is attached to the harness, this on a quick release mechanism so it can be jettisoned if you are unlucky enough to be about to land in trees or water.

When we were sat down on opposite sides of the helicopter fuselage, us eight British guys with the big uncomfortable containers in front of us, I leant forward and shouted to one of the Airborne guys above the din of the noisy rotor blades, which were increasing in speed prior to take off, asking where his container was with all his gear. He told me a truck would be meeting them at the drop zone and they would pick their kit up there after they had landed. I paused for a second, stopped myself from asking the obvious questions, just nodded, smiled and said, "Oh… Okay."

Eventually clearing Brize Norton customs and fortunately not having clobbered the jobsworth customs official, I walked off the base and sat alone in the bus shelter on a reasonably quiet road outside the perimeter fence, soaking up the crisp morning sun. Leant back on the bench, my face bathed in the warming glow, I found myself pondering on my journey to arrive back here, and how different things are in a 'normal' environment (whatever normal might mean?)

Only weeks earlier I had been up on the Dyer Plateau with only one other person in an area the size of Wales, then had returned to the base at Rothera and had to re-adjust to being around about eighty people, onto the *Endurance* with a ship full of sailors and being packed in tightly with the Marines, then into Stanley on the Falklands, and the very busy military base at Mount Pleasant. Now I was on my way to arrive in Oxford, a town with a population of over half a million, which felt to me like an enormous city; this 'large crowd acclimatisation' was feeling a bit tricky indeed. Other people I have spoken to who have travelled and lived in Antarctica have also felt a similar emotion, feeling a little overwhelmed when returning to busy developed areas. I imagine this also applies to people arriving home after spending a significant amount of time in any wilderness areas; but I guess it isn't the same for people who are resourceful and courageous enough to make the wilderness their permanent home (a choice which would be impossible, though, in somewhere like the Dyer Plateau with absolutely no natural food sources). I have always found it easy enough to get accustomed to relative isolation; this is probably because I find remote mountain ranges spectacularly beautiful, and as mentioned earlier, while the average city dweller, dependent on having consumer goods and luxuries at their fingertips might comment, 'But there's nothing there', my philosophy is quite the opposite.

The bus journey into a very busy Oxford did allow some time to adapt, but when I found myself weaving through a crowded and bustling train station I was drawn sideways to a quiet platform that I had noticed, just to escape the chaos for ten minutes, gather myself, then re-engage in the bedlam to find my train north. The train journey was quiet enough, and before long I found myself pulling into Leeds City station. I had used the train loo to spruce myself as much as possible and dab on some aftershave I had bought in Birmingham train station when I changed trains. Sandra was waiting for me on the other side of the ticket barriers as I approached during the busy rush hour human traffic, laden down with a large rucksack and an even bigger holdall; I could not miss her beautiful beaming smile, jet black hair and sparkly brown eyes standing out amongst a moving sea of commuters. As I bundled my gear past the ticket guard, she leapt at me, threw her arms around me and pressed her face and lips to mine, her eyes welling up with tears, I held her tightly in my arms and felt the love and warmth emanating from her. Rather than go back to my dad's place that evening, she had booked us into the Queens Hotel for a couple of nights; it is right in the centre of Leeds, adjoining the train station and is one of the more upmarket hotels in the city. I was so looking forward to a slice of luxury, and spending some quality intimate time with her. We quickly, and with a tangible sense of urgency, went through the formalities of checking in and got the bags into our room. We were immediately in a passionate embrace and I have to admit that after being away from her for so many months, the duration of our intimacy was all too brief and certainly wouldn't qualify me for 'stud of the year', which we both thought was quite amusing, but I guess to be expected. That evening we went out for dinner and drinks. She asked me for all the details about my adventures down south and relayed what had been happening at home. It was a fantastic night filled with laughter and hugs and after dinner got quite tipsy bar hopping in the busy Leeds nightlife. When we were slowly waking next morning in our luxurious bed, both suffering from a bit of a hangover, my mind was wandering back to Antarctica. I had told Sandra that my trip south was a one off. However, as I lay there half asleep, with her snuggled softly against my chest, my mind began to wander and turned back to the awe-inspiring beauty of the great white continent, wondering about how great it might be to do a deep field full season for three months in the mountains, guiding a geologist. As those who have worked or been fortunate to travel in Antarctica can attest, it does leave a lasting impression; its magnetism was certainly evident in my mind right then; *Let me just leave those thought alone for a while* I thought, and enjoy the present moment. After a wonderful cooked breakfast in the hotel's dining room, we arrived by taxi outside my dad's house on the council estate in Leeds and carted most of my gear in, having left some clothes and toiletries back at the hotel. It was Saturday lunchtime and he was sitting in the lounge doing his newspaper crossword. "Hi Dad, I'm back," I said enthusiastically.

In his soft Dublin accent, he replied, "Oh Jaysus, that's great, hi Sandra... What's another word for a wide river mouth, seven letters, third letter is 't'?" Although he didn't really express it to me in an overt way, I knew he was hugely proud of what I had been doing; some of my aunties in Leeds would often tell me he had been enthusiastically relaying all my tales of adventure to them over Saturday night drinks at the Catholic Club or Irish Centre. I also think he was very sad that my mother was not around to witness my global travels. She was hugely influential in all our lives, but unfortunately and tragically we had lost her five years previously. She and my Dad were true soul mates who met in an army barracks in County Kildare as teenagers; he never really recovered from her passing.

"Estuary," I replied.

"I see all that cold hasn't frozen your brain, clever clogs. Do you both fancy a quick pint up at the local?"

We went to the local bar which was situated just up the street to find it hosting its usual mix of people; the Connemara and Mayo guys in their work suits enjoying their few well-earned cold beers having undertaken the Saturday morning shift; the functioning alcoholics getting their bloodstream topped up from the night before, sitting around talking a lot, but not really saying anything; some Jamaican lads playing dominoes in a very animated fashion sat at a table at the far end of the bar; and of course, as is the case with all bars in the middle of large council estates, the ubiquitous dodgy crew in the corner. I knew these characters did not work in regular full-time jobs, but seemed always to have plenty of cash for drinks and cigarettes; somehow, I felt sure that zero percent of the money they 'earned' would ever contribute towards our taxation system. I chatted with some of the Irish guys, as I knew them quite well from labouring with them years ago; they were a great bunch, always smiling, and had a fantastic work ethic. I remember previously while toiling away with them laying water mains, I was also competing in short course triathlons; one morning when I was being picked up by the transit van outside my dad's place, I put my road bike in the back of the van with the intent of cycling the thirty miles back home from our work location to utilise the journey and 'get it out of the way'.

On seeing this, the foreman Martin looked over his shoulder into the back of the van, "Jaysus Con, get that fecking thing out, if you can cycle all that way back here after a day's work, ye haven't been fecking working hard enough," happy days.

What was clear to me as I soaked up the atmosphere and environment surrounding us was that nothing had changed; I had grown up in this area and spent time in this bar in my late teens and early twenties. Although I had not frequented the place for a long time (if I was in England and was seeing my dad, I would normally pick him up and take him for a bite to eat and give him a change of scenery) it was the same people, sat in roughly the same place, talking about the usual things, but all looking slightly older – each to their own I guess. I had a great catch up with my dad over a couple of pints of delicious cold Guinness. He is a wonderful, gentle kind man and he and Sandra got on very well; she had been liaising with him occasionally in my absence to update him on how things were after I had contacted her by airletter. After a couple of hours, we parted company with my dad and taxied back to the hotel. I would be returning to stay with him for a while to keep him company and decide my next steps; although I did jointly own a property in Leeds with an ex-partner, it was currently rented out to people (who probably wouldn't approve of me camping in the garden), and although he probably wouldn't admit it, my dad liked having someone around. I was now back home in the environment I had often missed when up on the Dyer tent-bound in ferocious storms for days on end, but I was beginning to experience unusual feelings within me that I found difficult to analyse; I had even found myself momentarily staring into space while in the bar, nudged gently back into the present by my dad's elbow. Months later, I met someone who had also been to the Antarctic and he said exactly the same thing had happened to him on numerous occasions when he had returned home; he referred to it as 'the fifty metre Antarctic stare'. It was fantastic to be back into familiar surroundings, with Sandra and seeing my wonderful family and friends, but I felt that something had changed in me as a result of my experiences on the great white continent. I had been tested to my limits on just about every level and I'm sure this in itself had altered me, but in a positive way. I now felt much calmer than ever and my positive approach to life felt even more entrenched, but there was something niggling at the back of my head that I initially couldn't understand. After having been home for just a couple of days, I managed to find time for a little introspection (I think it was when I was sat on the loo in the hotel room); within the calm I was feeling, some contradiction was revealing itself. I sensed this calmness was ready for more adventure and adrenalin rushes, and I was beginning to acknowledge where I was going to get this excitement; there seemed to be a desire for further challenges surfacing, and these challenges were likely to entail having to travel many miles in a southerly direction. Adapting to a 'normal' day to day life in England was something I was maybe not ready for just yet. Over lunch with Sandra in a pleasant enough bistro bar by the River Aire in Leeds, we were having a general conversation about a variety of things; however, the thing uppermost in my mind seemed to be that I felt I had already made the decision about returning south; this was in no way a reflection of my feelings for her, it was something I really needed to do, and so there was a painful question burning a hole in my brain. The first season in the field had given me a real taste of the Antarctic, allowing me to experience both its breath-taking beauty, and its dangerous harshness. As with many who are fortunate enough to visit the great white continent, the place had left a lasting and significant impression on me. It is interesting how, when reflecting on my time there, I tended to forget those moments of bone chilling cold on the Dyer Plateau that seemed to freeze me to the core. It was instead the memories of awe-inspiring stunning natural beauty that stuck with me; maybe optimists subconsciously cherry pick the best bits to retain. I knew I needed to go back and do a full field season with a geologist, spending three months in the mountains as a mobile research unit. However, at the forefront of my mind right now was one simple question, *How the hell do I broach the subject of me returning to Antarctica for a second season later in the year?* Life is indeed a journey.

Glossary

Beaufort Scale – a scientific measurement that relates wind speed to observed conditions at sea or on land; its full name is the Beaufort wind force scale (devised in 1805 by Irish-born Francis Beaufort)

Bergschrund – a crevasse that forms where moving glacier ice separates from the stagnant ice above (from the German for *mountain cleft)*

Crampon – a steel alloy or lightweight aluminium traction device that is attached to mountaineering boots, the spikes underneath and front points improve mobility on snow and ice.

Crevasse – a deep crack, or fracture, found in an ice sheet or glacier, these cracks are formed by the stresses to the glacier as it moves over undulating ground below.

Hypothermia – reduced body temperature that happens when a body dissipates more heat than it absorbs; in humans, it is defined as a body core temperature below 35C.

Ice axe – a multi-purpose climbing tool used by mountaineers and hill walkers in snow and ice conditions, both in the ascent and descent of routes. An ice axe can also be used as a means of self-arrest in the event of a downhill slip.

Karabiner/Carabiner – a metal loop with a spring-loaded mechanism (often with a locking device) that is widely used in rope-intensive activities (from the German *Karabinerhaken* meaning 'spring hook').

Nansen sledge – a sledge with a strong, flexible, lashed wood construction named after Fridtjof Nansen, the Norwegian scientist, explorer and humanitarian; it can carry just over 450 kilogrammes in weight and has been used in the polar regions since Nansen's expeditions in the 1890s.

Pack ice – any area of sea ice (ice formed by freezing of seawater) that is not land-fast; it is mobile by virtue of not being attached to the shoreline or something else. It can be of varying thickness, often restricting the movement of vessels.

Primus stove – a pressurised paraffin burning stove that performs especially well under adverse conditions and has earned a reputation as a reliable and durable stove in polar regions.

Seracs – a block or column of glacial ice, often formed by intersecting crevasses on a glacier; commonly house-sized or larger, they are dangerous to mountaineers as they may topple with little warning (from the Swiss French *sérac*)

Skidoo – a type of motorised toboggan that is used for travelling on snow and ice.